A Union Officer in the Reconstruction

A
UNION OFFICER

IN THE

Reconstruction

———◆◆———

BY

John William De Forest

EDITED, WITH AN INTRODUCTION AND NOTES,

By James H. Croushore and David Morris Potter

———◆◆———

LOUISIANA STATE UNIVERSITY PRESS

Baton Rouge and London

Manufactured in the United States of America

Louisiana Paperback Edition, 1997

06 05 04 03 02 01 00 99 98 97   5   4   3   2   1

Library of Congress Cataloging-in-Publication Data

De Forest, John William, 1826–1906.
    A Union officer in the Reconstruction / by John William De Forest
; edited, with an introduction and notes, by James H. Croushore and
David Morris Potter.–Louisiana pbk. ed.
        p. cm.
    Includes index.
    Previously published: Hamden, Conn. : Archon Books, 1968, c1948.
    ISBN 0-8071-2183-5 (p : alk. paper)
    1. Reconstruction–South Carolina–Greenville region. 2. De
Forest, John William, 1826–1906. 3. United States. Bureau of
Refugees, Freedmen, and Abandoned Lands. 4. Freedmen–South
Carolina–Greenville Region–History–19th century. 5. Social
classes–South Carolina–Greenville Region–History–19th century.
6. Greenville Region (S.C.)–Social conditions. I. Croushore,
James H. (James Henry) II. Potter, David Morris. III. Title.
F279.G79D44 1997
975.7'27–dc21   96-29715
                                                                CIP

The paper in this book meets the guidelines for permanence and durability of the Committee on
Production Guidelines for Book Longevity of the Council on Library Resources. ♾

INTRODUCTION

IN recent years literary criticism has begun to recognize John William De Forest as one of the neglected figures of nineteenth-century American letters. A native of Connecticut, born in 1826, De Forest became a professional writer and reached his prime in the period known as New England's Indian Summer. But instead of conforming to the genteel attitudes which, though becoming autumnal, were still the safest way to popularity, he wrote in a vein distinctively his own, so direct, so stripped of illusion, so trenchant in its perceptions, that it forfeited the approval of a sentimental public. Although his worth was acknowledged by a mature critic like William Dean Howells, his last years were marked by personal frustration and literary barrenness. Only since the re-publication in 1939 of *Miss Ravenel's Conversion from Secession to Loyalty,* and the belated publication in 1946 of *A Volunteer's Adventures* have his literary merits begun to attain recognition.

In *A Volunteer's Adventures* De Forest turned, for a time, from fiction to non-fiction, as he wrote his personal record of participation in the Civil War. His account displayed an unusual gift for vivid, accurate, perceptive factual reporting. Although there have been more than enough personal memoirs of the Civil War to jade the public taste, the especial merits of this account have secured for it unusual acclaim, and it has been compared more often with Stephen Crane's *The Red Badge of Courage* than with the reminiscent narratives with which, in form, it belongs. Even amid many analogous narratives, therefore, De Forest's record has distinctive value.

A Union Officer in the Reconstruction illustrates further the qualities which distinguish De Forest as a writer. But there is another value in this record of personal experiences, and that is its importance as history. If his Civil War narrative is of value, in competition with uncounted writings of similar character, his account of experiences during Reconstruction is of much

more importance historically because of the paucity of informed, reliable, intelligent commentaries upon that troubled
phase of American history. Few subjects have a literature as
bulky and at the same time as disappointing as this one, where
so much has been written in a partisan, war-embittered spirit;
and so much more, in a narrow concept which regarded Reconstruction as a series of political transactions, rather than as
the story of a people defeated, a race enfranchised, and a society
overturned. Thus every item, such as carpetbag corruption or
Ku Klux outrage, which could be used to discredit an adversary,
has been pursued into its *minutiae,* and every legislative step has
been dutifully set down in the monographs. Francis B. Simkins
and Robert H. Woody, who have transcended the limitations of
such sources in their history of *South Carolina during Reconstruction,* characterize the historical narratives as "narrowly
political," the journalistic treatments as sensational, the
memoirs of natives as "dominated by the Southern sense of
reticence," and the accounts by outside observers as un-
distinguished and clouded by preconceptions.

These sharp phrases, measuring the deficiencies of the bulk
of the literature, furnish also, by indirection, a measure of the
value of the observations made by De Forest as an agent of the
Freedmen's Bureau at Greenville, South Carolina, in 1866 and
1867. For De Forest, in his post far up in the Piedmont, was
but distantly aware of political activities, either at Washington
or Columbia. He was so free of sensationalism that his comment,
though it was published in a series of articles in leading magazines, became lost even to specialists in the period, was used in
none of the histories, and appears in none of the bibliographies.
Scorning a politic reticence, he stated his individualistic con-
clusions with a vigor that probably offended both Northern and
Southern readers in the 'sixties, and may retain this double
effectiveness even today. Least of all was his work undis-
tinguished or clouded by preconceptions. In fact, De Forest was
already a skilled professional writer, who had by this time
published a history of the Indians of Connecticut, two travel
narratives, and two novels. He was a man of markedly superior
intellectual talent, and one of the salient features of his literary
skill was his impatience with stereotypes and his readiness to

acknowledge, without regard for current intellectual fashions, the merits of the individual man or the individual situation.

De Forest's service at Greenville extended over a period of fifteen months. Since the three counties in his district were the westernmost in the state, he did not witness Reconstruction where the Negro population was thickest. And since he left at the end of 1867, he did not witness carpetbag and Negro government. But though he missed these melodramatic phases, it was his lot to watch a characteristic region of the southern Piedmont under the impact of emancipation, defeat in war, military rule, and social and economic disorganization. It was his lot also to serve the United States in one of its earliest attempts at military occupation, and in its very first experiment with a vast administrative agency for social reform. Of the hundreds who knew the work of the Bureau at first hand, he seems to be the only person who wrote a full and realistic account of its operation at the level where it touched the daily lives of the freedmen. Of the thousands who saw and experienced the conditions of ordinary life in the South during the period of Reconstruction there was perhaps not one who left so readable a record, or a record in which breadth of experience, accuracy of observation, fairness of judgment, and sheer capacity of intellect were so notably combined. It is this combination of qualities which gives to *A Union Officer in the Reconstruction* a distinctive value in the literature of Reconstruction.

Before turning to De Forest's record of his experiences in the South, the reader may wish to know, in a general way, what developments in that region, what policies of the national government, and what personal circumstances in De Forest's own life led to his becoming sub-assistant commissioner for the Greenville District of the Freedmen's Bureau.

When the Confederacy collapsed in April, 1865, President Lincoln and Congress were already deeply divided. Lincoln, as is well known, wished to restore the South to the Union quickly and painlessly, while the Radicals in Congress desired to follow a more punitive policy, assuring themselves of the irrevocable overthrow of the old ruling class before they reinstated the seceded states. Clearly Lincoln needed all his tact and political mastery for the approaching struggle with the Radicals, and when Andrew Johnson succeeded to office, sharing Lincoln's views but not his ability, the ultimate triumph of Congress was already foreshadowed. But Johnson had one great tactical advantage in that Congress did not sit during the first eight months of his Presidency, that is, from April to December, 1865.

Before Congress could act, therefore, Johnson was able to launch a program based wholly on his own policy. His purpose was first to restore local home rule as soon as he could find a nucleus of white Southerners who would take an oath of loyalty, and then to recognize the state governments established by these citizens as soon as they had enacted measures repudiating secession and affirming the abolition of slavery. Since the war itself had prepared virtually all Southerners to accept these conditions as inevitable, the Johnson program moved very rapidly. After the administration of the amnesty oath, Johnson appointed provisional governors for the various states, with instructions to hold elections for constitutional conventions. When these conventions had done their work, a second series of elections would designate the officials of government under the new constitutions, and at this point, according to Johnson, the reorganized states would resume full membership in the Union. In accordance with this plan Johnson had completed, by July, 1865, the process of appointing provisional governors for the eleven seceded states. By October, elections had been held, conventions had met, and constitutions had been adopted in all these states except Texas. It required less than two months more for the election and installation of officials for these new governments. Thus, as early as December, 1865, ten Southern states had completed a process of reorganization, and fondly supposed that Reconstruction was complete.

South Carolina was, of course, one of these ten. For the first three months after defeat, with her war-time governor imprisoned at Fort Pulaski, she had remained under military rule, but in June President Johnson had appointed Benjamin F. Perry provisional governor of the state. A native of the district over which De Forest was later to become administrator, Perry was, moreover, a resident of De Forest's headquarters town,

Greenville.* He will appear again, therefore, in De Forest's narrative. The new governor was qualified for his post by his record as an aggressive Unionist who had excoriated secession until the last moment and had then acquiesced in the decision of his fellow citizens with the grudging assertion: "You are all going to the devil, and I will go with you." But though loyal enough, he was handicapped by certain doctrinaire attitudes, and by a failure to recognize that the denial of civil rights for the freedmen would invite Congressional rejection of the reorganized government.

Perry called an election, to be held in September, for a constitutional convention, which met during the same month. At this convention, the Ordinance of Secession was repealed, but not declared void *ab initio,* the abolition of slavery was recognized by resolutions which paved the way for the later legislative ratification of the Thirteenth Amendment, and a new constitution was framed. The suffrage, however, was placed on a basis which excluded Negroes entirely, and Governor Perry openly asserted to the convention: "This is a white man's government and the white man's only." Because of this statement, and others like it, the new government began, at its very inception, to incur hostile criticism from the North.

Under the newly framed constitution, further elections were held in October, and James L. Orr was chosen governor. Orr was a man of long political experience and of considerable eminence, for he had at one time been Speaker of the national House of Representatives. He took office as governor in November, 1865, and remained in that post until July, 1868. Thus he was civil governor of the state during the entire period of De Forest's service in South Carolina. But as will appear, the powers of his office were in time reduced almost to negligibility by acts of Congress.

Orr was neither so tactless nor so intransigent as Perry, and indeed he later identified himself with the Republicans, but at the outset of his term his legislature further antagonized the Radicals in Congress by enacting the so-called Black Code. This series of laws, applying to the freedmen, limited the rights

* Lillian Adele Kibler's *Benjamin F. Perry, South Carolina Unionist* (Durham, 1946) is a definitive biography.

of Negroes to engage in stated occupations, imposed certain disqualifications upon them in the courts, gave sweeping powers to their employers (to be known as masters) when the Negroes were bound in a labor contract, and provided that when freedmen became vagrants (also sweepingly defined) they might be bound out to labor by the local magistrates. Such measures as these, both in South Carolina and in other states, led to the belief in Republican circles that the South intended to restore a condition of servitude approximating slavery. The Black Codes, therefore, contributed to the further alienation of a Congress which was already hostile.

As a result of these and other factors, a second process of reconstruction, under the direction of Congress, began very gradually to take form. It was first ominously foreshadowed in December, 1865, when the Senate and House refused to seat the claimants sent to Congress by the new Southern governments. For the rest of the winter and spring, these new governments marked time, while the President fought Congress with his veto, and the Joint Committee on Reconstruction developed the strategy of Congressional attack upon the President. Then, in June, Congress presented the South with what was to prove a fatal dilemma: it submitted the Fourteenth Amendment for ratification by the states. This lengthy addition to the Constitution not only conferred citizenship upon the Negroes; it also confronted the states with a choice either of enfranchising the freedmen or of having representation in Congress reduced; and, worst of all in the eyes of Southerners, it disqualified from public life all citizens who, having once taken the oath to support the Constitution, had later participated in rebellion. Since this involved practically every prominent person in the South, the result threatened to be almost revolutionary.

When De Forest went to South Carolina in October, 1866, the people of the state faced this question of the Fourteenth Amendment. To ratify meant to destroy their own ruling class; to reject meant to expose both ruling class and government to destruction by the act of Congress. The people of this state, like other Southerners, were not yet aware of the cost of military defeat, and with both President Johnson and Governor Orr openly encouraging resistance, the legislature voted in December, 1866, almost unanimously against the amendment. When nine other Southern states took similar action, ratification was temporarily defeated. Two of the key figures in producing this result were President Johnson for the South as a whole, and Benjamin F. Perry for South Carolina; both were to be sharply criticized by De Forest.

Northern resentment of Southern action on the Fourteenth Amendment gave Congress the opportunity to move from mere passive non-recognition to the active destruction of the governments in the South. The instruments of this destruction were the two so-called Reconstruction Acts which were passed in March, 1867. (De Forest had at that time been in the South for six months.) These acts declared that "no legal state governments" existed in the "rebel states," and that the existing governments were "provisional only." Accordingly, they divided the ten states into five military districts with a general in command of each, vested with extensive though ill-defined governmental powers. Moreover, they provided that no state could be admitted to representation in Congress until it had held a new constitutional convention chosen "by the male citizens . . . of whatever race," had adopted a new constitution incorporating this same principle of suffrage, and had ratified the Fourteenth Amendment. As a means to these ends, instructions were also included for the military governors to hold new elections, to convoke the conventions, and, in short, to supervise the entire process of this second reconstruction.

In reluctant compliance with these acts, adopted over his veto, the President appointed military governors for the five Southern districts. For Military District Number Two (North and South Carolina) he named General Daniel E. Sickles, who was, in his day, famous for a certain strenuosity of temperament. In 1859 Sickles had shot and killed Philip Barton Key, son of Francis Scott Key, because of improper attentions to Mrs. Sickles, whom he had married when she was the seventeen-year-old daughter of an Italian music master. Later he was to be engaged with General Meade in a very warm and very public dispute over the strategy at Gettysburg, where Sickles had lost a leg. Johnson's appointee, then, was something of a stormy petrel, and all things considered, his administration of the Carolinas was surprisingly moderate. He permitted Governor Orr to continue in office, though with functions much restricted, and when he left the state some months later, the good wishes of the Carolinians attended him. The most drastic act of his administration had been the issuance of his General Order Number Ten, a measure on which De Forest had some occasion to comment. This famous decree abolished the death penalty for burglary and horse stealing, prohibited flogging as a penalty for crime, did away with imprisonment for debt, created a homestead exempt from seizure in debt proceedings, and, most important of all, suspended the legal collection of debts contracted between December 19, 1860, and May 15, 1865. Actually, this stay-law was highly acceptable to South Carolina, for the economic distress of the times was acute, and the legislature under Orr had already attempted to enact such a stay of execution, only to have it thrown out by the state supreme court. The fact that the military governor could do by decree what the legislature could not do by law was a testimony to his power.

Because of certain actions in the affairs of North Carolina which alienated President Johnson, Sickles was removed in August, 1867, after a tenure of five months, to be replaced by Major General E. R. S. Canby. Canby removed from office many local officials and, by indirection, prevented the legislature from holding its regular session, but, like his predecessor, he left Governor Orr undisturbed. His principal activity was the holding of elections for the new constitutional convention. For these elections, the enrollment of voters was completed by mid-October, 1867, and showed, for the state as a whole, a total of 46,346 registered whites and 78,982 registered Negroes. In De Forest's district, consisting of Anderson, Greenville, and Pickens counties, 5,953 whites and 3,734 Negroes were registered. The election took place in November, and as De Forest noted for his district, it was so quiet and orderly as to be almost lackadaisical. When the votes were counted, it was found that De Forest's district had chosen 7 whites and 3 Negroes, and that the state as a whole had elected 48 whites and 76 Negroes.

De Forest left South Carolina in January, 1868, at the very time when this convention met. Therefore he did not witness the new phase of Reconstruction which was to follow. For nine years the Radicals were to remain in the ascendancy, through their control of Negro majorities in the electorate and in the legislature. They were to plunder South Carolina so thoroughly as to earn for it the appellation, "The Prostrate State." Then, in 1876, the Democrats, resolved upon white supremacy, were to form a semi-military organization of "Redshirts," and were to place themselves under the leadership of General Wade Hampton, who was a perfect exponent of the planter tradition. Thus, challenging the Radicals and claiming victory in a tensely disputed governorship election, the Democrats were to attain uncontested control in 1877 when President Hayes withdrew all Federal troops from the South. But though De Forest did not witness these dramatic developments, he had for fifteen months observed the operation of Presidentially sponsored government and of military government. These months were critical, of course, in shaping the issues of Reconstruction and in developing the conditions of the postwar South.

While the administrations of Orr on one hand, and of Sickles and Canby on the other, represented the coinciding and sometimes conflicting jurisdictions of the state of South Carolina and of Military District Number Two, De Forest was himself the local agent of a third jurisdiction, that of the Bureau of Refugees, Freedmen, and Abandoned Lands.

The Freedmen's Bureau, as it was customarily called, in fact antedated the other two jurisdictions, for it had been established by act of Congress, with President Lincoln's approval, on March 3, 1865. As originally planned, this agency was an administrative branch of the War Department, vested with the "supervision and management of all abandoned lands, and the control of all subjects relating to refugees [that is, Unionist refugees] and freedmen." Its first Commissioner, chosen by Lincoln but appointed by Johnson, was Major General Oliver O. Howard. Howard combined an outstanding military record with a deep personal piety and an unflagging zeal in the anti-liquor, or temperance, cause. Under Howard, ten assistant commissioners were appointed for each of the ten unreconstructed states. For South Carolina, the Assistant Commissioner during De Forest's service was General Robert K. Scott of Ohio, who

later advanced from this strategic post to the governorship.
The final subdivision of Bureau functions was attained by
creating a number of districts within each state, each district to
be administered by an official cumbrously known as a sub-
assistant commissioner. It was in this capacity that De Forest
served at Greenville.

On December 2, 1864, after three years of strenuous cam-
paigning in the Union army, De Forest had been mustered out of
the Twelfth Connecticut Volunteers as captain and, according to
his own statement in *A Volunteer's Adventures,* had gone home
to Connecticut "with what then seemed a totally ruined constitution." Almost immediately he began to translate his war experiences into fiction in the novel, *Miss Ravenel's Conversion.*

Though he acknowledged upon his discharge that he was too
weak for active duty, he soon discovered, after two months of
recuperation, a branch of service where he could turn to account
his military training without enduring the physical hardships
falling to the lot of a line officer. In February, 1865, having
secured recommendations from Generals Sheridan, Weitzel,
Emory, and McMillan, he applied for a commission in the In-
valid Corps.

The purpose of this organization, subsequently called the
Veteran Reserve Corps, was to keep in the armed forces experienced soldiers who were disabled for active service. Thus
the Corps relieved able-bodied men for front-line duty, formed
a reliable body of military police, and sometimes acted as
garrison troops. De Forest's commission as captain in the
Veteran Reserve Corps was signed by President Johnson in
May, 1865. After serving a few months in Washington with
Company I, Fourteenth Regiment, De Forest was ordered, in
September, 1865, to report to Provost Marshal General Fry,
who, on October 2, appointed him Acting Assistant Adjutant
General in the Veteran Reserve Corps Bureau. In charge of nine
clerks, he was responsible for keeping up to date the records of
the officers and men who enlisted in, or were transferred to the
organization. One of his first tasks was to draw up a report on
the operations of the Corps from the time of its inception until
September 30, 1865. Prepared at a time when General Grant
vigorously opposed the retention of this unit within the army,

the report was an attempt to justify the existence of the organization. De Forest himself realized the uncertainty of his prospects in the Veteran Reserve, for he wrote in a letter to his brother, "But for the Secretary of War, it [the Corps] would have been mustered out before now." *

Two advantages of his service in Washington, however, were that De Forest retained his rank as captain and that he came constantly under the notice of the officials of the War Department. No doubt the careful performance of his duties was partly responsible for his being promoted to brevet major in recognition "of gallant and meritorious services during the war." Though not conferred until May 15, 1866, the rank was to date from March 13, 1865. Since his clerical tasks probably were not onerous, he had time in that year to complete *Miss Ravenel's Conversion* † and to write several magazine stories.

General Grant finally succeeded: the Veteran Reserve Corps was disbanded in July, 1866, and the Veteran Reserve regiments were absorbed, for limited service, in the regular army. De Forest, however, escaped its collapse by being transferred to the Freedmen's Bureau, the authority for this and similar assignments being the third Freedmen's Bureau bill, enacted on July 16, 1866, which, in addition to continuing the existence of the Bureau, empowered Commissioner Howard to appoint as clerks and assistant commissioners men detailed from the army. For the next two months De Forest served on a board for revising the regulations of the Bureau, now directed to assume increased responsibilities. The new law stipulated that the Commissioner and the Bureau officers should "extend military protection and have military jurisdiction over all cases and questions concerning the free enjoyment of . . . rights and immunities." This authority, however, was to be exercised only in the districts where the judicial processes of civil law had been interrupted either as the result of the war or as the result of "unreconstructed" interpretations of prevailing laws.

* A. L. S. John William De Forest to Andrew De Forest, October 22, 1865 (in the De Forest Collection, Yale University Library).

† Although Harper and Brothers bought the novel, in December, 1865, for serial publication in *Harper's New Monthly Magazine,* the firm changed its plans and decided to print De Forest's work in book form. A new agreement was signed in October, 1866, and *Miss Ravenel's Conversion* finally appeared in May, 1867.

In practice the Bureau never had enough men for the fulfill-
ment of the duties assigned to it. Where there was only a handful
of officers available to administer a state, such as South
Carolina, with 700,000 inhabitants and an area of 31,000
square miles, even the regions of dense Negro population were
wretchedly understaffed; and in regions of sparser Negro population a very extensive area was often placed under the control
of a lone officer, with not even a corporal and a squad of men to
support him. Thus De Forest had charge of three large counties,
which he called his "satrapy," and he would, no doubt, have
agreed heartily with a correspondent of the *Nation,* who wrote
from South Carolina that "an officer of the greatest ability and
activity, with the best intentions, would find it almost impossible
with the means now in his control, to protect all the negroes in one
of these wide-extending districts." This comment implies that
not all officers were men of the highest capacity, and, indeed,
lack of training and merit among the officials of the Bureau
seems to have been its second major weakness. Sidney Andrews,
after traveling across South Carolina in 1865, wrote of the
Bureau agents: "The probabilities are that half the aggregate
number on duty at any given time are wholly unfit for the work
entrusted to them." He cited the official at Orangeburg as an
example: "His position . . . is a difficult one; and he brings
to it a head more or less muddled with liquor, a rough and
coarse manner, a dictatorial and impatient temper, a most remarkable ability for cursing, and a hearty contempt for 'the
whole d—n pack o' niggers.' " Such men as these bore varied
responsibilities that would have taxed the combined capacities
of a social service worker, an administrative official, a labor con-
ciliator, and a judge. They were required to supervise labor contracts between employers and freedmen, to administer rations
and clothing to the destitute freedmen, to promote and supervise
schools for the Negroes, to provide transportation where it
would serve a beneficial purpose, to investigate complaints and
disputes between the Negroes themselves or between Negroes
and whites, to forestall any acts of violence against the Negroes,
or any unfairness to them in the courts, to report such cases as
could not be forestalled, and to maintain industry and good
conduct among the Negroes themselves. These duties they must

perform within the inflexible routine of the Army, with its elaborate system of reports and its rigid requirements of accountability for equipment and supplies. These objectives they must achieve through their own jurisdiction, without transgressing upon the ill-defined authority of civil officials or military government, for their administration was quite separate from that of the military governor of the district.

It was to this exacting duty that John William De Forest came on October 1, 1866.

In coming to Greenville, De Forest was renewing an old acquaintance with South Carolina. Eleven years previously, in the spring of 1855, he had met in New Haven Harriet Silliman Shepard, daughter of Charles Upham Shepard. Shepard, a cousin of Ralph Waldo Emerson and a widely traveled man, enjoyed an international reputation as a geologist. At this time he was serving both as professor of Chemistry and Natural History at Amherst and as professor of Chemistry at the Medical College in Charleston, South Carolina, in which state he became a founder of the phosphate industry. When he and his family went south for the winter term, De Forest, who was courting Harriet, accompanied them. In the year following, he married her, and, for most of the next two years, they lived in South Carolina. After their return to Connecticut in 1858, they made frequent southern visits. In fact, they were in Charleston in January, 1861, and sailed north on the last steamer to leave before the fall of Fort Sumter. Thus De Forest, when he arrived in Greenville in 1866, was already thoroughly acquainted with Southern society, its manners and its traditions.

During her husband's tour of duty in South Carolina, Mrs. De Forest remained in New England where she was better able to watch over the education of their son, young Louis Shepard De Forest. In fact, the uncertainty of his prospects in the Veteran Reserve Corps had discouraged De Forest from sending for his family even while he had been stationed in Washington. "It is not worth while," he had written to his brother, "to bring them on at a considerable expense, merely to take them back again." * Similar uncertainty about the length of his stay

---

* A. L. S. John William De Forest to Andrew De Forest, October 22, 1865 (in the De Forest Collection, Yale University Library).

in Greenville, and also his knowledge of the inadequate living accommodations which would be available in a community struggling desperately to recover its social and economic equilibrium were probably two important considerations which kept him from bringing his family with him to South Carolina. No doubt he felt that his wife and his son would be better taken care of in New England where they could turn to his brother, Andrew W. De Forest, in New Haven or to Dr. Shepard in Amherst.

In the initial enthusiasm for his new duties, De Forest was accustomed to begin his workday at eight in the morning. Then he delayed until nine o'clock, and finally until ten. Remaining at his hotel across the street from his office in the courthouse to smoke his after-breakfast pipe and to read the Charleston papers which had arrived on the previous evening, he watched for the arrival of his constituents. In spite of the clerical work necessary in reporting the official business of his district, and in spite of the number of people who came to him for advice and help, De Forest soon found that from three to five hours of labor were usually sufficient to discharge his daily duties, but he did not seek, during his leisure time, to secure a position in Greenville society. Fearing lest the ties of hospitality should hamper him in urging complaints against some of the citizens, he remained aloof and consciously refrained from incurring social obligations.

De Forest's position in Greenville was not enviable. Except for mere civilities, he was not generally accepted by what aristocracy was left after the war. How objectionable a person he was to the "high-toned" gentleman of South Carolina he acknowledges in his remark: "To my native infamy as a Yankee I added the turpitude of being a United States military officer and the misdemeanor of being a sub-assistant commissioner of the Freedmen's Bureau." There can be no doubt, however, that De Forest performed his duties faithfully, and it was probably in recognition of his work among the freedmen that he was offered a first lieutenancy in a colored regiment of the regular army. Since he wished to return home to resume his literary labors, he refused the offer and was content merely to finish his term of service. At length, on January 1, 1868, six years and one month after he had entered the Twelfth Connecticut Volunteers, he was mustered out of the army for the second and final time.

De Forest's impulse to write about South Carolina can be dated from his first visits there in 1855. On November 7 of that year, for instance, he wrote from Charleston to his brother: "I should like to have my letters preserved, as I mean to make them a sort of book of travels, as far at least as Charleston is concerned." * Nor is this the sole indication of De Forest's careful habit of keeping alive impressions which might later be useful in his career as an author. Additional evidence that he added to his reservoir of observations at every opportunity is contained in a chance remark in *A Volunteer's Adventures* concerning an interview with General Benjamin F. Butler: "In my character of novelist I made a study of him."

If, therefore, De Forest did not begin to write the account of his experiences as an official of the Freedmen's Bureau while he still was on duty at Greenville, he certainly studied carefully the region and the people and probably made notes, either in the form of memoranda or in the form of letters home, with a view to preparing some kind of narrative. Such a narrative was not long delayed in appearing, for as early as May, 1868, only five months after the expiration of his service, *Harper's Monthly* published an article entitled "Drawing Bureau Rations." Eight other articles on other aspects of Reconstruction or of Southern society appeared in rapid succession in *Harper's,* the *Atlantic Monthly,* and *Putnam's Magazine,* so that, by February, 1869, the series had reached completion. Although published at random, and without sequence in the order of their appearance, these articles naturally fell into a logical pattern and were potentially material for a book. In later years, therefore, probably in the 'eighties, De Forest collected them, rewrote paragraphs here and there, and grouped them into a connected whole. Just as he had sought to preserve his personal record of the war by gathering his letters and periodical articles into a single manuscript which he entitled, "A Volunteer's Adventures," so also, he sought to preserve his personal record of

* A. L. S. John William De Forest to Andrew De Forest, November [7], 1855 (in the De Forest Collection, Yale University Library).

Reconstruction by gathering his articles into a companion manuscript entitled "The Bureau Major." It is this second manuscript which forms the text of the present volume, though the editors have ventured to substitute another title in place of one which would be almost meaningless today. At the beginning of each chapter in this volume, a note is appended showing the exact date of the original article and the magazine in which it appeared.

If, at any time, De Forest offered either his war or his Reconstruction manuscripts for publication in book form, they were not accepted. *A Volunteer's Adventures* remained unpublished until 1946, and the articles on Reconstruction have lain dissevered and forgotten in the files of old magazines. Thus the organic form which De Forest intended to impose on them has never been shown.

This neglect is especially regrettable in view of the carefully developed organization in the final account. For the series of articles, in fact, undertook to make a comprehensive report on two things—the practical operation of the Freedmen's Bureau in a specific district, and the structure of Southern society.

In reading De Forest's account, written as it is in easy, spontaneous, and effortless prose, one thinks of the discussion as being casual, almost conversational, in its quality. Yet it is remarkably accurate and detailed, despite this apparently offhand manner, and it describes, in turn, all the various functions of the Freedmen's Bureau, as carefully as if a formal treatise were intended. To appreciate this thoroughness, one need only compare this account with some of the monographic literature which examines, in series, the various phases of Bureau administration, such as the program to protect the freedmen from violence or official injustice; the relief measures to alleviate distress by the free distribution of food and clothing; the supervision of labor relationships through the regulation of contracts binding freedmen to certain terms of employment; the long-range plans to develop the capacity of the freedmen by providing elementary education for them; the policy, which today would be called a resettlement program, to encourage Negro workers to remove to places where free land or attractive wages were available; and the granting of free transportation to facilitate such removal. These and certain subsidiary activities constituted the legitimate province of the Bureau, though there were, of course, instances where it was used, as any relief agency may be, to build a political machine. So far as its proper functions were concerned, however, it will appear, upon examination, that De Forest has, in his disarmingly easy style, provided a systematic and thorough coverage of every significant category of Bureau business. And where the more academic treatise tends to show only what policy existed, De Forest explains also what result was attained. Since no institution becomes in practice what it was intended to be in theory, De Forest's study of the actual operation and the day-to-day business of a Bureau office assumes especial value. Despite the copious supply of official reports, and the various analyses of Bureau activities as viewed from the top, it is doubtful that there can be found anywhere a more revealing account of what this vast government agency was like at the critical point where its policy was translated into action.

This account of the Bureau occupies De Forest's first four chapters. In the six that remain, he turns to a topic which would prove thorny enough at any time, but which in the 'sixties presented a maximum of difficulties—that is, to an analysis of the classes of society in the South.

Of the scant realism which cast its light upon the discussion of any subject in that decade, almost none, it is safe to say, had illumined the understanding of this topic. For well over a generation, as Clement Eaton has shown in his *Freedom of Thought in the Old South,* the South had placed an embargo on free inquiry—an embargo which De Forest himself mentions in Chapter X. This taboo, centering on the slavery question, also extended to tangential matters. If slavery were, as asserted, "a positive good," the society built upon it must also be above reproach, and, as a result, Southern writers, maintaining this view, had indulged in the wildest extravagancies of flamboyant romanticism. Intent upon believing that their system of landed estates and social stratification had re-established in the Cotton Belt the very distillation of the values of the Age of Chivalry, they had fallen to depicting themselves, both in their fictional and their non-fictional literature, as embodiments of knighthood and the feudal age. In this process some of the very substantial merits of their society became intermingled with such exaggerations and posturings as to render the composite picture incredible.

As an offset to this dominant tradition, it should be added that there were a few Southern writers like Augustus B. Longstreet, Joseph G. Baldwin, J. J. Hooper, and H. E. Taliaferro, who held a strong enough grip upon actualities to recognize that the illiterate, non-slaveholding farmers of the Southern backwoods were far too earthy to be considered cavaliers, and far too bumptious to be regarded as serfs in a chivalric society. These writers, therefore, had begun to exploit a secondary theme: the robust vigor of the hardy, boisterous, independent spirited farmers who flourished beyond the charmed circle of the gentry. Yet, as if in deference to a caste tradition which holds that kings speak blank verse, while clowns speak prose, that only those of noble class merit serious literary treatment, these writers customarily presented their subjects as picaresque and comic figures, in whom the genteel reader might condescend to find amusement. Longstreet, in fact, showed signs of regret, that he, a clergyman, had ever stooped to such a theme

While this was the Southern view of its own society, the anti slavery crusade had gone far to crystallize a contrasting view which was, in its own way, even more of a stereotype, and quite as exaggerated in its romanticism—though here the romantic theme employed diabolic, rather than chivalric properties. It is true that Mrs. Stowe had attempted to record the merits as well as the evils of Southern society, but Northern writers, for the most part, placed major emphasis upon a portrayal of a brutal, overbearing master class—monsters of sadistic lust and heartless exploitation. In their characterization, the non-slaveholding white existed chiefly to execute, as an overseer, the evil purpose of the master, or to illustrate, as a victim, the arrogance of the master class. Thus, Northern authors as well as Southern denied the non-slaveholding class recognition in its own right.

Although there may be some who, by modern standards, will question De Forest's impartiality as a social critic—for he is severe in his strictures both upon the chivalry and upon the Negroes—his analysis appears astonishingly accurate and discriminating in contrast to stereotypes which surrounded him. At the top of the social scale, as he saw it, was that limited group whom he accepted as being "chivalrous Southrons." The best representatives of this class enjoyed advantages of tradition and breeding, and had responded to the challenge of *noblesse oblige* in a way that led De Forest to speak approvingly of their consideration for others, their unpretentious dignity, their grace of bearing, their genuine courtesy, and their personal courage. Even here, however, he appraised their hot tempers—their pugnacity as he termed it—and their emphasis upon virility, with an astringent disregard of romantic values.

Next below the gentry, he identifies a class of "semi-chivalrous Southrons," men who in his own district had opposed secession, but who in the larger sense represented the class of small farmers. Often illiterate and painfully limited in experience, they had in some cases picked up the hot-tempered behavior, if not the courtesy, of the gentry, so that there was a basis for calling them semi-chivalrous. The best of them were "honest, worthy, generous, hospitable" folk, and they were sometimes rich in terms of land, but not in those of money or education.

Though De Forest deals with these "poor, uncultured, and, in some cases, half-wild people" primarily as Unionists, it is significant that in them he observes a distinct gradation between the chivalry and the miserable class usually known as "poor-whites." Inasmuch as some of the most important analyses of recent years * have been devoted to the overthrow of the concept of a complete duality in Southern society, it is striking to note that De Forest, more than seventy years ago, recognized an intermediate element. He probably did not look upon it as being either as important or as respectable a class as some modern investigators believe it to have been. Be this as it may, however,

---

* *e. g.*, Benjamin B. Kendrick and Alex M. Arnett, *The South Looks at Its Past* (Chapel Hill, 1935); "Middle Class and Bourbon" by Clarence E. Cason, in W. T. Couch, editor, *Culture in the South* (Chapel Hill, 1935); Frank L. and Harriet C. Owsley, "The Economic Basis of Society in the Late Ante-Bellum South" and "The Economic Structure of Rural Tennessee, 1850–1860," in *Journal of Southern History*, VI (1940), 24–45, and VIII (1942), 161–182; Blanche Henry Clark, *The Tennessee Yeoman, 1840–1860* (Nashville, 1942); and Herbert Weaver, *Mississippi Farmers, 1850–1860* (Nashville, 1945).

one will hardly find so mature, fully developed, and perceptive a survey of this level of Southern society until the social sciences began to concern themselves with such matters in recent years.

On a level below the "semi-chivalrous Southrons" were "the low-down people," the term applied in Greenville District to the "poor-whites." Here, almost for the first time, this anomalous class is accorded serious rather than comic treatment. It is not respectful treatment, to be sure, for having little faith in the typically Northern hope that the "low-downer" could be reclaimed, De Forest described the type with a frankness that bordered on contempt. As Shields McIlwaine has suggested in *The Southern Poor-White from Lubberland to Tobacco Road,* De Forest's account was the first to depict this class as it later appeared in twentieth-century fiction when the vogue of the sharecropper became widespread.

The Negroes, so recently freed, were, of course, the most controversial class of all. Concerning them, De Forest might have been expected to share the abolitionist view so prevalent in New England. But, in fact, he had rejected it long before becoming a Bureau official, for when he first visited South Carolina in 1855, he had written home to his brother Andrew that the Southern blacks "are not worth all the hul[l]abaloo that is made about them. They are kept ignorant and animal, say the abolitionists. Granted. But their great, great grandfathers in Africa were four times as ignorant and at least twice as animal. . . . So much for my present feeling and ideas with regard to slavery. They may change on further observation." *

His attitude did change, probably in response to his original zeal as a Bureau Major. At first he told the people of Greenville "that soon their finest houses would be in possession of blacks," but he was forced to abandon this expectation of Negro progress when he observed what he saw as the freedman's shiftlessness his lack of responsibility, and his failure to conform to the moral code of the white race. De Forest's final censure was not directed against the Negroes, but against the circumstances which brought the race "to sharp trial before its time." "This new, varied, costly

* A. L. S. John William De Forest to Andrew De Forest, November [7], 1855 (in the De Forest Collection, Yale University Library).

life of freedom," he prophesied, "this struggle to be at once like a race which has passed through a two-thousand-years' growth in civilization, will probably diminish the productiveness of the Negro and will terribly test his vitality." Holding this somewhat deterministic view, De Forest showed an equal readiness to recognize either the defects or the merits of Negro character as he found it–the unreliability and lack of industry on one hand, the unselfishness and the zeal for education on the other. Without palliating the exploitation of the Negroes, he constantly refused to accept predictions of progress which did not allow for the way in which slavery had conditioned the character of the first generation of freedmen. It is perhaps indicative of his objective approach that he attributed both the good and bad qualities–the generosity and the unscrupulousness–to the same source, namely, "an imperfect moral education as to the distinction between *meum* and *tuum:* the Negro learned slowly that he had a full right to his own property, that his neighbor had a full right to his."

This was the range of Southern society as De Forest observed it. Allying himself neither with those who regarded the Southern gentleman as the epitome of a gracious society, nor with those who prophesied that the Negro possessed potentialities which needed only a short period of nominal freedom to flower, De Forest restrained his personal prejudices and described accurately and candidly the people with whom he came in contact when he served as a Bureau Major. Though his unpretentious record was confined to one agency, one officer, and the population of one district, the justice of his appraisal gives his account pertinence in the evaluation of the entire reconstruction program and in the understanding of the passing of one social order and the advent of another.

The original manuscript of *A Union Officer in the Reconstruction* is preserved in Yale University Library among the De Forest papers which the owner, L. Effingham de Forest, kindly allowed the editors to consult. De Forest's official correspondence and reports as an agent of the Freedmen's Bureau are now deposited in the War Department files in the National Archives, and the editors have been permitted to use them freely.

These documents have provided supplemental information on parts of De Forest's work and have validated innumerable statements in the manuscript.

In preparing De Forest's text for the press, the editors have made no changes except to regularize punctuation and spelling and to rectify about ten of De Forest's oversights in correcting proof. They have retained his notes with the abbreviation De F. as a distinguishing mark, and have included additional notes only when these seemed necessary for a clearer understanding by a twentieth-century reader. In the division of editorial duties, in general, Mr. Croushore has prepared the text and has contributed those parts of the Introduction and notes which relate to De Forest or to literary points, while Mr. Potter has been responsible for the parts of the Introduction and notes which deal with the history of Reconstruction, or with Southern society.

CONTENTS

AUTHOR'S PREFACE

I HAD been adjutant-general of the Veteran Reserve Corps, and when that ceased to exist I was placed on duty in the Bureau of Refugees, Freedmen and Abandoned Lands, commonly called the Freedmen's Bureau.

On the 2^d of October, 1866, I took charge of the sub-district of Greenville, South Carolina, with the official title of Acting Assistant Commissioner. My satrapy consisted of the two counties of Greenville and Pickens, and was subsequently increased by the addition of the county of Anderson, the whole including a surface of some three thousand square miles and a population of perhaps eighty thousand souls. My capital was the little borough of Greenville, situated in the northwestern part of the state, two hundred and seventy miles from Charleston, and within sight of the lower extension of the Alleghenies.

In population and wealth Greenville was then the third town in South Carolina, ranking next after Charleston and Columbia. It boasted an old and a new courthouse, four churches and several chapels, a university (not the largest in the world), a female college (also not unparalleled), two or three blocks of stores, one of the best country hotels then in the South, quite a number of comfortable private residences, fifteen hundred whites and a thousand or so of other colors.

The neighboring scenery is varied and agreeable, and picturesque highlands are not far away. In a latitude of rice and cotton, but with an elevation of one thousand feet above the sea, the climate has a winter which resembles a Northern November, and a summer which is all June.

The officer whom I relieved said to me, with an expression of good-natured envy, "You have the best station in the state."

His eulogium referred more particularly to the inhabitants. He went on at some length to declare that they were orderly, respectful to the national authorities, disposed to treat the Negroes considerately, and, in short, praiseworthily "reconstructed."

"The worst social feature is the poverty," he added. "There

are numbers of old Negroes who are living on their bankrupted former masters. There are four hundred soldiers' widows in the district of Greenville, and six hundred in that of Pickens. You can imagine the orphans."

Such was my field of duty.

CHAPTER I

A REPORT OF OUTRAGES [1]

AT the close of every month a Bureau officer made out a report of "outrages committed by whites against freedmen," and another of "outrages committed by freedmen against whites." As each of these papers was in triplicate —one copy for the Assistant Commissioner of the state, one for the military commandant of the district, and one for retention —it follows that during my fifteen months of duty, I ruled and filled out and certified to just ninety documents of this nature. In this period there were, if I remember aright, seven outrages, which makes very nearly one-thirteenth of an outrage to each paper. For the more convenient information of the public I will consolidate my ninety reports into one.

THE CASE OF CATO ALLUMS

The first morning after my predecessor had turned over to me his records and left me alone in my South Carolina pashalic —at six o'clock on that morning of new responsibilities and untried power, a timorous yet persistent rap roused me from bed. Hastening to the door in such drapery as could be secured at once, I set it ajar and looked out upon a Negro of about thirty-five, medium in height, but singularly muscular in build, whose eager face and somewhat crouching carriage indicated strong anxiety for protection.

"Good morning, Sir," he said in better English than was common to our manumitted slaves. "I wants very much to see you, Sir, right away."

"Wait till I have dressed," I answered. "I will be out in ten minutes."

1. Published originally in *Harper's New Monthly Magazine*, XXXVIII (December, 1868), 75–84.

"But it's mighty pressin', Boss," he insisted. "It's something that's following me up mighty sharp. I wants to speak to you now."

"Go on," I assented and, letting him into the room, proceeded to dress in his presence.

"Did you ever hear of me—Cato Allums?" he asked. "Cap'm Bray was a mighty good friend to me, and holped me powerful. If you've got his papers, I reckon you'll find my name on 'em. I'm the man that was robbed by a gang from old Jimmy Johnson's house last year; robbed of two thousan' poun's of meat and a heap of other things. Cap'm Bray took up for me—the Lord A'mighty bless him for his friendship to me! I wish he was here now. That was some of old Jimmy Johnson's mischief. But I won't talk about that ar. I've got a worse trial on hand. It's been a bad night for me, Boss—I don't know what your title is. I'll tell you how it happened. Last night, after we was all in bed—me and my brother-in-law and his wife and children—comes a rap at the door. Well, ye see I've been so hunted and robbed by these yere bushwhackers that I wasn't gwine to let nobody in without knowing who 'twas; and so says I, 'Who's thar?' I couldn' make out much what they said, though they said something—kind o' muttered, like they didn' want to show who they was. Then I gets up and goes to the door with my revolver in my hand: Cap'm Bray give me the revolver; he did, Boss, and told me to shoot any man, white or black, that attacked me; he said he'd see me out in it. 'Who's thar?' says I. They kep' knocking, and didn' speak. Then I looked out of the cracks in the logs and made out by the moon that thar was five or six of 'em. Says I, 'You can't come in yere unless I know who you be.' Then they begun to drive at the do' with a log, and jest as it give in I heard one of 'em say, 'Break it down and shoot every boogar of 'em.' Well, Boss, when the do' come down I jumped out to run; I reckoned they was the same men that had robbed me befo', and had come now to kill me; for many and many has said to me, 'Cato, they'll bushwhack you yet for following 'em up so.' Jest as I jumped out, one of 'em fired and missed me. Then I saw another aiming at me, with his pistol resting on his arm. Boss, I—" (Here his face quivered, and he looked at me with indescribable anxiety.) "I shot him."

"You did?" I answered. "It's my belief that you served him perfectly right."

He drew a long breath, sat down in a chair to which I had previously signed him, seemed to rest his jaded soul for a moment, and then continued his story:

"Boss, you don' know how I felt that minute; I never shot a man befo'. But I couldn' stop to think about it. I run with all my might for the road, they a-shooting after me, and one bullet hitting the fence as I jumped it; and in a minute or two I was in the woods and out of their sight. I don' know whether the man is dead; all I knows is that he fell over when I shot; I don' know who he was—don' know any of 'em."

"Where did this happen?" I inquired.

"Over in the edge of Pickens District, about ten miles from yere, and two miles from old Jimmy Johnson's settlement; and that's whar all my troubles has started from, Boss; that old Jimmy Johnson has been a sore neighbor for me."

An hour later, seated in my office, I made a further investigation into the case of Cato Allums. I found a file of papers, signed by Captain Bray, one of my predecessors, showing that Cato had indeed been robbed about a year previous and that the efforts of the military authorities had not been able to discover the malefactors, although "old Jimmy Johnson," the supposed instigator of the mischief, had been arrested and confined for a season in Castle Pinckney at Charleston. While I was studying into these by-gone matters Cato stepped out in search of an acquaintance to vouch for his character. He returned with one of those devil-may-care, dissipated-looking youths whom one so frequently meets at the South, and who have the air of being a cross between the plug-ugly, the fine gentleman, and the professional gambler.

"Major, this boy is sound," asseverated the stranger, with many oaths. "He's a square, decent, sensible, polite nigger. I've known Cato ever since I was a baby, and I never had but one thing against him. He's just as civil a nigger as need be. No gentleman ever had cause to quarrel with him in no way, shape, nor manner. Wherever Cato goes, if he meets a gentleman, he offs hat and says, 'Good morning'; and if he sees a gentleman coming across the fields he puts down the bars for him; just as polite, decent a nigger, Major, as you can find! I'll allow that Cato is sharp on a trade; if you go to swapping horses with him you've got to keep your eye skinned; he an't a-going to make money for you out of his own pocket."

"Well, I s'pose a man has a right to look out for himself," suggested the Negro apologetically.

"That's so, Cato," assented the youngster. "I ha'n't got a word to say against you on that account. If ever you trade horses with me you are welcome to cheat me, if you can. I tell you, Major, I've only one thing against Cato. They do say he kept a white woman for his wife or something. I don't know how it is, whether it's so or not; only I do say that if he did that he did wrong. Yes, Cato, if you did that you did wrong, and I can't uphold you in it."

"They said so," admitted Cato, who had looked monstrously uneasy under this charge. "But when the woman had a baby a while ago it was just as white and pretty a baby as ever you saw. It wa'n't no nigger's baby."

"Well, if that's so, it's all right. I an't down on you, Cato, about it, if it an't as they say 'tis. As for killing this man last night I don't know anything about it, in no way, shape, nor manner. I don't know who the man is, nor what he was thar for. But I'll bet ten dollars, Major, that Cato served him right in shooting him. I'll swap horses even with Cato on that. I say, Cato, whenever you want to trade your sorrel mare, let me know."

Meanwhile I was pondering as to what I should do with my homicide. A few months later I should have suspended my judgment with regard to the truth of his story until after I had heard the other side and examined somewhat into the evidence. But in my present state of inexperience I believed Cato Allums; believed that his house had been broken open by men who might be assassins, and were unquestionably burglars; believed that he was a worthy applicant for such protection and counsel as lay in the Freedmen's Bureau.

It was a dubious and critical matter to handle. On the one hand, I wanted to make sure that this man should not fall a victim to any burst of popular fury, and that the bushwhackers who had outraged him should be brought to condign punishment. On the other hand, I so interpreted my orders as to believe that my first and great duty lay in raising the blacks and restoring the whites of my district to a confidence in civil law, and thus fitting both as rapidly as possible to assume the duties of citizenship. If the military power were to rule them forever— if it were to settle all their difficulties without demanding of them any exercise of judgment or self-control, how could they ever be, in any profound and lasting sense, "reconstructed?" If there were to be any beginning in this essential work, it might as well come at once. Leaving Cato locked up in my office, I called on the leading lawyer of the Greenville bar, well known throughout the country as Governor Perry,[2] but not then noted as an opponent of the Congressional plan of reconstruction; and after relating to him the case of Cato Allums, asked him if the civil authorities could be trusted to manage it with firmness and justice.

"They can," he assured me. "If the magistrate of this man's neighborhood is not fit for his post, you can refer it to the solicitor of the district court, Mr. Jacob Reed of Anderson. You may be sure that he will do the same justice by a Negro as by a white man."

Returning to Cato, I told him that he must go home, apply to his magistrate as an injured and innocent man, make a formal complaint against the persons who had molested him, and demand an investigation. He looked exceedingly gloomy and answered, "But, Boss, what if they should arrest *me?*"

"You must let yourself be arrested, if they do it according to the forms of law. Killing a man is serious business and can not be passed over without grave notice."

"Oh, if you knew how many men had been shot up our way, and nothing said! Jest shot down, Master, right in thar own do's, and no law about it! I tell you, Boss, I don't like to be tried. They'd make believe try me, and they'd jest hang me. I tell you, it's mighty resky."

"We must see," I replied. "I could protect you now, no doubt; but my protection would not last for long; in a year or two the

2. See Introduction, p. vi f.

Bureau and the garrisons will go.[3] If your case is not brought to a settlement now, it will be then. Settle it at once, while the Yankees are here to see that you have justice. Don't put yourself in the position of an outlaw, subject to be hunted for life."

After a long discussion he consented to return home and report himself to the nearest magistrate. I gave him a letter to the official,[4] in which I stated the matter as it appeared to me, representing it as an attack of burglars upon the house of a peaceful citizen and demanding that the gang should be traced, arrested, and punished.

"The point now is to reach your magistrate before any further bloodshed takes place," I said to him as he rose to leave. "Can you get home safely?"

"Oh, yes!" he laughed. "I knows every road and cross-cut. It would be mighty hard to trap me, Boss. And if any man does git a holt on me," he added, pointing to his revolver, "he'll let go agin in a hurry."

During the next three days I had many fears for Cato Al-

3. On December 31, 1868, all the Freedmen's Bureau except the educational department withdrew from South Carolina, as required by act of Congress, but at the time when De Forest wrote, the Bureau was operating under an act which extended its operations only to July 16, 1868. Laura J. Webster, "The Operation of the Freedmen's Bureau in South Carolina," pp. 91–92, in *Smith College Studies in History*, Vol. I, Nos. 2–3.

4. The text of this letter to James Parsons, October 4, 1866, is preserved in the official letter book which De Forest kept, and is now part of the large collection of Freedmen's Bureau material in the National Archives. The letter book and the official reports which form part of the same collection give full details on the case of Cato Allums and on De Forest's action in connection with it. He reported the matter on October 4 to Lieutenant Colonel H. R. Smith, A.A.G., at state headquarters; on October 6 he wrote to J. P. Reed, solicitor for the Pickens District, requesting action against the attackers; on October 10 and October 30 he wrote additional letters to Parsons, expressing satisfaction with the treatment accorded Allums and inquiring whether the attackers had been arrested; he sent inquiries, on November 23, to J. P. Reed, and to the Clerk of Court, Pickens Court House, inquiring whether Allums had been released; and he sent a message to Thomas Dillard, magistrate, May 6, 1867, requiring to know whether Dillard had at any time refused to issue a warrant on an affidavit concerning the robbery of Allums. In addition to corroborating the account given in the text, these letters show that Allums had been a free Negro before the Civil War. Five of the six men who attacked Allums's house are specifically named, and Joseph Williams is mentioned as the man whom Allums shot.

The editors wish to thank Miss Elizabeth Drewry of the War Records Office in the National Archives for her help in making available De Forest's official reports and correspondence.

lums. Pickens District was a vast region of hills and mountains, wild in its landscape, and hardly less wild in the character of many of its inhabitants, always noted for displays of individual pugnacity, and stained since the advent of secession with the blood of several Unionists. I feared that I had sent this man to sure destruction at the hands of the bushwhackers who then infested South Carolina, or of a mob of citizens roused to fury by the spectacle of a white slain by a Negro.

On the fourth day my anxiety was somewhat relieved by the appearance of a Pickens farmer, in homespun, who delivered a letter from James Parsons, the magistrate of the "beat" in which Cato lived. From the letter and the messenger I gleaned the following facts with regard to the outrage. The gang which attacked Cato's house consisted of five "mean whites" from Anderson District, who, with the usual disregard of their caste for Poor Richard's axiom that time is money, had ridden no less than twenty-four miles to effect their picayune stroke of business. Of course they had their side of the story to tell; they had gone to Cato's place, they said, to recover a pistol which he had stolen from one of their number; they had knocked civilly at his door and had only broken it in when he threatened to shoot them.

The letter added that Jack Williams, the injured man, had received a ball through the intestines and was lying at the house of a neighbor of Parsons, in great agony and near to death. He had made his affidavit that he meant no harm to Cato Allums and that, so far from aiming a pistol, he was endeavoring to escape when overtaken by the fatal bullet.

"It's a tough lot, I reckon," commented the messenger. "Willums's wife has come up to see him, an' she told him it served him right for meddlin' with a nigger."

The letter went on to state that, as soon as Williams should die, a coroner's jury would be empaneled and that, according to the civil law, the verdict of the jury would decide whether Cato should or should not be prosecuted as a criminal.

"What is the feeling in your district with regard to this affair?" I asked the messenger.

"Well, we think the nigger ought to be tried. Shootin' a white man an't no joke. If they get a notion that they can do it whenever they think they ought to, they'll think they ought to oftener than will be comfortable."

"Do you mean to give him a fair trial? Or will you get up a mob and lynch him?"

"We're bound to give him as fair a trial as a white man would have," he replied somewhat indignantly. "We ha'n't no use for lynching. We're a law-abiding people, Major."

Somewhat doubting this last assertion, I nevertheless resolved to continue my experiment, knowing that, if it ended well, it would be the best ending possible.

"See that you do give him a fair trial," I exhorted. "Obey precisely the instructions of your magistrate, who seems to be a judicious and conscientious man. Do the thing justly, and you shall be sustained in it. Tell your neighbors that; tell them that the United States Government wants nothing but justice; tell them that I am here simply to see justice carried out."

I wrote another letter to Parsons, approving of his course, directing him to call on the military for assistance if necessary to prevent a mob, and urging him not to neglect using the law against the whites if they should prove to be burglars, as well as against the black if he should prove to be an assassin. In a day or two a reply came, stating that Williams was dead and that the coroner's jury had charged Cato Allums with willful murder.

"Under the circumstances I must issue a warrant for his arrest," added the magistrate. "I do not see how else I can carry out even the appearance of civil law. I trust that you will make no objection. And if you meet up with him I hope you will be so good as tell him not to make resistance. He has not yet been to see me. He sent me your first letter, instead of bringing it to me; and I hear that he is lying out and says he won't be tried."

The next morning Cato arrived on his sorrel mare, revolver in belt.

"Well, Master, they're boun' to be the death of me," he said. "They've brought me in guilty without tryin' me. And now, if they kin ketch me, they'll hang me up to the first tree. That's the way courts is for niggers."

So I was obliged to explain the mystery of law to this man who had never lived under the law, and who knew little more of it than if he were a native of the Marquesas. It was hard work to make a fellow whose neck was in danger understand the deliberate wisdom of that sequence of the coroner's jury, the grand jury, and the criminal jury; and Cato had more objections to the safety and sagacity of the process than I can now remember; but the substance of them was that he did not believe in the good faith of Southern jurors.

"Ef they once git me in Pickens Court House jail, I'm a gone nigger," said he. "I'll go in jail yere, with this garrison close by and a big village full of 'spectable people. But Pickens Court House is no place at all. It's jest a few houses. The bushwhackers will come in and take me out o' jail and hang me."

"If you are injured unlawfully I will see that those who do it are severely punished," I replied. "But you must take the risk, if there is any. I should demand that of a white man. Look here, Cato, can you fairly ask anything more than a white man's chance?"

"No, Master, I can't," he replied after a moment of reflection. "I'd scorn to ask more'n a white man's chance. Well, Master, I'll do what you say; I'll go back to Mars Parsons and give myself up."

He had scarcely been gone twenty minutes before Parsons's constable arrived in search of him, accompanied by two assistants, all armed with revolvers.

"Cato has gone to surrender himself," I assured them. "I am surprised that you did not meet him."

"Gone to surrender himself!" exclaimed the constable with some indignation at the absurdity of the story. "You won't catch him doing that without a fight. He's a bad, hard nigger, Sir. He's gone to Tennessee, most likely. Which road did he take, Sir?"

"The road to Pickens, as I believe. If you want to find him, go back to Mr. Parsons; that is the best advice that I can give you."

The men looked at each other doubtfully; they were perfectly respectful, but they did not trust me. Noting the hard, pugnacious expression of their faces, an expression very common in the wilder districts of the South, I thought it best to advise them against violence.

"If you meet him, treat him gently," I said. "Make no threats or threatening gestures, and I will be bound that he will offer no resistance."

"We won't hurt him unless he tries to fight or escape," they answered. "If he sets in for anything of that sort we must do our sworn duty. I hope you wouldn't ask anything less of us, Major."

A day or two later Mr. Parsons paid me a visit, bringing the information that Cato had surrendered himself and was in Pickens Court House jail.

"Now then," said I, "let us see if the whites of your district are worthy of living in the same region with this Negro. He has shot a man, as he believes, justifiably and in his own defense; yet he surrenders himself to trial, as becomes a good citizen. Do you show that you can protect him in your jail and try him justly before your courts. The Northern people doubt whether you can give a Negro a white man's chance. Show that you can do it. It will be a great triumph for you; it will disprove a grave suspicion. You can not take a surer step toward recovering your rights as citizens."

My magistrate was a farmer, a plain and apparently a poor man, dressed in homespun, mild and grave in manner and, I judged, thoroughly honorable in his intentions.

"I understand the importance of doing this matter justly and according to the forms of law," he said. "I am very much obliged to you for trusting me with it, instead of managing it by means of the garrison. I believe we can show you that we mean to be as fair to a nigger as we know how to be to a white man. There is some excitement among us now; there are some fellows who are right mad at the idea of a nigger shooting a white man; and I told Cato that it was best for him to go to jail for that reason. You see, if he was not sent to jail, people would say niggers have a better chance than white folks, and would get madder than they are now, and perhaps lynch him. Yes, I allow there's some excitement; but it will blow over before long. Some folks are mighty pleased with Cato already for surrendering himself."

"But what have you done about the bushwhackers?" I asked. "Have you tried to arrest them?"

"They have put back to Anderson, where they belong, and that is out of my jurisdiction. I have sent on a statement of the case to the magistrate of their settlement, and asked him to take action in it. I can't do more."

"But don't you think your coroner's jury was a little severe on Cato?" I continued. "Don't you think Cato would have been cleared at once, if he had been white and Williams black?"

"No, Major, I don't think so," he answered firmly. "Killing a man is severe business anyhow, and ought to be thoroughly looked into. At any rate, the process has all been according to law, and even a nigger can't ask more, nor less."

This being irrefutable, I could only express my commendation of Mr. Parsons's course and urge him to be energetic in keeping the affair within the legal channel. Meantime I had forwarded a statement of Cato Allums's case to Brevet Major General Scott, the Assistant Commissioner of South Carolina,[5] and had received a reply approving my action. A month or so later the Circuit Court of Special Sessions and Common Pleas convened at Pickens Court House. There had been an inflammatory paragraph or two from those veteran blowhards and professional mischief-makers, the "sound Southern editors"; the manly act of Cato Allums in shooting a burglar had been described as the unprovoked murder of a worthy citizen by a black ruffian; but the men of Pickens District had shown themselves to be a law-abiding race, and the prisoner had not been lynched.

The case waited; the state solicitor was anxious to get it off the docket; but where were the witnesses for the prosecution? No one had been present at the tragedy but the five friends of the dead man and Cato Allums's own relatives; and from the nature of the circumstances, as well as from the ties of blood and race, these last would undoubtedly testify in favor of the prisoner. The five gentlemen from Anderson had been duly summoned, and in vain; a bench warrant was issued for their apprehension—still in the character of witnesses. But Mr. Jack Williams's nocturnal comrades were that kind of men who, to use a Southern country phrase, "have no use for a courthouse." The more they were called on to "come to court," the

5. See Introduction, p. xi f.

further and faster they went from it. The constable dispatched to find them returned to say that they were "lying out in the swamps"; and presently it was reported that they had "done gone out of the country."

This fact turned public opinion at once; the tale of the stolen pistol was dismissed from popular credence, and Cato Allums was decided to have done the duty of a good citizen in shooting a scoundrel. As Pickens District had shown itself law-abiding, so did it show itself amenable to reason and considerate in sentiment; many of the men who had insisted upon the prosecution now besieged the court to have the prisoner dismissed from further action; and among the most urgent of these was the magistrate who had committed him—Squire Parsons.

"I can not throw the case out at once," replied the solicitor. "It is my duty to hold it over till the next sessions, and see if these witnesses can not be made to appear. But the man shall be admitted to bail. I will advise that any bail be accepted which he can give."

So Cato Allums was bailed out for the low amount of one thousand dollars, on the security of his brother-in-law, a mulatto, who probably was not worth half that money. This was substantially the end of the matter, for Jack Williams's friends persisted in keeping themselves retired from the public gaze, and at the next sessions Cato was informed that he need not trouble himself further about coming to court. Somewhat disgusted at having been imprisoned and put to various costs in his own defense, he removed to East Tennessee; but, having farmed it there during one season, he got homesick for his native settlement and came back to live among his old neighbors.

"How are you treated?" I asked him when he called upon me after his return.

"I ha'n't nothing to complain of," he answered. "Everybody is friendly, and the men that wanted me tried is the friendliest of all. But, Master, I never was treated like most niggers was. Mighty few white men has tried to ride over Cato."

He was a fine, stalwart, vigorous fellow, as strong as a mule physically, and with plenty of moral muscle, all qualities which command the respect of the general Southerner. Even his sharpness in trading horses was calculated to win him the admiration

of the chaffering farmers of Pickens District. After telling
me, with some triumph, of certain of his successful dickers, he
added: "But I don't always get the best of it; I was mightily
come up with last spring when I was gwine to Tennessee. Ye
see, I sent over part of my traps by my brother-in-law and a
friend of his'n. They begged me to lend 'um my gun and one of
my revolvers, and hung to it so that I had to say yes, though I
was feared they wouldn't know how to take care of 'um. Well,
the fust night they camped out, a man in Yankee clothes came
into the camp and wanted to see their shootin' irons. Then says
he, 'It's contrary to the law for you to carry these, an' I mus'
take 'um.' And the big fools jes let him carry 'um off. If I'd been
thar, Master, he wouldn't have got 'um, not if he'd had on all
the soger clothes in the world. Of course he wasn't a Yankee; he
was some mighty smart Reb."

Then he had a couple of complaints to make: one about a
horse which had been stolen from him by bushwhackers, with
the connivance of a citizen of Abbeville; the other about a little
farm which a Pickens man had sought to swindle him out of,
on pretense of some old, uncompleted trade in Confederate
money. As General Sickles had authorized civil law in South
Carolina I advised him to try the courts, but to wait until the
stay-order [6] then in force was annulled, so as to be able to collect immediately on getting judgment. After some further talk
about the still mysterious robbery of his two thousand pounds
of bacon, and certain threats of legal vengeance against "old
Jimmy Johnson," whom he held to be somehow responsible
for it, he departed, and I saw him no more.

Such is the history of Cato Allums, as nearly as I am able
to state it from memory. So far as concerns the homicide, I considered the result a triumph of justice, public conscience, and
public sense. It had been decided, with the consent of Southern
law and Southern public opinion, that a Negro has precisely
the same right of self-defense as a white man; and thence-
forward every ruffian and bushwhacker in the region would
understand that in trespassing on the property or threatening
the life of a black he did it at his peril. The great point gained
was that the Southerners had of their own accord come to this

6. For General Sickles and this stay-order, see Introduction, p. ix f.

decision. It was far better than if the release of Cato Allums and the expatriation of his assailants had been attained by military interference.

LARGENT AND JOLY, BUSHWHACKERS

In consequence of the complaints of Cato Allums I made inquiries about "old Jimmy Johnson" (not his true name) and learned the secret of his evil reputation. From the time of the surrender down to a little before my arrival in Greenville, this northwestern portion of South Carolina had been disturbed by the misdemeanors of two noted bushwhackers or desperadoes named Largent and Joly, ex-soldiers of the Confederate army. Joly, a native of Spartanburg District, South Carolina, and a farmer by occupation, had lost a brother in the war and had avenged his death by taking a hand in the murder of some straggling Union soldiers after the proclamation of peace. Largent had been, it was reported, a Baltimore plug-ugly; but when I inquired about him of a fighting gentleman who had formerly known that city well, he could not recollect such a person.

"He must be," he said, "one of the latter-day saints; he must have come on after I left."

As is usually the case with desperate characters, both these men were under thirty years of age. This fact, that violent crime is generally youthful, seems, by the way, to be unknown to novelists; they paint their bloody-minded villains as men of mature development, fearfully grizzled and haggard with a long life of wickedness. Although Largent's motive in his murders and maraudings was apparently nothing but a love of mischief, he was much the most troublesome and formidable of the two. Small, agile, muscular, ready with his weapons, as full of stratagems as a fox, and as audacious as a wolf, he for months defied the pursuit of the garrisons of the region and made himself the terror of Union men and Negroes. He sent threatening messages to the former, bullied the latter with cocked revolver, and plundered both. Certain citizens were called to their doors of dark nights; there would be a pistol shot and the fall of a corpse; then a clatter of hoofs through the night; then silence.

Some of these atrocities were imputed to Largent and others to Joly, although there was no proof. The two scoundrels lived on the farmers of the region, sometimes remaining several weeks in one lurking place, sometimes changing their den every night. The inhabitants gave them shelter, partly from admiration of their defiance of the Yankees and partly from fear of their vindictiveness. One of their favorite resorts was the house of the above-mentioned Jimmy Johnson; and hence Cato Allums's charge that the old man connived at the robbery of his two thousand pounds of bacon.

Some of Largent's escapes from the soldiery were remarkable. Overtaken by a squad of volunteers, he fell down as if intoxicated, lay perfectly still until his pursuers were close upon him, then shot two or three men in a breath, leaped to his feet, and got away unhurt. On another occasion a company surrounded him by night in old Jimmy Johnson's house, and several were already in the veranda, blocking up his exit, when Largent rushed out with a pistol in each hand, firing right and left, and disappeared in the darkness. Twenty cartridges or more were burned in this curious *mêlée,* and yet neither pursuers nor pursued were injured.

Tired at last of being hunted, and finding that the farmers no longer received them joyfully as the redeemers of the South, the two reprobates vanished. Their departure from the district happened before my arrival, and I tell their story as I heard it, without vouching for its correctness in particulars.

TEXAS BROWN AND HIS GANG

A more impudent, pertinacious, and ferocious desperado was one Brown, called, on account of his supposed birthplace, Texas Brown, and believed to be a deserter from Wheeler's cavalry. Before I reached Greenville it was reported that a cantankerous old farmer named Ezra French, furious at two of his former slaves for quitting his employment immediately on their emancipation, had hired Brown to murder them for the consideration of two hundred dollars. Aided by two or three mean whites of the rougher sort, the Texan caught his victims, took them into a swamp, tied them to saplings, prepared and ate his supper in their presence, and then deliberately shot one of them. The other, inspired with maniacal strength by this spectacle, broke his bonds, rushed through the thickets unharmed by the bullets which were sent after him, told his tale to a terrified friend who for long kept it secret, and immediately fled from the state. This adventure led to a quarrel between Brown and his employer; for as the former had but one corpse to exhibit, the latter refused to pay more than one hundred dollars for the job; and in the constant bickerings between the two worthies the atrocity became public.

Like Joly and Largent, this scoundrel considered the world his oyster and opened it without scruple. If he saw an article that he wanted in a crossroads grocery, he took it, merely saying to the proprietor, "This suits me." If he needed lodging, he entered the house of a farmer, told his awe-inspiring name, and was entertained. If he fancied a horse, he traded for it pretty much on his own terms, or he stole it. If he met a Negro with a bundle or a cart, he appropriated therefrom whatever he fancied, made the poor, scared darkey take off his hat or get on his knees, and then dismissed him with perhaps a kicking. He had a kind of ferocious humor in his composition and delighted as much in terrifying people as in harming them. For instance, seeing three Negroes engaged in mending the roof of a barn, he amused himself with firing balls by their heads to make them dodge. Meeting a Negro with a new hat, he forced him to toss it in the air, and sent a shot through it; then ordered him to drop it in the mud and to dance upon it; then departed, saying, "Next time make a bow."

Incomprehensible and almost incredible was the imbecility, indeed I hardly know how to call it less than cowardice, with which the inhabitants, white and black, submitted to the insults and extortions of this blackguard. For months he resided in a considerable hamlet of Abbeville District, called Cokesbury, without any molestation except from an occasional and always unsuccessful raid of the neighboring garrisons of Aiken and Anderson. What with a small minority which admired him, and a vast majority which feared him, there were always men to warn him of the approach of the bluecoats, and other men, dark-minded farmers of one secluded locality or another, who would receive him into their houses until the search was over. He rode through the country with impunity; he even came into Greenville, where there was a garrison of a full company; indeed, it is my belief now that I have seen him there.

Brown was described to me as twenty-three or twenty-five years of age, of medium height, slender, sinewy, and agile, with a dark complexion, piercing black eyes, a jaw disfigured by a pistol shot, and an expression of brutal ferocity. Such a man, dressed in gray homespun, his trousers tucked into long boots, a blanket hanging from his shoulders, and a broad-brimmed black hat slouched over his ill-favored countenance, met me one winter morning in the main street of the village, eyed me with such a savage and steady glare that I turned to look at him, gave me one searching backward glance as if to see what purpose I had, and then passed on with a swagger. At the time I knew nothing of Brown's personal appearance and was not aware that he was in the habit of making such bold ventures. I simply paused to face this individual because his demeanor was offensively defiant. After all, he may not have been the Texan desperado, but some "bomb-proof"[7] hero who would not have fought a mouse.

Brown's shot in the face was the result of an "unpleasantness" with a person named Foster, against whom he had some grudge of an unknown nature, and whom he invited out on a ride, with the intent, as was supposed, of assassination. Not an innocent lamb himself, the selected victim had suspicions of danger and kept on his guard. Arriving at a narrow path which entered a forest, Brown told his companion to take the lead.

"Go ahead yourself," replied Foster, reining up his horse.

The Texan dashed on thirty yards, leaped from his saddle, and ambuscaded himself behind a tree, at the same time drawing one of his revolvers. Foster fired as the other ruffian peeped from behind his cover, and Brown fell with a ball through his head, apparently lifeless. The lucky marksman put himself to the superfluous trouble of getting out of the country, as if Southern justice were at that time likely to notice such a trifle as the homicide of an outlaw. Brown recovered his senses, crawled to

7. Secure from the dangers of combat. The term was applied, in the Southern states particularly, to one who held a position of safety during the Civil War.

the house of a neighboring farmer, and was as carefully nursed back to health as if he were a benefactor to the human race.

The most curious of this ruffian's adventures occurred in a store at Cokesbury and was related to me by an eye-witness. While Brown was in the salesroom, conversing on equal terms with two or three respectable citizens, among whom was a clergyman whom I shall venture to style the Rev. P. V. Nasby,[8] a Negro named Lewis entered to make some trifling purchase. Not knowing the desperado by sight, or not being aware of the deferential respect which would be exacted by him, Lewis approached the group of colloquists without offering any profound salutation.

"Take off your hat," shouted Brown. The Negro stared, but lifted his hat.

"Now get on your knees," ordered the Texan, at the same time advancing with a threatening air. Instead of obeying, Lewis sprang forward, seized the wrists of this menacing instructor in deportment, and held them in a grasp of iron. Brown struggled violently to free himself, pouring out a torrent of oaths, calling on the storekeeper to hand him a pistol and threatening murder. The Reverend Nasby, driven by his cloth and his conscience to interfere, patted the outlawed scoundrel on the shoulder, and said in a meek voice, "Don't, Mr. Brown! Mr. Brown, I beg you, don't! I know this boy Lewis. He is a good, quiet, decent-behaved nigger. He has always been civil to white men. I haven't the least idea that he meant to be disrespectful. I beg that you won't hurt him."

"I will!" screamed the Texan, still struggling. "By —! I'll kill him. I'll cut his d—d throat."

"Well," answered the heroic Nasby, "I am a minister of the Gospel, and if there is to be a murder done here I am not going to stay and see it."

With which sublime words, worthy to be engraven on his forehead with a pen of iron, he picked up his hat and left this scene of ungodly strife.

8. Cf. *The Nasby Papers* (1864) by D. R. Locke. Petroleum V. Nasby, the fictitious author of this series of letters first appearing in the Findlay *Jeffersonian* (March 21, 1861), is an illiterate country preacher whose defense of the South is purposely made foolish in order to satirize the Confederate cause.

What followed? The citizens of Cokesbury wanted to get rid of Brown; only a few days later they secretly petitioned for a garrison to drive him out; here they had him bound in two fists as firm as fetters; what did they do? Doctor Vance, one of the proprietors of the store, whose name deserves and shall have wide publicity, mustered up all his heroism and said: "Mr. Brown, if you will pledge your word as a gentleman that you won't harm Lewis I will make him let go of you."

After a long scuffle, after finding that he had not strength to free himself, this hired murderer of Negroes gave the required promise—on his word of honor, be it understood—and obtained his release. It was confidently predicted that he "would find some chance to kill the nigger"; but either from fear of so muscular an antagonist, or because other matters occupied his valuable time, he never tried it.

Sullivan and Birkett, two young Southerners of respectable connections, one of them the son of a leading lawyer in Laurens District, were so captivated by Brown's exploits in bullying Negroes and defying the Yankees (and doubtless also by that wonderful horsemanship and marksmanship which could strike a sapling with a pistol ball at full gallop) that they became his open adherents and joined him in his villainous knight-errantries. These three youths, the eldest twenty-five and the others barely twenty, were an incubus upon four large districts, containing a population of near a hundred thousand souls. Not a citizen dared to arrest them, or scarcely to give information about them. Men who had a complaint to make against Brown's gang came to me in private and whispered their story under strenuous injunctions of secrecy. Sullivan called on a certain high civil official, boasted of his affiliation with the Texan bushwhacker, and was suffered to depart with a fatherly remonstrance. Birkett was to the last countenanced and protected by his relations, as merely a wild boy whose only fault was a passion for reckless feats, more or less pardonable in a youth of spirit. The general imbecility of public opinion with regard to these ruffians was inexplicable, unless it can be attributed to a secret sympathy with them as exponents of Southern independence, or to a languor of feeling resulting from the exhaustion produced by the war. Sullivan's father, I must state, was a noble exception to this despicable feebleness, disinheriting his unworthy offspring and driving him from his house.

The story of the gang was hurried to a *dénouement* by a circumstance which resulted from the murder of Ezra French's Negro. It will be remembered that French had promised Brown two hundred dollars for two assassinations, and that, only one having been accomplished, he refused to pay more than half the price of blood. To punish the old farmer for his niggardliness, and also by way of collecting interest on the debt, Sullivan called at the house of the defaulter, put a pistol to his head, and forced him to sign a note for five hundred dollars. French advertised the note in the papers, forbade any one to pay it, and fled to Mississippi. As he left secretly, not even confiding his departure to his family, it was generally supposed that he had been murdered; and now at last Governor Orr [9] took official notice of this series of outrages, offering a reward of three hundred dollars each for the apprehension of Brown, Sullivan, and Birkett. A few days later Birkett rode into the village of Anderson with the avowed intention of killing Lieutenant Loeche of the garrison, whom he suspected, very justly, of an attempt to entrap him. Trotting up to the headquarters of the post and seeing an officer in full uniform mounting a horse, he asked a Negro, "Is that Lieutenant Loeche?"

"No," said the man. "That is Colonel Smith, the commandant."

"He will do just as well," observed Birkett coolly; and resting his revolver on his left arm, fired at the colonel, narrowly missing him. Smith dashed toward him, but the desperado had the swiftest horse and, after a short chase, disappeared in the forests near the village. Then followed a successful raid upon one of his haunts, and he was sent in irons to Castle Pinckney in Charleston Harbor, there to be tried by a military commission and sentenced to hard labor upon the fortifications of Tortugas.[10] It will scarcely be believed that one of this rogue's cousins had the impudence to ask Colonel Smith to join in a petition for his release. The pretense was that the youngster was

9. See Introduction, p. vii.

10. During the Civil War a penal station was established at Fort Jefferson on one of the coral reefs of Dry Tortugas in the Gulf of Mexico.

insane; the colonel's reply was that there was too much method in his madness.

Alarmed by this arrest and by a certain show of activity which the governor's reward had aroused among the civil authorities, Birkett's comrades left Cokesbury and sought shelter in Greenville District, at the house of a drunken farmer whom I shall christen John Jones. Brown was as boastful as ever; he offered to kill any man, white or black, for five dollars; he robbed Negroes, made them take off their hats, and get on their knees. Hearing of these outrages, I reported them to Brevet Major M'Clary, commandant of the infantry garrison at Greenville; and a corporal was sent with four men, mounted on quartermaster animals, to arrest the bushwhackers. Reaching John Jones's house at sunrise and meeting the proprietor at his gate, they asked him if he had seen any strangers.

"You want Brown and Sullivan, I s'pose," said he. "I don't mind telling you all about them. I'm tired of them, by —! They've just left here. They ain't more than a mile off at this minute. But you can't catch 'em—with your creeturs; they've got the best horses around here. And if you do catch 'em they're too many for you; they've got two revolvers apiece, and that's twenty shots to your five. If you go for 'em, I advise you to begin firing as soon as you lay eyes on 'em. At long range you have the advantage, but at short range they'll have it."

Having given this advice, in the spirit of a man who didn't care much which whipped, John Jones walked away to his bottoms and left the result to Providence. To his great disappointment, doubtless, the detail did not come up with the bushwhackers, and nobody was killed. Brown and Sullivan reached North Carolina; remained there until they supposed that the excitement against them had abated; returned in some mysterious manner, probably by long night marches, to Cokesbury; then, finding that they were still unpopular, vanished for good.

A HARBORER OF BUSHWHACKERS

Shortly after the fruitless expedition to John Jones's house that gentleman held with me a dialogue which is curiously illustrative of the ideas of honor and gentility prevalent among many of our Southern brethren. Clad in homespun, loutish and yet fearless in carriage, red in the face with forty years of whisky, his breath profusely scented with that vigorous fluid, his expression indicative of nothing worse than drunken braggadocio, he stalked into my office, took a chair, and observed, "Major, I hear you haven't a high opinion of John Jones."

"You have been harboring Texas Brown," I replied, "and I sent a detail to your house to arrest him there. We may as well be frank in this matter. I knew where he was; I knew precisely where John Jones could be found; I gave the corporal full instructions about his road; I told him the number of your milestone."

For a moment he was silent, utterly disconcerted and probably fearful of arrest.

"Well, Major, I'll tell you how it is," he said at last. "John Jones is a gentleman. He never refused a man the use of his roof. A gentleman comes along and says, 'Give me a lodging for the night.' What can I do? I can't shut my door on him. I take him in, let him eat what's on the table, and charge him a dollar in the morning. That's my way. I never refused any man a night's lodging or a meal of victuals. If he can pay for it, well and good; if he can't, he's welcome. That's John Jones, Major. If you'll come to his house you shall have the best he can furnish, and not a dollar to pay."

"But this Brown is an outlaw and a scoundrel; he has no claim on the hospitality of a good citizen."

"Major, I know it; that is, I know it now. I used to think a good deal of Brown; I thought he was a lively, smart, wild fellow who would settle down some day; I allow I thought a good deal of Brown. But he's no-account, Major. I tell you, Brown has ruined himself—as a gentleman."

Was there ever anything more deliciously absurd than this intoxicated farmer declaring that this vagrant cutthroat had "ruined himself as a gentleman?" It was inexpressibly refreshing to hear him, and I let him go on with his boozy maunderings.

"John Jones has done with Brown," he continued. "He has no use for him. I've no use for anybody that won't work, Major;

I don't want 'em round my place; I told Brown so. He didn't stay at my house when you thought he did; he stayed at another house that I can't tell you of. But he come over to me at daybreak and wanted to buy my best horse. I sold it, Major, because I knew that if I didn't he would steal it. That's the reason I knowed your men couldn't catch him; I knowed he was astraddle of the best stock in this district. Yes, I sold Brown a horse and got my money. But that was all—that time; I didn't lodge him nor feed him. I don't want to set eyes on him again. Major, you mustn't do injustice to John Jones; he an't of the same sort with Texas Brown in no way, shape, nor manner; nor he an't of the same sort with some other folks. John Jones is a gentleman. If he wants to kill you, Major," —here he rose and laid his hand impressively on my shoulder—"if he wants to put you out of his way, he won't hire another man to take you into the woods and murder you in cold blood—you know what I mean? John Jones won't do that. He'll take a crack at you with his own pistol, and, if he misses you, you shall have your crack."

With this magnanimous declaration and with a further warm invitation to partake of his hospitality ("No dollar in the morning, Major"), he departed.

Numberless, and for the most part ludicrous, were John Jones's oddities. While the volunteers garrisoned Greenville his favorite amusement was to ride up to the camp, defy the "d—d Yankees" to fight, and, when they came out after him, gallop away laughing.

It seems incredible, but nevertheless it is a fact, that this curious being was kind and generous to Negroes, as is proved by the circumstance that his slaves did not desert him on the emancipation, and continued to labor contentedly on his plantation. His last visit to me was for the purpose of getting a teacher for a freedmen's school which he had resolved, he said, to set up on his place at his own expense. What came of it I can not say, for I left Greenville shortly after.

After the bushwhacking gangs of Largent and Texas Brown had disappeared from my pashalic the outrages which I had to report dwindled into petty squabbles, in which the Negroes were quite as often the aggressors as the whites.[11] There would be a seizing of guns, a picking up of bludgeons, a deal of loud threatening, and occasionally a blow. The civil law generally took these affairs in hand, and they are not worth inserting in a "report of outrages."

11. In addition to the case of Cato Allums De Forest reported a total of only five other outrages (complete file of monthly reports in the National Archives). Three of these are described in subsequent chapters of the present work: they involve Miles Hunnicutt (p. 127 f.), Thomas Turner (p. 109), and the Stigalls (p. 110 f.). The other two were the flogging of a Negro woman, Sally Charles, and the infliction of a bullet wound upon a Negro man, Terry Benson. See reports of outrages, December, 1866, and August, 1867, and letter of De Forest, December 29, 1866, to D. Moore, magistrate, in connection with the case of Sally Charles.

CHAPTER II

A BUREAU MAJOR'S BUSINESS AND PLEASURES [1]

AS Brevet Colonel Niles,[2] my predecessor in the sub-district, sat in his office one summer morning of 1866 an old colored woman entered and, with a pleading voice and smile which should have persuaded eggs from an anvil, inquired, "Is you got a bureau, Mas'r?"

"What do you mean?" responded the colonel. "No, I don't keep bureaus, aunty."

"Oh, yis you doos!" persisted the visitor. "An' I wants one mighty bad, I doos, Mas'r."

"Somebody has been fooling you, old lady. You mustn't suppose that I keep sure-enough bureaus, with drawers and knobs, to give out. A bureau here means an office. You don't want me to give you my office, do you, aunty?"

"Oh, no!" laughed the old creature, good-humored, patient, and determined to win. "I doesn't want your office; I wants a bureau. Please, Mas'r, let me have one."

After a few minutes of teasing the colonel's temper showed signs of breaking loose, and, as a consequence, the applicant began to doubt whether she might not be on the wrong track.

"Mas'r Wil'm Graves sont me yere," she explained. "He said you had ever so many bureaus; an' he said you'd say you didn't have none, cos so many folks is after you for 'um; an' he tole me to stick to you an' you'd give me one. An' ef you would *please* give me one, Mas'r, I'd be so glad, cos I wants one powerful."

"Ah, old lady! Mas'r William Graves has been playing a joke on us," said the colonel, with a solemnity which carried

1. Published originally in *Harper's New Monthly Magazine*, XXXVII (November, 1868), 766–775.

2. On October 31, 1866, De Forest reported to Brevet Lieutenant Colonel J. P. Low that, on October 2, he had relieved Brevet Lieutenant A. E. Niles in charge of the Greenville office. National Archives.

conviction and sent the aunty away in her habitual content and poverty.

I do not insinuate that all Bureau business was like this; but I do say that a good deal of it was light and matter of laughter. At the commencement of my fifteen months of duty I went to my work at eight o'clock in the morning; but after a while the hour became nine, and eventually ten. My hotel faced the old court-house of Greenville, in which was my office, so that, while smoking my after-breakfast pipe and reading the Charleston papers which had arrived the evening previous by railroad, I could keep an eye out for the advent of my constituents. The appearance of one or more freedmen, sitting on the stone steps or leaning against the brick columns of the old courthouse, and looking up and down the street with an air of patient, blank expectation, was the signal for me to lay down my *Courier,* pick up such official documents as I might have received by mail, and repair to my various though not often ponderous duties.

A SHAM BUREAU OFFICER

I sometimes doubted whether a sham Bureau officer, acting simply under instructions of "how not to do it," would not have answered as good a purpose as a real one. The Mr. William Graves above mentioned seemed to prove, by one of his experimental jokes, that such a scarecrow might serve very acceptably on ordinary occasions. A lawyer, having an office next to mine and having often enlightened me in such mysteries of civil statutes as I needed to know, and being, moreover, subject to many intrusions from my blundering clients, he was tempted at times to let his jocose temper wander into the solemn sphere of my duties. During one of my brief absences a Pickens farmer and a Negro, both a little "corned" and in high good-humor, entered his office and asked, "Which is the Bureau man?"

"There he is," replied Graves, pointing to one of his own clients, a gentleman from Laurens District named Jackson, who happened to have on at the time a blue blouse, the spoils perhaps of his Confederate service. "But I must tell you," he added in a whisper, "that he never does any business without a drink. You had better step round to the corner store and buy a bottle of the best North Carolina whisky; it is the only way to get anything out of him.''

This was a most slanderous insinuation as far as it touched me; but nothing could seem more rational to the visitors, especially in their present grogginess; they were accustomed to men who could not do "a lick of work" without alcoholic assistance. Out they went and presently returned with a bottle, not, indeed, of North Carolina old rye, but of the stinging corn whisky of their native Pickens, good to take your hair off as clean as a scalping knife, and probably drawn from some surreptitious keg which they had brought to market in defiance of the revenue laws. Meantime Jackson, who was all abroad and did not even know that Greenville boasted a Bureau officer, had been informed as to the nature of the emergency and instructed in the part which he was to play. Accordingly the offering was accepted graciously; glasses were produced and all hands took a drink. Then followed some conversation on the "craps" of Pickens, after which all hands took another drink. The bottle being now finished, and the extempore Bureau officer warmed up to his work, he announced that he was ready for business.

"Now, to avoid confusion, Major," said Graves, "I suggest that you hear one at a time."

"Very good," answered the make-believe major. "One at a time."

"And as the white man owns the land he had better speak first," continued the self-constituted secretary. "You, Sir, stand up and state your case."

The farmer got on his legs with some difficulty and told his story; but, being a good-humored, generous man in his cups, he made out very little cause of difference; "mought be five dollars betwixt us, Sir, and mought be less. I ha'n't nothing, Major, to say aginst Jim, in general. He's jist as good a boy as I want to see. But when he says he's entitled to half the fodder instead of one third he's bearing down on me a little too hard."

Then came a speech from the Negro, which, as I was assured, was so exceedingly funny as to be unreportable.

"Now, Major," said Graves, "it seems to me that both these

men are so nearly right that they couldn't be more so without splitting the difference. My opinion is that you had better order them to split the difference."

"Very good," decided the sham dignitary. "Split the difference."

Human wisdom could no further go, and both the complainants were perfectly satisfied.

"Now you see that I put you up to the right way of doing the thing," whispered Graves, as they left the office. "If ever you get into any future trouble bring your whisky straight to me, and I'll put you through."

Had I been there I could not have rendered a wiser judgment and should not have left the Pickensites so convinced of the convivial and amiable nature of Bureau officers.

NATURE OF COMPLAINTS

Most of the difficulties between whites and blacks resulted from the inevitable awkwardness of tyros in the mystery of free labor. Many of the planters seemed to be unable to understand that work could be other than a form of slavery, or that it could be accomplished without some prodigious binding and obligating of the hireling to the employer. Contracts which were brought to me for approval contained all sorts of ludicrous provisions.[3] Negroes must be respectful and polite; if they were not respectful and polite they must pay a fine for each offense; they must admit no one on their premises unless by consent of the landowner; they must have a quiet household and not keep too many dogs; they must not go off the plantation without leave. The idea seemed to be that if the laborer were not bound body and soul he would be of no use. With regard to many freedmen I was obliged to admit that this assumption was only

3. Bureau officials were authorized to approve all written labor contracts between freedmen and their employers, but it is evident from the scant number of contracts approved that many labor agreements must have been made without such formal sanction. Most labor contracts ran from the beginning of the year, for a one-year term. De Forest's official reports (National Archives) show that in 1867—largely during January and February—he approved 151 contracts for the labor of 322 people. A typical contract of the kind endorsed by the Bureau is given, with attention to variant forms and to the whole problem of contracts, in Webster, "Freedmen's Bureau in South Carolina," pp. 106–108, 112–117, 152–154.

too correct and to sympathize with the desire to limit their noxious liberty, at the same time that I knew such limitation to be impossible. When a darkey frolics all night and thus renders himself worthless for the next day's work; when he takes into his cabin a host of lazy relatives who eat him up, or of thievish ones who steal the neighboring pigs and chickens; when he gets high notions of freedom into his head and feels himself bound to answer his employer's directions with an indifferent whistle, what can the latter do? My advice was to pay weekly wages, if possible, and discharge every man as fast as he got through with his usefulness. But this policy was above the general reach of Southern capital and beyond the usual circle of Southern ideas.

One prevalent fallacy was the supposition that the farmer could, of his own authority, impose fines; in other words, that he could withhold all or a part of the laborer's pay if he left the farm before the expiration of his contract. The statement, "You can not take your man's wages for July because he has refused to work for you during August," was quite incomprehensible from the old-fashioned, patriarchal point of view.

"But what am I to do with this fellow, who has left me right in the hoeing season?" demands a wrathful planter.

"You have no remedy except to sue him for damages resulting from a failure of contract."

"Sue him! He ha'n't got nothing to collect on."

"Then don't sue him."

Exit planter, in helpless astonishment over the mystery of the new system, and half inclined to believe that I have been making game of him. I could, of course, have sent for the delinquent and ordered him to return to his work; but had I once begun to attend personally to such cases I should have had business enough to kill off a regiment of Bureau officers; and, moreover, I never forgot that my main duty should consist in educating the entire population around me to settle their difficulties by the civil law; in other words, I considered myself an instrument of reconstruction.

The majority of the complaints brought before me came from Negroes. As would naturally happen to an ignorant race, they were liable to many impositions, and they saw their grievances with big eyes. There was magnitude, too, in their manner of statement; it was something like an indictment of the voluminous olden time—the rigmarole which charged a pig thief with stealing ten boars, ten sows, ten shoats, etc. With pomp of manner and of words, with a rotundity of voice and superfluity of detail which would have delighted Cicero, a Negro would so glorify his little trouble as to give one the impression that humanity had never before suffered the like. Sometimes I was able to cut short these turgid narratives with a few sharp questions; sometimes I found this impossible and had to let them roll on unchecked, like Mississippis. Of course the complaints were immensely various in nature and importance. They might refer to an alleged attempt at assassination or to the discrepancy of a bushel of pea vines in the division of a crop. They might be against brother freedmen, as well as against former slave owners and "Rebs." More than once have I been umpire in the case of a disputed jackknife or petticoat. Priscilly Jones informed me that her "old man was a-routin' everybody out of the house an' a-breakin' everything"; then Henry Jones bemoaned himself because his wife Priscilly was going to strange places along with Tom Lynch; then Tom Lynch wanted redress and protection because of the disquieting threats of Henry Jones. The next minute Chloe Jackson desired justice on Viney Robinson, who had slapped her face and torn her clothes. Everybody, guilty or innocent, ran with his or her griefs to the Bureau officer; and sometimes the Bureau officer, half distracted, longed to subject them all to some huge punishment. Of the complaints against whites the majority were because of the retention of wages or of alleged unfairness in the division of the crops.

If the case brought before me were of little consequence, I usually persuaded the Negro, if possible, to drop it or to "leave it out" to referees. Without a soldier under my command, and for months together having no garrison within forty miles, I could not execute judgment even if I could see to pronounce it; and, moreover, I had not, speaking with official strictness, any authority to act in matters of property; the provost court [4]

4. In June, 1865, the commander of the Department of the South issued orders establishing courts, consisting of an army officer and two citizens, to adjudicate

having been abolished before I entered upon my jurisdiction. If the complaint were sufficiently serious to demand attention, I had one almost invariable method of procedure: I stated the case in a brief note and addressed it to the magistrate of the "beat" or magisterial precinct in which the Negro resided. Then, charging him to deliver the letter in person and explaining to him what were his actual wrongs and his possibilities of redress, I dismissed him to seek for justice precisely where a white man would have sought it. Civil law was in force by order of the commanding general of the department; and the civil authorities were disposed, as I soon learned, to treat Negroes fairly. Such being the case, all that my clients needed in me was a counselor.

"But the square won't pay no sawt 'tention to me," a Negro would sometimes declare. To which I would reply: "Then come back and let me know it. If he neglects his duty we will report him and have him removed."

Of the fifty or sixty magistrates in my district I had occasion to indicate but one as being unfit for office by reason of political partialities and prejudices of race. New York City would be fortunate if it could have justice dealt out to it as honestly and fairly as it was dealt out by the plain, homespun farmers who filled the squire-archates of Greenville, Pickens, and Anderson.

But the Negro often lacked confidence in the squire; perhaps, too, he was aware that his case would not bear investigation; and so, instead of delivering my letter in person, he often sent it by a messenger. As the magistrate could not act without the presence of the complainant, nothing was done. A week or fortnight later the Negro would reappear at my office, affirming that "dese yere Rebs wouldn't do nothin' for black folks no-how."

"What did the squire say?" I would ask.

"Didn' say nothin'. Jes took the ticket an' read it, an' put it in his pocket."

"Did you see him?"

---

cases in which a freedman was either plaintiff or defendant. For a time these courts functioned as one of the most important parts of the judicial system, but civil law was fully restored in October, 1866, that is, during the same month in which De Forest went to Greenville. Webster, *idem*, pp. 109–113.

"No. I was feared he wouldn' do nothin'; so I sont it roun' to him."

"Now then, go to him. If you have a story to tell, go and tell it to him, and swear to it. I shall do nothing for you till you have done that."

And so the process of education went on, working its way mainly by dint of general laws, without much regard to special cases. As this is the method of universal Providence and of the War Department, I felt that I could not be far wrong in adopting it. But even this seemingly simple and easy style of performing duty had its perplexities. Magistrates rode from ten to thirty miles to ask me how they should dispose of this, that, and the other complaint which had been turned over to them for adjudication. Their chief difficulty was to know where the military orders ended and where civil law began; and here I was little less puzzled than they, for we were acting under a hodgepodge of authorities which no man could master. I had files of orders for 1865, and 1866, and 1867; files from the Commissioner, and from the Assistant Commissioner, and from the general commanding the department; the whole making a duodecimo volume of several hundred closely printed pages. To learn these by heart and to discover the exact point where they ceased to cover and annul the state code was a task which would have bothered not only a brevet major but a chief justice. My method of interpretation was to limit the military order as much as might be, and so give all possible freedom of action to the magistrate.

SPECIMEN CASES

Occasionally my office was the scene of something approaching to the nature of a disturbance. Once I heard an uproar in the outer passage; and then appeared two farmers leading a tall Negro by a long rope which secured his hands, the three closely followed by a small mob of expostulating and threatening Negroes belonging to the village. The white men were tremulous with astonishment and alarm, and at the same time not a little indignant.

"Putty rough talk for black 'uns," said one of them, indicating with a toss of his head the menacing freedmen who now filled my doorway. "Some of 'em may git a knife into 'em if they don't keep their distance."

Meanwhile Edward Cox, a mulatto of convivial habits, and disposed, like many white men of similar tastes, to take a leading part in public affairs, was vociferously questioning the prisoner: "What you been doing? Have you done anything?"

"Took a pair of trousers," confessed the long, ragged, stupid-looking subject of arrest.

"Were they yours? Did you steal 'em?" persisted Edward. "Oh, you stole 'em, eh? Then I've got nothing to say for you. Come, boys, get out o' the way; clar out now, I tell ye; don't be bothering the Major. When a man steals, I've got nothin' to say for him, no matter how black he is."

Closing the door on the rabble, I heard the statement of the captors. The Negro, it seems, was a stranger in the district, who had called at the house of one of the farmers to beg and had been furnished with a dinner of cold pieces. Immediately after his refreshment he had disappeared in company with a newly washed pair of homespun trousers, which had been hung out to dry. Enraged by the "meanness of the critter," by ten miles of hard riding to overtake him, and by the noisy interference of the Greenville Negroes, the prosecutor was bent upon severe punishment. I took captors and captive to a magistrate's office and left them there. In half an hour I went back and found that, on the intercession of the squire and on the darkey's solemn declaration of penitence, the farmer had not only forgiven him, but had hired him as a laborer.

My worst perplexities arose from cases in which I had to deal with respectable white citizens. Just imagine the North conquered by the South, Confederate officers stationed in every community as agents of the "Copperhead Bureau," and all the Bridgets of the land flowing to them with complaints against their masters and mistresses. Would not the "Copperhead Bureau Agent" find himself very often in a quandary? Would he be able always to satisfy both his clients and his own sense of justice and social propriety?

Mr. John Doe, one of the leading citizens of Greenville, complained to me that he had hired a colored woman named Sarah to work for him and that she had failed to come, to the detriment of his household affairs. I sent a note to Sarah informing her that she must fulfill her contract. An hour later Mrs. Richard Roe, the wife of another leading citizen, then absent at the North, entered my office in her best robes and gave me the soundest scolding that I have had since my boyhood.

"This Sarah lives in my yard," was her story. "I only received her out of charity, as she is sickly and has a small child. I gave her the rent of a cabin on condition that she should do my washing. Then I found that she could not earn her food otherwheres, and I allowed her rations weekly—as a charity. This week she has neglected her washing and is aiming to get off without doing it. I can hire other people easily enough, but I do not wish to be imposed upon. I insist that she shall do that washing. She shall not leave, Sir, until it is done. To make sure of my point I have locked up her things in my cabin, and I have the key in my pocket. I am not going to be deceived and cheated by Negroes."

Then followed a series of sharp scoffs at the interfering disposition of Bureau officers, which my regard for myself forbids me to repeat. What could I do? The imperfect information of Mr. John Doe and the imbecile laziness of this colored Sarah had put me in a ridiculous position. Falling back on the fact that I had been assigned to duty for the benefit of Negroes rather than of whites, and remembering that Sarah was to get wages at her new place, whereas now she was barely earning a subsistence, I shut my eyes to justice and refused to withdraw my order. I attempted to silence Mrs. Roe by remarking that it was a very small affair; but she replied with tart pertinency, "It was not too small, Sir, for you to meddle with it."

So I remained dumb, in all the greatness and meanness of despotic power, and persisted in having my stupid way. With no small satisfaction I learned next day that Mr. John Doe had had his share of humiliation. Meeting him on her way homeward, Mrs. Roe descended from her buggy and gave him a piece of her mind.

"To think of a Southern *gentleman* appealing to these Yankees!" she sneered. "I thought that it was a point of honor among us Southerners to stand by each other and not to turn informers against each other before our conquerors. It may do for niggers and mean whites, Sir; but have Southern gentlemen come to this?"

"Mrs. Roe! Mrs. Roe!" shouted the wounded and inflamed Doe, panting to get in a word in his defense; but the torrent of feminine sarcasm was too much for him, and he was as glad to finish the combat as had been the Bureau officer. When Sarah came to his house he sent her back to Mrs. Roe; then Mrs. Roe, satisfied with so much of victory, sent her back to Mr. Doe; then Sarah lived a fortnight with the Does, did next to nothing, as usual, and was turned away.

Of course there were numberless little disturbances which were not brought up for my official action. Mr. Peter Cauble [5] was a blacksmith, nearly eighty years of age, but still vigorous, who had acquired by industry, economy, and wise investment a fortune of seventy thousand dollars, and had seen it disappear in the grand hocus-pocus of the Confederacy. A rough, high-tempered, but kindhearted and generous nature, he was one of the men to whom the poor and outcast of his district chiefly resorted for help. White or black, good or bad, Peter Cauble gave them food, found them shelter, and went bail for them. Society had pointed out his proper place in it and made him chairman of the Commissioners of the Poor. One misty spring morning Peter Cauble arose at four o'clock, as was his hale custom, and, taking a hoe on his shoulder, went out to work in his garden. He was threading a pathway which led along a little bank, when some unknown person ran against him and, at the same moment, hailed him with the impudent salutation, "How are you, Pete?"

Who it was Peter Cauble could not see, for his spectacles were in his pocket, and the morning was still darkness; but he raised his hoe with both hands and brought the staff of it across the stranger's head, rolling him off his feet and down the bank. The prostrated individual then bounced up and ran away.

It was a Negro. For three or four days the adventure made a great noise in the village. The reactionaries declared that this man was on his way home from a Union League meeting, and

5. Peter Cauble is listed in the census of 1870 (National Archives) as a blacksmith, aged 78, native of North Carolina with real property valued at $1,000.

that there was a widespread conspiracy to address all the respectable whites by their Christian names. The Radical Negroes called Peter Cauble a Reb and talked about confiscating his land. But the two parties chiefly interested in the affair settled it amicably.

"Bill—" said Peter Cauble, on discovering that the man whom he had floored was one of his colored acquaintance, "Bill, I knocked you down the other morning. I think I served you right; but if you don't think so, we'll go and settle it before the Major; you shall tell your story, and I'll tell mine; what do you say, Bill?"

"I ha'n't no use for the Major," replied Bill sheepishly. "I'm ready to call it squar. I'd been drinkin' that night and didn' know what I was about. I don't want nuffin to do with the Major."

TRANSPORTATION [6]

For nothing were the Negroes more eager than for transportation. They had a passion, not so much for wandering, as for getting together; and every mother's son among them seemed to be in search of his mother; every mother in search of her children. In their eyes the work of emancipation was incomplete until the families which had been dispersed by slavery were reunited. One woman wanted to rejoin her husband in Memphis, and another to be forwarded to hers at Baltimore. The Negroes who had been brought to the up-country during the war by

6. After the war many freedmen were, in effect, displaced persons, having been carried as slaves to places where they would not fall under the control of Federal armies. To return them to their original places of residence, and also to enable them to reach places where employment was available, the Freedmen's Bureau furnished transportation on a large scale. In December, 1865, the *Nation* estimated that more than one thousand Negroes monthly were in transit through Columbia, S.C. Later, under orders from General Howard, transportation was furnished less freely, as is shown by the fact that in 1866 only 1,829 freedmen received transportation in South Carolina, and in 1867 only 881. De Forest, as he indicates here, personally approved of the restriction of free travel, and his own grants were extremely sparing. In October, 1866, he issued transportation to no one; in November, to 8 people; in December, to 10; in January, 1867, to 19; in February, to 3. The March and May records are lacking, and the April, June, July, and August reports show no transportation issued. Reports in the National Archives; report of Major General O. O. Howard in *Annual Report of the Secretary of War for 1868*, p. 1019; and Webster, "Freedmen's Bureau in South Carolina," pp. 139–141.

white families were crazy to get back to their native flats of ague and country fever. Highland darkeys who had drifted down to the seashore were sending urgent requests to be "fotched home again." One aunty brought me her daughter, who suffered with fits, and begged me to give them "a ticket" to Anderson so that they might consult a certain famous "fit doctor" there resident. Others desired me to find out where their relatives lived, and send for them.

In short, transportation was a nuisance. I believed in it less than I believed in the distribution of rations and in modes of charity generally. It seemed to me that if the Negroes wanted to travel they should not insist on doing it at the expense of the nation, but should earn money and pay their own fare, like white people. I learned to be discouragingly surly with applicants for transportation papers and to give them out as charily as if the cost came from my own pocket. I claim that in so doing I acted the part of a wise and faithful public servant.

From the class properly known as refugees—that is, Unionists who had been driven from their homes during the war by the Rebels—I had no requests for transportation. Not that they were few in number; the mountains near by Greenville were swarming with them; but they had the Anglo-Saxon faculty for getting about the world unassisted. The mean whites, those same "low-down" creatures who bored me to death for corn and clothing, were equally independent of aid in changing their habitations. The "high-toned" families which had fled to the up-country from the cannon of Dupont and Gillmore [7] also made shift to return to their houses in Charleston or their plantations on the sea islands, without any noticeable worrying of government officials. The Negroes alone were ravenous after transportation.

I soon found that many of my would-be tourists were chiefly anxious to enjoy that luxury, so dear to the freedman's heart, "going a-visiting." A woman would obtain transportation of me

7. On November 7, 1861, Captain Samuel F. Du Pont of the Navy had executed a successful attack on Fort Beauregard and Fort Walker at Port Royal Sound. The capture of these positions had brought an extensive part of the sea-island region under Federal control. In 1863 General Q. A. Gillmore landed a force near Charleston and conducted a bombardment of Fort Sumter, lasting intermittently from August to October and resulting in the devastation but not the capture of the objective.

on the plea that she wanted to rejoin a child in Charleston whom she had not seen for ten years and who was suffering for her care; then, having enjoyed a sufficient amount of family gossip in the city, she would apply to the Bureau officer there to save her from starvation by returning her to Greenville. I became wickedly clever in fathoming this deceit and used to ask in a friendly way, "When do you want to come back?"

"Well, Mars'r, I doesn't want to stop mo'n a fo'tnight," would perhaps be the answer.

"Ah! if that is all," I would lecture, "you had better wait till you want to stay for good, or till you have money enough to pay for your own pleasure excursions."

It was necessary, I thought, to convince the Negroes of the fact that the object of the government was not to do them favors, but justice; and of the still greater fact that there is very little to get in this world without work.

Planters who were about to remove to more fertile regions sometimes asked transportation for their Negroes, on the ground that these latter would be benefited by the change of locality and that it could not be effected without government assistance. Of course this seemed rational; and I understood that aid of this sort was freely rendered by some Bureau officers; but I rejected all such applications. Grant one, grant a thousand; and the government would be bankrupt. At last a general order from the Commissioner sanctioned transportation for this purpose; but the planter's application must be approved by the Assistant Commissioner of the state where he resided and by the Assistant Commissioner of the state to which he proposed to emigrate; he must give satisfactory security that he would feed and pay his hands; he must then get the approval of the Commissioner. What with postal and official delays these preliminaries generally consumed at least a month; and as the planting season pressed, this complicated circumlocution was usually abandoned before it was completed, the applicant either giving up his migration or conducting it at his own expense. Whether the result were intended or not, it was a good one. In so vast and fertile a region as the South the industry which can not succeed alone rarely deserves success. Charity is either an absolute necessity or an absolute evil.

Although I received no precise instructions as to visiting the various portions of my district, it was probably presumed by my superiors that I would make occasional tours of inspection, and so attend to local disorders on the spot where they occurred. I did not do this; I made but a single journey of above fifteen miles; I did not absent myself more than a single night from my station, except once when summoned to Charleston. My satrapy, it must be remembered, contained two state districts or counties, and eventually three, with a population of about eighty thousand souls and an area at least two thirds as large as the state of Connecticut. Consider the absurdity of expecting one man to patrol three thousand square miles and make personal visitations to thirty thousand Negroes.

Then I had no assistant to attend to the complainants who constantly presented themselves at my office. They averaged five a day, or a total of something like two thousand during my fifteen months of duty. Moreover, they came from distances of five, ten, twenty, and even thirty miles. I planted myself firmly in Greenville and let my world come to me. Toward the end of my term of service an order was promulgated to the effect that Bureau officers should thereafter "travel more" and that they should regularly visit the important points of their districts, giving previous notice of their tours to the inhabitants. Knowing what labor this signified and how impossible it would be to perform it in any satisfactory manner, I welcomed the decree from the headquarters of the army which mustered all volunteer officers out of the service, and declined an appointment as civilian agent of the Bureau. How far and with what good result my successors performed their tourist labors I should be glad to know.

RED TAPE

Reports, returns, correspondence, and records formed no small part of my duty. The papers for which I receipted to my predecessor included over two thousand contracts, and the addition of Anderson to my district considerably increased my documentary library. Then there were files of letters, files of indentures of apprenticeship, files of orders from various superior officers, files of retained copies of reports and returns. Everything must be recorded: the contracts must be entered alphabetically in the book of Contracts, with statement of employer's name, number of employees, date of signature, date of closure, and terms of agreement; letters forwarded must go in the book of Letters Sent, and letters received in the book of Letters Received; indorsements in the Indorsement Book; so with transportation; so with orders. If a document appeared in two books, each entry must be marked with reference numbers, so that the subject could be hunted from volume to volume. Along the margin there was a running index, by which every name might be traced from beginning to end. In short, the system of army bookkeeping is a laborious and complicated perfection.

My letters to magistrates concerning freedmen's complaints were so numerous that I only recorded the most important, leaving the vulgar herd of insignificant injuries to the uncertain labyrinths of my memory. Had I undertaken to put every matter on paper in duplicate, I should neither have eaten nor slept during some considerable periods, and should have had Main Street blocked up with waiting applicants. It was quite clerical duty enough to book my most strenuous cases of outrage and the august documents which passed between me and my superiors.

My reports were not numerous, but I had to rule several of the forms, and thus they occupied me three or four days of every month. They consisted of a report of contracts; of outrages committed by freedmen against whites; of outrages committed by whites against freedmen; of officers and civilians on duty in the district; of persons and articles employed and hired; of rations, clothing, and medicines issued; of refugees and freedmen; of transportation; of schools. The reports of outrages were required in triplicate, and the others in duplicate. The report of schools was eventually left to the teachers. The report of refugees and freedmen was a letter in which I was expected to consolidate everything of importance that had transpired with reference to those classes during the month. The total of these documents, it will be observed, amounted to about two hundred and forty a year, to which may be added, as a finishing work of grace, twelve letters of transmittal, every one commencing, "I have the honor to forward," etc., and closing with, "I am, General, very respectfully, your obed't serv't." It is my impression that the Bureau sub-district of Greenville, South Carolina, was abundantly reported.

But this is not all. Every few weeks special documents were required, such as a census of the blind, the deaf-mutes, the deformed, and other natural unfortunates; a statement of the amount and nature of the crops of my district; a table of the number of Negroes in the almshouses; a list of indigent freedpeople; a list of colored orphans. How did the lonely Bureau Major, without a soldier or a clerk to aid him, satisfy this incessant hunger for information? He gathered such knowledge of each subject as he could, and trusted that no one was wise enough to detect his shortcomings. To obtain my report of orphans and unfortunates, I addressed a circular to the magistrates of my district and got it published in the local papers gratuitously, not being allowed to advertise. For my estimate of crops I went to the United States Census of 1860 and subtracted therefrom or added thereto at discretion, under advice from knowing citizens. There was no other method of arriving at a result, unless I went a-harvesting in the depths of my subjective.

Then there were my property accounts: four regular monthly returns of clothing, and three ditto of Bureau stores; now and then a triplicate return of rations for the Commissary-General; receipts, certificates, and vouchers *ad infinitum*. What would the War Department do if we should drop back to the era of parchment? The heads of the various military offices ought to thank Heaven every morning for the miraculous continuance of the supply of paper. Now that I have got done with it all, it is delightful to think that the annual total of my reports and returns amounted to something like three hundred and fifty, without counting letters of transmittal. And yet there were men, calling themselves patriots and Christians, who abused the Freedmen's Bureau!

Indeed, a Bureau officer was an official jack-of-all-trades. He must understand the Army Regulations; he must be able to lead troops on occasion; he must have an idea of civil law; he was a Poor Commissioner; he was a statistician. With all this multifarious knowledge, he must be a man of quick common sense, with a special faculty for deciding what not to do. His duties and powers were to a great extent vague, and in general he might be said to do best when he did least.

The citizens were, of course, even less informed than I was as to the limits of my authority; and consequently I was bored with applications for all sorts of favors, countenancings, and counsels. People waylaid me in secluded places to ask leave to put up a little distillery, "just for family use." Others wanted me to collect their debts, to evict their delinquent tenants, to stop the sheriff from selling their lands. I was consulted upon points of law concerning which judges are at variance. If I pleaded ignorance or lack of authority, the reply would be, "Oh, you can fix it just as you think it ought to be"; or, "Can't you issue an order now?"

I was greatly aided in my perplexed wanderings among the civil statutes by four young lawyers who occupied offices in the same building, and who placed their professional knowledge at my disposal with an unrequited liberality for which I here tender them the thanks of the government. In return for their advice I turned over to them various Negro lawsuits, from which they reaped little pecuniary profit, but an experience of which the value can not be estimated, unless perhaps in fractional numbers.

BROTHER OFFICIALS

I have remarked that I had no assistance in my duties; but it must not be understood that I could not have had it. During the first six or seven months of my stay in Greenville, Company H of the Sixth Infantry was stationed there as a garrison; and I could undoubtedly have obtained from it any temporary detail which might appear to be necessary; for the officers were not only under orders to further the operations of the Bureau, but they were personally friendly and obliging. I did not obtain aid from them, merely because I did not need it. My great labor, that of the corn distribution, during which I should have been most glad of help, came on after the company was transferred to Newberry. I anticipated some trouble from refractory citizens on being thus left alone, with no troops nearer than Anderson, forty miles away, and with no United States official at hand excepting the postmaster and two or three revenue agents. But I met with none; the population had not a spark of rebellion left in it; not even enough to make it sympathize with the Fenians and Garibaldi.[8]

The revenue officers, by the way, were, with one exception, small comfort to me, as well as small help to the government. There were two inspectors and a collector, natives of the soil and reputed Union men, who could not write ten lines without bushwhacking our mother English. There was a wretched little Northerner, a fair specimen of a New York City Johnson man, who stayed drunk from morning till night, falsified his returns, and solicited bribes. This youth was thoroughly demoralized; he believed that the ethics of New York aldermen extended the world over; he suggested conjoint peculations to me or to whomsoever else came in his way; he had entirely disconnected the ideas of rascality and punishment. I never shall forget the knowing nods and winks with which he offered me a share in a proposed extortion which he calculated at a profit of twelve hundred dollars. He must have judged me a monster of ingratitude when I subsequently advised his arrest, and locked him up in my office until the warrant could be made out for his apprehension.

The inspector of the revenue was another curiosity. He was a German, with a vast deal of that grandiose air which is so vexatious in the petty officials of continental Europe, but also with a frank, bold military bearing which made me for a time think well of him. It was quite startling to see him shake his forefinger at a simple citizen who had been ignorantly breaking the revenue law, and to hear him thunder out, "I'll make an example of you, Sir!"

He certainly acted with energy and courage, even to the point of exceeding his instructions. Obtaining a detail of mounted men from the garrison of Anderson, he swept over Greenville

8. Both of these allusions were highly contemporary in their flavor, for in June, 1866, the Fenian attempt to invade Canada across the Niagara River had been repelled; and in the autumn of 1867 Garibaldi had been arrested by the Italian authorities for his invasion of Roman territory.

and Pickens districts like a whirlwind of honest severity, confiscating stills by the hundred. He separated his escort and set every man to work individually. He did incalculable good to a region in which whisky was ruinously plentiful and corn at famine scarcity. I had a pang of sincere regret when I was informed that he too was a peculator, gobbling up horses and cattle for his own profit and pocketing considerations. No great space of time elapsed before he was in the same jail with the assessor who had fallen before justice. Both were tried at the same court, and both convicted. One wonders that the South did not rebel anew when one considers the miserable vermin who were sent down there as government officials. But things had improved before I left, and the Greenville revenue district was in the hands of a respectable man.

THE PLEASURES OF OFFICE

Thus far I have sketched my duties; I must now describe my pleasures. At two o'clock, after from three to five hours of labor or lounging, I closed my office and rarely had positive need to open it again during the day. Having breakfasted at eight on beefsteak, bacon, eggs, and hominy, I now fortified myself with a still more substantial dinner and looked forward to a sufficiently solid tea. The manner in which my host of the Mansion House kept up his hotel and supplied a praiseworthy table on a clientage of five permanent boarders and from five to ten weekly transients was to me one of the greatest financial phenomena of the age. The same amount of "faculty" exerted in New York City during the last seven or eight years would have made Mr. Swandale [9] a Crœsus. In a region of miserable hotels, where the publican seems to consider it a part of his contract to furnish his boarders with dyspepsias, I considered myself amazingly lucky in finding such fare as honored the Mansion House.

It was a large building and had been a flourishing stand of business in the prosperous old times of Greenville, when the merchants of Charleston and the planters of the low country

9. Simon Swandale is listed in the census of 1870 as a hotel keeper, aged 58, native of Hamburg, Germany, with real and personal estate valued at $40,000.

came up every summer to breathe the wholesome air and enjoy the varied scenery of this mountain district. There had been a great ballroom—later an apothecary's shop—and in it there had been gayeties of proud ladies and "high-toned gentlemen"—later paupers. Occasionally a representative of this impoverished gentility, a transitory Rutledge, Pinckney, Grimke, Hayward, or Ravenel, passed a night under the roof, finding cause, doubtless, for sad meditations in the contrast of the present with the past. The Trenholms, a comparatively parvenu race, but famous since the days of secession, were there repeatedly, on their way to and from their country seats in western North Carolina.

Laying down the huge and sorrowful volume of the past, I emerge from the Mansion House and proceed upon my constitutional. There were some sights worthy of a glance, and perhaps of a smile, in the eight or ten brief streets of the village. There were the two or three leisurely gentlemen who "did the heavy standing round," one in front of his favorite grocery and another at his pet corner. There were those wonderful acrobats, the cows, who climbed into market wagons after ears of corn and bunches of fodder. There were occasional soldiers— staggering, noisy, quarrelsome, and slovenly, if they had been lately paid off; otherwise, quiet even to demureness, buttoned from waist to chin, and brushed as clean as dandies. Women of the low-down breed, in the coarsest and dirtiest of homespun clothing, and smoking pipes with reed stems and clay bowls straddled by with so mannish a gait that one doubted whether they could be hipped after the feminine model. The young ladies of the respectable class were remarkably tall, fully and finely formed, with good complexions, and of a high average in regard to beauty. The men were of corresponding stature, but in general disproportionately slender, and haggard from overuse of tobacco. At least half of the villagers and nearly all of the country people wore gray or butternut homespun; even Governor Perry, the great man of the place, had his homespun suit and occasionally attended court in it.

The Negroes are not so numerous as the whites, but there is a wonderful number of variously colored youngsters about, generally in an uproarious excitement of playing or fighting.

These youth are getting to be nuisances, and I am on the lookout for the first punishable malefaction among them, meaning to call on the Council to fine and imprison the noisiest. Twice, late at night, I have been so infuriated by their persistent screaming and swearing that I have opened my window and ordered them to go home and, on receiving a hoot of defiance, have sallied out, cane in hand, only to find the street solemnly quiet. Many of them are children without parents, who have run away from farm labor to enjoy the festivities of the village, and are living Heaven alone knows how and growing up to be merely vicious and indolent.

One urchin of eight or ten presents a fearful example of what may come from overmuch happiness. He has his hat half full of brown sugar and is eating it with an ecstatic rolling of the eyes; discovering some boys at the next corner, he is taken with the idea of joining them and claps his hat upon his head; then, seized with dismay, he snatches it off and exhibits an embarrassing topknot of commingled wool and sugar. Whether the Negro will not use his newly won social and political blessings with some equally discomforting result is a grave question.

The country around Greenville is hilly, sufficiently wooded, and affords a number of pleasant walks. I established three or four rounds for myself, going out on one road and returning by another, the trips varying from three to eight miles. I walked alone; no young man would like to be seen much in my company; the Southerner so forgetting himself would not be smiled upon by woman. I do not think that the hatred of Northerners was seriously bitter; but it was a fashion set by the aristocracy, and Mrs. Grundy is everywhere potent. However, I could not personally complain of inhospitality on the part of the elder and solider citizens. Yankee, military officer, and Bureau agent as I am, I was invited to breakfasts, dinners, teas, and picnics. It is my belief that, if I had set my heart upon it, I could have made a footing in Greenville society. I did not, because my chief did not want his officers on familiar terms with the citizens, and because I dreaded to be hampered by the hospitality of men against whom I might be called upon to urge complaints.

A certain judicious and popular post commandant once said

to General Robinson, temporarily in charge of the department, that he should consider it a favor to be allowed to remain at his present station, adding that he could easily have the request supported by a petition of citizens.

"By Jove!" answered the general, "you bring me such a paper, and I'll order you off immediately. I don't think, by Jove! that it looks well for an officer to be such a favorite with people whom it is his business to govern. It may be all right, but it doesn't look well."

One of the hospitalities offered to me was so great a temptation that I could not decline it. There was a literary club in Greenville; it had weekly essays and discussions and provided the public with lectures; it had a reading room also and a list of some thirty American and English periodicals. To this library I was made welcome and allowed to draw as a member. It must be noted that a Southern village differs from a Northern one of the same magnitude in possessing a larger class of leisurely people; and consequently, notwithstanding its mania for politics and cotton, Southern society has a considerable element which is bookish, if not literary. Besides this set, Greenville had the professors of a university and of a female college, so that it was able to claim rank as the Athens of the up-country, thereby exciting much envy and bitterness among less pretentious communities.

There were other amusements in Greenville. There were concerts of native talent, in which I noted two unusually fine singers of operatic music, one of them a pretty girl of barely fourteen. There were two circus visitations, various afflictions of Negro minstrelsy, a series of grievances from a vagrant dramatic company, a wizard, and a magic lantern. The Baptist church, a most aggressive and money-getting institution, had two admirably managed fairs and a succession of ice-cream entertainments, for the purpose, as I was given to understand, of paying off a mortgage on its steeple. At one of these fairs there was exhibited a fabulous beast called the Gyascutus,[10] who howled

---

10. A current term, having variant spellings, for a fictitious or fabricated animal. According to the *Dictionary of American English* the expression was first used in 1846 in a story in *The Knickerbocker;* see also De Forest's *Kate Beaumont* (Boston, 1872), p. 33.

and shook his chains to the great terror of an audience of freed-men, but also with much pecuniary benefit to the cause of religion. Whether he was one of the beasts seen by Daniel I did not learn.

Knowing the general poverty of the citizens, I wondered at this succession of recreations. I thought of the desperate Florentines, in the time of their plague, who put on their best apparel and passed their days in festivity. I am inclined to believe that in eras of supreme misfortune the mass of men are disposed to become wasteful and to seize recklessly upon every chance of enjoyment. The Negroes, who were the poorest class in the community, were the most given to entertainments. It was wonderful to see the great circus tents crowded with this bankrupt population, and especially wonderful to note that fully one half of the spectators were freedmen, all screaming in happiness without a cent in their pockets.

The drollest evening that I passed in Greenville was at a magic-lantern exhibition. The pictures illustrated Bunyan's *Pilgrim's Progress* and were horrible enough to have been designed by Apollyon himself in mockery of that almost sacred narrative. The exhibitors were two "muscular Christians," who had precisely the tone and bearing of professional roughs, and whom I suspected of being Baltimore plug-uglies. The contrast between their blood-tub intonation, as they explained the designs, and the pious gravity of the story which was illustrated kept me in a paroxysm of laughter. The climax was reached when we beheld a blue and white Christian meeting three greenish angels.

"Here you see the three shining ones," expounded the plug who stood beside the curtain. "As Christian goes up the hill with his burden he meets the three shining ones. One of them takes him by the hand and says to him— What the h-ll are you doing?"

This last phrase was a loudly whispered aside, addressed to the operator in rear of the curtain, who at that moment extinguished the lantern, perhaps in lighting a cigar from its hallowed flame.

CHAPTER III

APPLICANTS FOR BUREAU RATIONS [1]

ALTHOUGH October, it was beautiful summer-like weather when I commenced my duties in Greenville. My office, a vaulted room on the ground floor of the old courthouse, was so warm that I had opened both door and window and was sitting in the draught, when my first visitors of the impoverished classes entered.

TWO SISTERS

They were two tall, lank, ungainly women, one twenty-three, the other twenty-seven, dressed in dirty, grayish homespun, with tallow complexions, straight, light, dead hair, broad cheek bones, and singularly narrow foreheads. One of them was made a little more repulsive than the other by a deformed hand.

"Mornin'," they said, sat down, stared at me a while, and then asked, "Anythin' for the lone wimmen?"

" 'Pears like I oughter git, if any one does," added the elder. "My husband was shot by the Rebs because he wouldn' jine their army."

Supposing that they might object to the smell of tobacco, I had laid down my pipe on their entrance. Presently the eldest one inquired,

"Stranger, is your pipe a-smokin'?"

"It is," I replied, wondering at such extreme sensitiveness. "But I can put it out."

"Ef it's a-smokin', I should like a smoke," was her only comment.

I may have cringed at the idea of putting my pipe between

1. Published originally as the first installment of "Drawing Bureau Rations" in *Harper's New Monthly Magazine*, XXXVI (May, 1868), 792–799.

those broken teeth, but I of course made haste to do what was hospitable, and I went into the entry before I allowed myself to smile. She smoked tranquilly and passed the luxury to her sister; then they thanked me, "Much obleeged, stranger"—and departed.

MOTHERS AND DAUGHTERS

Next came a mother and daughter. The mother was forty-three, looking sixty, short and broadly built, haggard, wrinkled, filthy, with desperate gray eyes and unkempt gray hair. The daughter, fifteen years old, with a white, freckled face and yellow•hair, had but one garment, a ragged frock of cotton homespun, unbleached, uncolored, and foul with long wearing. Not large enough to meet in front, it was tied with twine in a loose fashion, exposing entirely one of her breasts. This child had in her arms another child, a wretched-looking baby of six weeks old, tied up in an old rag of carpet, her own illegitimate offspring. Her first words were, "How you git'n 'long?" Her next, "Got anythin' for the lone wimmen?"

A few days later, while on my afternoon constitutional in the neighborhood of the village, I was overtaken by another couple, likewise mother and daughter. The former, dressed in coarse white cotton, ghastly, wrinkled, and eager in face, stooping and clumsy in build, slouching forward as she walked, might have been forty-five, but seemed sixty. The daughter, nineteen years old, as I afterward learned, but looking twenty-seven in the precocity of squalor, had a form so tall and straight and shapely that it could not be otherwise than superb in bearing, despite her miserable poverty of life and raiment. Her face too was almost handsome, notwithstanding its broad cheek bones, narrow forehead, and mustang-like wildness of expression. The first words which I heard from this Juno were, "Mam! don't go so fast. Thar's my shoe ontied."

The mother slackened her speed and opened conversation with me.

"Good evenin'. Git'n cold for the season. Goin' to be a mighty hard winter for poor folks."

After some further complaint they pointed out their cabin to me, and I promised to inquire into their circumstances. A little sleet had fallen, the ground had been more than once stiffened by frost, and the long blue ranges visible from Greenville were white with winter before I chanced to fulfill my promise. The cabin consisted of one large room, with a fireplace, two doorways, and two windows. As in all dwellings of the people of this class, the windows were merely square openings, without glass or sashes, and closed by board shutters. The logs of the walls were unhewn, and on two sides the chinking of mud had entirely fallen out, leaving some fifty long slits, averaging two inches in width, through which the wind drove the inclemencies of winter. The moisture which came through these hencoop sides and through the porous roof drained off through the rotten and shattered floor. No furniture was visible beyond two broken chairs, two or three cooking utensils, and a pile of filthy rags which seemed to be bedding.

The family consisted of the mother, two daughters named Susie and Rachel, a son of about five, and a grandson of two, named Johnnie. No man; the father had died years ago; the husband of Susie had fallen "in one of the first battles." Johnnie, flaxen-headed, smiling with health and content, as dirty as a boy could desire to be, squatted most of the time in the ashes, warming himself by a miserable fire of green sticks. His mother, Susie, sat in a broken chair in one corner of the chimney, her eyes bloodshot and cheeks flushed with fever. When I uttered a word or two of pity—it seemed such a horrible place to be sick in!—a few tears started down her cheeks.

"What makes me sick," she said, "is going bar'foot in the winter. I an't used to't. I had a husband once, and no call to go bar'foot."

"Oh, mam!" she presently groaned, addressing her mother, "this is an awful house!"

When I asked her how old she was she confessed ignorance. To the same question the other girl answered with a sheepish smile, "You are too hard for me."

The mother, after some reflection, gave their ages as nineteen and thirteen; but, looking in their worn faces, it seemed impossible that they could be so young. There was an elder sister "who had married and gone way off"; and she had carried away the family Bible with all their names and ages. Their father "used to think a heap of the family Bible."

The remembrance of departed days—not very fine, it may be, but still better than these—revived the sick girl's sentiment of self-pity. "Oh!" she groaned, "I've been through a power in the last two years."

"He's a powerful bad boy," she said, twisting Johnnie's flaxen curls with a smile and looking kindly into his sunny face. "I don't know how I can keep him. I've been all over the village and can't git no work. I can put him in the poorhouse," she added, after a brief silence of desperation.

As she talked with me she turned her head from time to time to spit out her tobacco juice.

"POOR-WHITE TRASH"

Such is the destitute class of the South, familiar to us by name as the "poor-white trash," but better known in Greenville District as the "low-down people." It is the dull, unlettered, hopeless English farm laborer grown wild, indolent, and nomadic on new land and under the discouraging competition of slavery. The breed, however, is not all Anglo-Saxon. Among the low-down people you will find names of Irish, Scotch, French, and German origin. Whatsoever stock of feeble or untamed moral nature settles in the South descends rapidly into this deposit of idleness and savagery. The Celtic race seems to possess a special alacrity at sinking; and Irish families left on the track of Southern railroads become vagrant poor-whites in a single generation. The class, in short, is composed of that tenth of humanity which the severe law of natural selection is perpetually punishing for the sin of shiftlessness.

It seems probable that once the poor-whites were small farmers. The great planter bought them out and turned them into "trash," just as the Roman patrician turned the plebeians into a populace. When Colonel Gresham sold 27,000 acres to a German colony at Walhalla, South Carolina, he delivered one hundred and fifty titles as proofs of ownership, showing the extraordinary fact that something like one hundred and fifty families, or a population of from six to nine hundred souls, had given place to one large landholder. Thus it seems to have been everywhere throughout the domain of slavery. The men who had few Negroes or none parted with their lots and cabins to those who had many; and, once cut loose, they went altogether adrift. They might have bought other lands in their old neighborhoods, but they did not. In the vigorous language of Sut Lovengood,[2] "they sot in to rovin' round."

Before emancipation the Negro supported nearly all Southerners. His daily labor produced the great staples which seemed to enrich the planter, and mainly enriched the factor, merchant, hotel keeper, lawyer, and doctor. After nightfall he stole the chickens, pigs, and corn which he sold to Bill Simmins and his tribe for whisky, or for some trivial product of a gipsy-like industry. The planter, aware of this contraband traffic, sometimes quarreled with Bill and drove him out of the neighborhood, but more frequently tried to bribe him into honesty by gifts and favors. Moreover, Bill had a vote and must be endured and even coaxed for that reason. On the whole, the Simminses were treated by the landholders much as the old Roman populace were treated by the patricians. They got no gladiatorial shows, but in one way or other they got hog and hominy. It was a life of rare day's works, some begging, some stealing, much small, illicit bargaining, and frequent migrations.

When the "black 'uns went up," or, in more universal English, when the Negroes were transfigured into freedmen, the "low-downers" were about as thoroughly bankrupted as the planters. No more trading with slaves, and no more begging from masters. Not only was there far less than formerly for the Negroes to steal, but they were far less addicted to stealing, having acquired some self-respect with their freedom and finding the jail more disagreeable than the whip. The planter, being reduced to his last crust, had, of course, nothing to spare for

2. Sut Lovingood is a fictional character created by G. W. Harris. The first of the stories about Lovingood appeared in *The Spirit of the Times* (New York, November 4, 1854), and a volume of *Sut Lovingood Yarns* was published in 1867. These tales of a "rough, lanky, uncouth mountaineer of the Great Smokies" are in the robust, comic, rustic vein first exploited by A. B. Longstreet in *Georgia Scenes* (1835).

the Simminses; and, furthermore, the male low-downer has roved away to a land whence he will never return, not even with his faculty for migration. Conscripted, much against his will, he was sent to the front, did a respectable amount of fighting, deserted, or died. If a morsel of him survives, it will be pretty sure to tell a Yankee what a Union man it was and how opposed it was to the war before it was "fo'ced in."

His death, although no great loss to him nor to his country, was a more serious matter to his family than one would naturally suppose. "Triflin' creetur" as Bill Simmins was, he was better to his wife than no husband, and better to his children than no father. It is a beggarly fate to be a poor widow or orphan, under any circumstances; but to be one of six hundred soldiers' widows or one of eighteen hundred soldiers' orphans, in a region so lean and so sparsely settled as Pickens District, was a cruel excess of poverty which even a pauper in New England might shrink from.

How to deal with this mass of destitution? Even before hostilities closed it had so far exacted public attention that the Confederacy had been forced to feed the families of its dead or unpaid soldiers.[3] The first Monday of the month, generally known in the South as "sale day" on account of its customary public auction, acquired the additional title of "draw day," because it was used for the issue of rations. Thus, when the Union resumed dominion over the revolted states, it found a population already habituated to corn distributions. "Draw day" disappeared under the first shock of conquest; but it revived as soon as our troops went into garrison; in fact, there came a saturnalia of "draw days." To some extent these monstrous public charities were necessary. There were not only the Simminses to be fed, but many families, once wealthy, who had been stripped by the war or the emancipation, and multitudes of old or infirm or juvenile Negroes who had been set adrift from their homes by the same causes.

3. The program of relief which the various states of the Confederacy provided, by legislative act, for soldiers' dependents is discussed in Charles W. Ramsdell, *Behind the Lines in the Southern Confederacy* (Baton Rouge, 1944), pp. 25–26, 61–68, 89–91. This relief was furnished entirely by state action and not, as De Forest supposed, by the Confederate government. South Carolina had levied a 3 per cent tax in kind, to provide such relief.

"POOR BLACK 'UNS"

I must be permitted to sketch two or three of the colored patriarchs of Greenville. Most curious on the list was Uncle Peter, otherwise known as Kangaboonga, a native African. As there was only one other aboriginal Congo in Greenville or its neighborhood, and as almost any distinction is matter of vanity to its human possessor, Kangaboonga was very conceited over the fact that he was "bohn in Africa, Sar." A withered little fellow, cramped and dislocated with rheumatism, his legs twisted in a style not suitable for traveling, he got himself about with the aid of two sticks, his wrinkled, old face grimacing with the effort, and perhaps with pain. When I heard two sticks and a shuffle on the brick pavement of the passage leading to my office, I knew that the next sound would be the deep, harsh bass of Kangaboonga, trumpeting, "He, he, good morning, Sar."

He had a delusion that his former master owed him five dollars, or some other similarly incredible sum, for services rendered "sence de freedom." I, who knew that the decrepit creature could not earn his salt and that he had been allowed to remain on the old place out of pure charity, sought to argue him out of his absurd complaint or, when fatigued with the useless labor, sent him to roar his grievances to my neighbor, the civil magistrate. In the memory of Kangaboonga I probably live as a "triflin' sort o' Booro man," although in course of time I issued him both corn and clothing.

Uncle March looked like a bald-faced ape in goggles. His small black visage was completely surrounded by snowy hair and beard, and he wore spectacles of such diameter that it seemed as if he might jump through them. Diminutive, stooping, rumpled, decrepit, eighty or ninety years old, he scratched about with a cane, having a laborious air of paddling or "poling." A more cheerful, smiling, sweet-tempered old Negro would be hard to find outside of Paradise. Yet he had a terrific specialty; he was the scarer of naughty children.

"Been down to Mars'r David's, frightnin' one o' his black boys," he relates, naming one of the leading white citizens. "Mars'r David give me fifty cents. Way I manages chil'n is, I has to be 'lone with 'um, locked in a room. Then I looks at 'um through my specs, and I talks to 'um. Ef the boy don't 'pear to come round, I tells him I has to put him up chimly; and sometimes I has to put him up a leetle. Yes, I makes boys good. It's my bisnis."

A mild development of "cussedness" Uncle March would treat for a quarter; but for cases of special depravity he felt that he ought to have half a dollar. We may infer from the liberality of Mars'r David's payment that his offending pickaninny was one of the "real hardened wicked."

Another patriarch, whom I never saw and whose name I have forgotten, came to my knowledge in the following manner: A sturdy, middle-aged Negro, called Cæsar, entered my office and inquired if he could not have his wife and children.

"Certainly," said I.

"But she's got another husband, and things is powerful mixed up."

"Let us hear the whole story."

"Ye see I was sold away from here fifteen years ago into the Alabarmers. Wal, ever sence the freedom I'se been workin' to get back, and last week I gets back and finds my wife all right an' powerful glad to see me. But she thought I was dead, an' so she's been married these ten year, an' thar's her ole man a-livin' with her now. He's a drefful *ole* man; he can't skasely see. She wants me, and wants him to go away, but he won't go."

It was a complicated and delicate case. According to the laws of South Carolina the first marriage was binding, precisely as if the parties had been white, while Bureau orders declared that such persons as were living in lawful wedlock at the date of emancipation were husband and wife, to the exclusion of all other claimants.[4] But looking at the hale, middle-aged man

4. This is almost the only point in the account where De Forest appears to err on his facts. According to the law of South Carolina, December 21, 1865 (*Statutes at Large of South Carolina*, XIII, 269), "Those [persons of color] who now live as such are declared to be husband and wife." The Freedmen's Bureau order, on the contrary, although recognizing the marriage of persons who were living together as husband and wife at the time of emancipation, declared that a husband might, with his wife's consent, leave a childless marriage to claim a previous mate by whom he had had children, if these children were still minors. *House Executive Documents*, 39th Cong., 1st Sess., No. 70, pp. 108–111.

before me and remembering the blind senility of his rival, I ventured to make this a special case and decided according to the civil statute.

"You can have your wife," said I. "If you have worked your way back from Alabama for her sake, you deserve her. I'll write an order to put you in possession."

"An' about the chil'n?" he asked.

"Why, take your own children, of course."

"I means *his* chil'n—the ole woman's chil'n an' *his*. She says she won't go ef she can't hev all her chil'n. An' when we offers to take 'um the old man he hollers an' says: 'What's to come o' *me?*' He's sich a *ole* man, ye see, he can't so much as see to light his pipe. Arter he's got it filled one of us has to put some fire on it 'fore he can git to smoke. That's so, as suah as you's bohn; he can't git to smoke ef some of us don' light some straw to put on his pipe."

"They are your children," I decided, cutting all knots with the statute. "All the children of the wife are the children of the husband. Tell the old man that. It will at least enable you to make good terms with him."

The result was that the wife clove to the younger husband, while the elder remained in the family as a sort of poor relation.

During this man's recital another Negro stood by laughing convulsively; for the race has a keen appreciation of fun and especially of humorous situations. His gayety ceased, and his face assumed a slightly sheepish expression when he came to state his own case.

"Boss, I wants to know ef I kin go roun' and git my chil'n?"

"Were you married to the mother?"

"Why, ye see, Boss—he! he!—thar's two or three mothers," he explained with an embarrassed drawl.

"Oh! but you shouldn't have children lying about loose in that way."

"That's so, Boss. But I'm done with that now. I'm gwine to quit that ar. What I wants now is to pick 'em all up, an' git 'em together, an' look after 'em, an' give 'em a little schoolin'."

"You can't do it. You haven't the slightest legal right to them. The mothers are the only persons who have a claim."

Thus it was. What with superannuated Negroes, families that had been separated by slavery, and families that had been created illegitimately, a large part of the colored race was incapable of self-support and without natural guardians. Where were the children whom Kangaboonga and Uncle March sent into the world scores of years since? Gone to the lowlands or to "the Alabarmers" or to some other undiscovered region. But for the pity of former owners, themselves perhaps bankrupt, and the habit of individual almsgiving prevalent in the South, as in all sparsely settled countries, multitudes of aged, infirm, and infantile blacks would have suffered greatly or perished outright. The freedmen themselves gave willingly, and even lavishly, to each other; but they were improvident, they were working under various disadvantages, and they had little to spare.

OBJECTIONS TO A DISTRIBUTION

But in spite of this mass of poverty I was unwilling to commence a distribution of rations. My predecessor had counseled me against it, assuring me that I would be surrounded by hundreds of claimants and that I would be unable to distinguish between really needy persons and sturdy beggars.

"It does very little good and much hurt," said one respectable citizen. "Where it feeds fifty people who are suffering, it sets a thousand crazy with the idea of getting corn for nothing. If there was a free granary in South Carolina I fear that a large part of our people never would do another lick of work."

Curious stories were told me of the scenes which occurred during my predecessor's distribution. On the last "sale day"— that is, on the first Monday of the month previous to my arrival —a crowd of a hundred people, some bringing bags, others driving carts and wagons, had collected around the Bureau office in the old courthouse. The officer, driven distracted by previous similar trials, had left town to escape his persecutors. The crowd filled the street, questioning, grumbling, quarreling, but waiting. Conspicuous in it, sitting in a cart drawn by two stout little mountain oxen, was a beautiful country girl, who loudly demanded the Bureau officer.

"I want ter settle with him for the way he worked it last draw day," said she. "Thar was folks in our settlement got corn that had no more right to it than nobody."

When informed by some bystander that no more rations would be issued, she replied: "I'm glad of it. You may tell him I wouldn't thank him for any. We've got corn enough of our own to go upon."

So I remained deaf to complaints and requests. I was a general principle, a law of nature; I went for the greatest good of the greatest number. It was useless to tell me that it was "draw day"; I replied that it was not, and that it never again would be.

Some one may suggest the poorhouse as a remedy for this clamorous and persevering mendicity. In one sense it was a remedy; the mere word was sufficient to frighten off all but the most helpless claimants; gaunt, filthy, barefooted women would answer, "Lord's sake! don't send us to the poorhouse." They would accept beggary from door to door, wintry life in a house of pine boughs, prostitution, and thieving, rather than sleep under the roof of public charity. It was a shadow which blighted self-respect and tortured the sensibilities of the meanest white and the most shiftless Negro. Only the decrepit, the sick, and children would go to the almshouse; and in many cases even they had to be carried thither by main force.

Moreover, this resource was altogether inadequate. In South Carolina there are no townships; the district, or county, is the lowest unit of government. Greenville District, a territory of fifteen hundred square miles, containing twenty-five thousand inhabitants, had but a single establishment of public charity— a farm, with one house and a few cabins, capable of accommodating fifty or sixty persons. At the somewhat urgent official instance of my predecessor, acting in accordance with orders from Bureau headquarters, it had been thrown open to Negroes as well as whites, and the cabins increased in number from four to six. There were also a few outside pensioners.

The institution was not only too limited in size, but it was dolefully short of funds. In that impoverished community taxes were practically a myth, and every public interest was fighting for a pittance of public money. In order to save the poorhouse from utter insolvency it had been found necessary to get an order from the governor appropriating to its use the fund of the district commissioners of public buildings. The prisoners were left in rags, the jail and courthouse unrepaired, in order that the paupers might not starve. But this scanty supply could not keep pace long with the current expenses, much less pay the debt which had been accumulating during the lean years of the Confederacy. With that private benevolence which in the South often struggles to stand in place of our Northern system of organization, the Commissioners of the Poor had furnished out of their own (by no means abundant) purse such moneys as were necessary to slide the poorhouse over its frequently recurring breakers. Justice bids me hold up for admiration the names of those tried and stanch friends of indigence, Peter Cauble, Alexander McBee, S. Swandale, and Henry Smith.[5]

I would have been glad to furnish rations to the institution; I thought that to do so would be the best method of getting food to those who absolutely needed it; but there was an order forbidding such application of public stores.[6] Either General Howard supposed that it would lead to frauds, or he wished to force Southern public charities to do their own utmost. At all events commissary stores were not to be dealt out to paupers or prisoners.

Thus I remained a general principle, merciless toward the few for the good of the many, refusing to feed the suffering lest I should encourage the lazy. If I had drawn rations for thirty old Negroes whose decrepitude could not be questioned, three hundred other old Negroes, whose claims were almost equally

5. Of the Commissioners of the Poor, Peter Cauble and Simon Swandale have been identified on pages 35 and 44. Alexander McBee is listed in the census of 1870 as a miller, aged 48, native of South Carolina with real and personal estate valued at $20,100. It is not possible, however, to identify Henry Smith from among the several men of that name listed in the census.

6. Because of complaints that Negroes were being fed in idleness, General Howard halted the issuing of rations in October, 1866, "except to the sick in regularly organized hospitals, and to orphan asylums for refugees and freedmen already existing." Shortly afterward he was persuaded, by petitions from his subordinates, to modify the order and to permit the limited distribution of provisions. "Circular No. 10," August 22, 1866, *Report of the Commissioner of the Bureau of Refugees, Freedmen and Abandoned Lands,* November 1, 1866, p. 8.

good, would have presented themselves. The watchword of "draw day" would have spread like a fiery cross over two thousand square miles of country, bringing into Greenville many hundreds of people who otherwise might remain at work. It would have been "lay down the shovel and the hoe," shoulder the begging-bag, and "try to git." To one who asked for corn because he was near starvation, three would demand it, "seein' 'twas a-gwine."

MORE "POOR-WHITE TRASH"

Dolefully amusing were many of the incidents of mendicity which were daily forced upon my notice. Once a stout woman of thirty-five and a singularly vigorous, rosy girl of nineteen arrived from a settlement in Pickens District, thirty miles distant, in search of rations, beguiled by a report that there was "a drawin'."

"There is nothing to get," I said, "and there will be nothing. You must give up this notion of trotting about the country after corn. You have wasted three days on this expedition, and in that time you could have earned more than you could hope to beg here. You must go to work. Regular labor is the only thing which will keep you from suffering. If you can't sew or spin, go into the fields and hoe. You are strong enough for it."

The girl laughed cheerfully and declared that she was strong enough for anything. The woman looked utterly disconsolate and remained silent for some minutes, apparently in a state of gloomy reflection over these novel and repugnant ideas.

"Oh!" she groaned at last, "I'll go back to Pickens, and I'll work—and I'll work—and I'll work! Nobody shall ever git me away from home again with talkin' about draw day."

"Come, let's start," answered her jolly comrade. "I'll devil you all the way back. I'll have some fun out of it."

A family of North Carolinians named Tony pestered me into more than one fit of snappishness. It consisted of two sisters of about forty, charitably supposed to be widows, of whom one had a son of twenty-two, the other a son of nineteen and a daughter of seventeen. As if their own poverty were not sufficient for them, the two boys married shortly after their arrival in Greenville, each taking to himself a disreputable "lone woman" several years his senior, the wife of the youngest having the additional burden of a stout boy. This horde of two men, five women, and a child would have outbegged a convent of Dominicans. Their first haunt was a deserted hotel which had been used during the war as a Confederate hospital and subsequently became a den for vagrants of all colors. Expelled from this, they took refuge in the racecourse and slept under cover of the Milky Way. Their next move was to a cabin on the land of a miller, seven miles below Greenville, where they worked a little for the proprietor, made a few baskets, told fortunes, and whence they went forth on begging excursions. Every Monday they inquired of me "ef thar was a drawin'," and on other days, "ef thar was anythin' to git."

The miller, a large landholder and one of the wealthiest men in the region, would have given them plenty of work if they would have done it. But work was not their ideal; they only desired to be supported while they slept, smoked, and gossiped; "their strength was to sit still." In the words of a worthy farmer who knew their ways, "them fortune-tellers was the meanest, most triflin', low-down, no-account lot a-goin'." It was useless to threaten them with prosecution as vagrants if they did not keep out of the village. They replied indignantly, and with a sort of pert tartness, "Hain't poor folks got a right to be nowhar?"

I have often laughed to think of the fierce charges which this tribe used to make upon me for rations. One Monday, when I had already been pestered into spitefulness by a course of mendicants, the Tonys appeared in full force, with their usual hungry eagerness of demeanor. The chubby boy, the pale daughter, the two yellow-faced youths, their burly wives, the gaunt and ragged mothers swept in, nearly filling the little room.

"Wal, I've got here," grunted one of the elder women, slapping down a large basket and two or three sacks. "I guess I've come fur enough for it."

"What do you want?" I demanded in high ill humor.

"It's draw day!" she snapped.

" 'Tain't!" I responded in the same tone; for life at that moment was a burden.

The look of disappointment which followed this pettish declaration was little less than ferocious.

"Wal, I should like to know what poor folks is to do," was the
next comment.

"An' thar's my dahter sick," broke in the other woman. "An't
no more fit to come up here than nothin'. An' nothin' to git!"

Then ensued half an hour of waiting and staring; it still
seemed possible that I might be looked out of the rations;
probably, too, I was not fully credited when I denied that there
were any. Another hour was spent on the steps of the courthouse,
and then the tribe departed for the day, hungrier but not wiser.
From such disappointments they never went home to work;
they simply wandered through the village to beg. Did they
obtain? Only too often; the habit of private charity is widely
diffused in the South; the "high-toned gentleman" gives as of
old, and much more than he can now afford. The better classes
despise and almost detest the "low-down people," but rarely
have the heart to refuse them. The thought of turning any one
away hungry is repulsive in almost all communities where a
sparse population forbids organized beneficence. I learned
during my stay in Greenville that many men whose incomes
were little more than nominal constantly contributed to the
support of their absolutely indigent neighbors, whether worthy
or unworthy.

"Colonel Towns helped me some," one vagrant would declare; "and ef I could git two dollars, I'd have enough to go
upon for a month."

"General Easely give me a dollar," confessed another; "Alec
McBee let me have a bushel of corn," was the story of a third;
and so on, an endless round of charities, not from overflowing
pockets. Oh! but that slavery was costly, with its breed of
parasite poor-whites and its remaining dross of decrepit old
Negroes! I do not think that I exaggerate greatly when I declare that two thirds of the people of my Bureau district were
burdened with the support of the other third. A Greenville
merchant assured me that, what with gifts outright and credits
to people who, as he knew, could never pay, it cost him five times
as much for the living of other people as for his own.

And such ungrateful recipients as many of them were! There

surely never was a more dissatisfied, crabbed, growling, un-appeased, unconverted set of poor folks than the "low-down people." It seemed probable to me that they would willingly join in any feasible scheme for confiscating the acres, if not for cutting the throats, of the property holders who fed them. "When's our folks gwine to git the land?" they sometimes asked me, passing themselves off for worthy and oppressed Unionists.

A clergyman of Greenville related to me an interview which he had with a woman of this degraded caste. She had come to his door to beg, and he had, after his custom, invited her into his parlor to talk; "for," said he, "I owe a duty to these people's souls as well as to their bodies." To his horror he discovered that she knew nothing about Christ and was, practically, a sound heathen. Her desire was not for the heavenly manna, but for hog and hominy—not to forget some smoking tobacco.

"You are a strong, healthy woman," said he. "You ought to be able to earn your own living."

"Poor folks ha'n't no chance," she asserted. "What's poor folks to do without land? I don't see why you should have such a big dooryard when I ha'n't got nothin'," she added, carrying the war into the enemy's country. "Ef I had your dooryard I mought raise a crop on it."

"This dooryard is not mine," he replied. "Still, I will give you a chance to make something off it. If you will clean it and my garden of leaves I will give you a dollar a day as long as the work lasts."

"Wal, I'll see about it," gloomily replied the inveterate old tramp and, departing with her bag and basket, returned no more. She had no fancy for a house where she was offered work and wages instead of meal and broken victuals. Had she come into possession of the parsonage dooryard she would simply have put a cabin or a brush house upon it, and thence gone forth on her begging excursions.

I presume that I saw more of these lazy agrarians than any one else. Citizens, whose patience or purses gave out under their exactions, naturally sent them to the United States officer, as a person who was supposed to have unlimited command of hog and hominy. Village jokers used to tell them, "You must come down to the Bureau next Monday. It's going to be a big draw day—corn and shoes and dresses and parasols."

IMPOVERISHED GENTRY

Besides the white trash and the old Negroes, there were suffering people of the better class, though not many. My district was an upland region, a country of corn rather than of cotton, cultivated by small farmers and middling planters. Containing few slaves compared with the lowlands, only a moderate proportion of its capital had been destroyed by emancipation. Sherman's bummers had never crossed its borders. Its poverty arose from the leanness of the soil, the imperfection of agriculture, the loss of hundreds of young men in battle, the exhaustion of stock and capital during the war, the lack of intelligent and zealous labor, and the thriftless habits incident on slavery. There were few families of landed gentry so reduced as to need rations, and those few were chiefly refugees who had fled from the seacoast during the Rebellion.

The condition of these persons was pitiable. A mulatto once came to me and said: "I do wish, Sir, you could do something for Mr. Jackson's family. They's mighty bad off. He's in bed, sick—ha'n't been able to git about this six weeks—and his chil'n's begging food of my chil'n. They used to own three or four thous'n acres; they was great folks befo' the war. It's no use tellin' them kind to work; they don't know how to work, and can't work; somebody's got to help 'em, Sir. I used to belong to one branch of that family, and so I takes an interest in 'em. I can't bear to see such folks come down so. It hurts my feelings, Sir."

Another claimant was a lady who had formerly owned six hundred and fifty acres on one of the richest of the sea islands. When Du Pont took Port Royal she had fled, carried away by the deluge of panic. Her house was burned, no one knows how or by whose act. In 1862 her estate was sold for delinquent taxes, one plantation falling into the hands of private purchasers, the other becoming a part of the city of Port Royal. Long before the war ended this lady, seventy years old, was an object of charity, supported by friends nearly as impoverished as herself, and frequently carrying her bag, like a poor-white, to beg corn of the miller. While I was in Greenville she lived in a little ruinous house, furnished her rent-free by a relative, himself ill able to support even so small a sacrifice. Her bed was a mattress spread on the floor, as far as possible from the broken window. She did her own cooking; it was not much to do. I have seen her trudging slowly up a long hill, at the foot of which was a spring, reeling under the weight of a pail of water.

This woman has already tasted greater bitterness than there is in death. Two sons—she could not have restrained them—if she could have done that she could not have sheltered them—joined the Southern army and fell. A daughter, an educated lady, worked for eight dollars a month at service little less than menial. A beautiful granddaughter, the heiress herself of a confiscated plantation, was surrendered at the age of seven to the adoption of strangers and was parted from her by the breadth of the Atlantic.

NATIVE VIEWS CONCERNING RATIONS

Had such cases as these been common in my Bureau district I should have been driven by my conscience into an early distribution of rations. But the fact that my poor were chiefly low-down whites who needed to be spurred to work, or venerable Negroes who were tolerably well cared for by charitable planters, enabled me long to resist that humane impulse which detests general laws and calls for special providences. In this policy I was sustained by the wisest and best of the inhabitants.

"There always was this mean lot about," affirmed one industrious farmer, who abhorred lazy people. "In the old times, when corn was twenty-five cents a bushel, you could see these same creeturs going around with their bags on their shoulders, tryin' to git. It would be God's good riddance if two thirds of them could be starved to death. The rest might set in to work."

"I wouldn't advise an issue," said one of my legal acquaintances, as pitiful-hearted a man as I ever knew. "If you begin, you won't know where to stop. I really think that many of our people will have to suffer severely before they will learn that they must support themselves. This distribution of food is an absolute injury to us."

Against the claims of the Union mountaineers of the Dark Corner [7] I was warned with something like ardor. "I tell you those Tories are the meanest people on God's earth," roared an old farmer who had hunted them, and been hunted by them, during the Rebellion. "They are nothing but robbers. They didn't care a shake of my cane for the United States. All they wanted was to plunder the people who had the rich bottoms and the full corn cribs."

And then the venerable "Reb" rushed into a long narration of how he had been despoiled of hams and yarn by a notorious Unionist after the proclamation of peace.

"I had him tried for it in the last court," said he; "and don't you think that they brought him in not guilty? The indictment was for stealing, and the judge charged that it wasn't stealing because it was done openly—it was robbery. And so they cleared him. What do you think of that for justice?"

"Oh! there are some good ones among them," he admits presently, for he is not destitute of fairness. "There's old Solomon Jones, he's an honest sort of an old feller; he's no robber. And there's a few more such—but mighty few, Major. It's about the meanest crap of humans that ever *was* raised."

And so the Bureau Major persevered in his refusal to have a "draw day." Do not be bitter upon him; he suffered somewhat for his obstinacy; he was perseveringly pestered. Day after day he took an unwilling part in such dialogues as the following:

"Mornin'. How you git'n 'long? Got anything for the poor folks?"

"Nothing at all. Not a solitary thing."

"Got any corn?"

"No."

"Got any shoes?"

"No."

"Got any close?"

7. The term Dark Corner had been applied to the Glassy Mountain District of Greenville County by the Nullificationists of 1832 because it gave them only one vote out of 170. Lillian Adele Kibler, *Benjamin F. Perry, South Carolina Unionist* (Durham, N. C., 1946), p. 487.

"No."

"Ha'n't got anythin'?"

"No. I told you so at first."

"Didn't know but you had *somethin'*. I thought I'd name it to you."

In my next chapter I will relate how I eventually had something, and how I got rid of it.

CHAPTER IV

DRAWING BUREAU RATIONS [1]

IT was February, 1867, and I had been over four months in charge of my sub-district, before I was driven to make a distribution of public stores.

The winter was an unusually cold one for Greenville, bringing with it ice two inches in thickness and one snowfall of three inches. I heard that the family of women and children mentioned in my former chapter as living in an unchinked log cabin had been evicted in consequence of inability to pay the rent of a dollar and a half a month, and was camping out in the snow under a shelter of pine branches. A barefooted Negro or two appeared, trampling down my sense of duty as a general principle. I slowly and unwillingly came to the conclusion that the greatest good of the greatest number must give way to the necessities of a poverty-stricken minority.

Accordingly, when an order came from the Assistant Commissioner at Charleston to make a requisition for such clothing as might be needed in my district, I remembered the aged Negroes, the soldiers' widows, and the orphan children, and demanded a supply of blankets, coats, trousers, boys' jackets, women's dresses, and shoes. Corn I would not ask for, because I considered it demoralizing. The very name of corn, the bare hope of being fed from the public crib seemed to be sufficient to change plowshares into begging-bags, and pruning-hooks into baskets.

In return for my requisition I received thirty greatcoats, forty blankets, thirty pairs of trousers, seventy pairs of large brogans, twenty women's skirts, and twenty dresses. Coats for men, jackets and shoes for boys, small dresses for girls were not to be had. The greatcoats, blankets, and trousers were stores originally bought for the army, but condemned as being either

---

1. Published originally as the second installment of "Drawing Bureau Rations" in *Harper's New Monthly Magazine*, XXXVII (June, 1868), 74–82.

of inferior quality or not in accordance with the uniform. The brogans were the sturdiest kind of clod-thumpers, such as planters formerly provided for their field hands. The skirts and dresses, also for plantation wear, were of the coarsest imaginable cotton stuff, stiff enough to stand alone, and of a horrible bluish gray. I was grievously disappointed over my stock of "winter goods," for I had especially wanted something for women and children. There were not a quarter dresses enough, and they were "perfect frights." But the Assistant Commissioner had sent what he could get and had portioned out the various articles impartially among his subordinates.

ARMY BOOKKEEPING

One word as to the method of accounting for these stores. From the moment that they were consigned to me they were on my official conscience and could not be wiped off without much paper. To get them it was necessary to have duplicate requisitions, duplicate receipts, and duplicate invoices. To issue them was far more serious. The skirts and dresses being furnished by the Bureau, and the other articles by the Quartermaster-General's Department, I had to settle matters with both those sublime authorities. If I issued but one blanket and one skirt, I must make out three Bureau returns and four Quartermaster returns,[2] supporting each set with duplicate invoices, duplicate receipts, and duplicate clothing-receipt rolls, the latter signed by the names of the recipients, and the signatures witnessed by another officer or a civilian. The returns must show what I had on hand at the beginning of the month; what I had received during the month, and from whom; what I had issued, and to whom; and what remained on hand. Each must have my name and rank in four places and must be certified to "upon honor." Even if I did not issue a solitary thing, I must still make out my seven returns, although without vouchers. On no account must I neglect to forward a letter of transmittal and copy the same in my book of Letters Sent.

2. De Forest's quarterly reports of Bureau Stores on Hand (National Archives) show the precise number of garments which he lists in the previous paragraph, and show also that quartermaster's stores were reported separately.

But the labor did not stop with me. All the returns must go to the Assistant Commissioner and the Commissioner. Under the eye of the last a division took place, the Bureau papers pushing on to the Third Auditor of the Treasury, the others to the Quartermaster-General, and thence to the Second Auditor. All these august officers peered and poked into them with severe eyes, searching for some error whereby to stop my pay.

Great as this wonderful "accountability system" is, it has by no means reached its majestic possibilities and is yearly, if not monthly, growing more perfect and impracticable. At the beginning of the war a company commander made annually but twelve returns of "clothing, camp and garrison equipage," whereas now he makes forty-eight, with an amount of vouching and certifying "upon honor" that was formerly unimaginable.[3] If somebody does not put a stop to the pranks of the paper-eating jugglers in the accounting offices, army affairs will soon be conjured into a clerkly paradise of "how not to do it," and patriotic souls will welcome whatsoever rebellion will take Washington and burn the War Department.

AN ISSUE OF CLOTHING

"Mornin'. How ye git'n 'long? Got anythin' for the lone wimmen?"

"Yes, ma'am. What do you need? How am I to know that you need anything?"

"Oh, Lord! I guess I'm poor enough. My ole man was killed in the war because he wouldn't jine the Rebs. They shot him in the swamp, right whar they found him. We was always for your side. And I've got two small children, and nothin' to go upon. Got any corn?"

Her old man was probably a "low-down creetur" who was executed as a deserter, having refused to join the Rebs just as he would have evaded joining any army or doing anything that implied work. But looking at her haggard face and ragged clothing, how could I find it in my heart to doubt that she was a "Union woman?" My stores, it must be remembered, were properly distributable only to freedmen and refugees, the latter

3. This statement applies to 1867; matters now may be better—or worse. (De F.)

term meaning Southern loyalists who had been driven from their homes by the Confederacy.

I had intended to procrastinate and be mercilessly conscientious in my distribution, giving nothing except to persons whom I knew by personal inspection to be the very poorest in the district. But the pressure of an instantaneously aroused horde of dolorous applicants rendered it impossible to be either deliberate or fastidious. Amidst such an abundant supply of poverty there seemed to be no choice; and after a few days of heroic holding on to my goods, I let go with a run. Only in the overcoat business did I make a firm stand; the weather having turned mild, I boxed them up for another winter; indeed, I counterfeited innocence of overcoats. The remaining articles, one hundred and eighty in number, were distributed among ninety-four applicants, consisting of eleven white women, forty-nine colored women, and thirty-four colored men. All but one or two of the whites were widows with families of small children; and nearly all the blacks were deformed, rheumatic, blind, or crippled with extreme age.

In vain I resolved to issue but one article to an individual, in order to make the supply go further. A venerable, doubled-up contraband would say, "Boss, I got shoes now, but dey won't keep me warm o'nights. Can't I hev a blanket, Boss?" A woman furnished with a dress would show her bare or nearly bare feet and put up a prayer for brogans. The wretched family from the brush house appeared and in its grasping distress carried off three dresses, three pairs of shoes, and two blankets. Widows of Confederates though they were, how could I look on their muddy rags and tell them that they were not refugees and had no claim upon Bureau charity? Had the Second Auditor and the Third Auditor discovered this pitiful rascality of mine, it would have been their duty to disallow my returns and stop my pay.

My little room, crammed with people of all colors elbowing each other in the equality of sordid poverty, looked as though it might be a Miscegenation Office. The two races got along admirably together; the whites put on no airs of superiority or aversion; the Negroes were respectful and showed no jealousy. There is little social distance at any time between the low-downer and the black. Two white women were pointed out to me as having children of mixed blood; and I heard that one rosy-cheeked girl of nineteen had taken a mulatto husband of fifty.

Now and then I was amused by a sparkle of female vanity. Two white widows of twenty-four or twenty-five—comely by nature, but now gaunt and haggard with the ailments which hardship surely brings upon women—charily exposed their muddy stockings of coarse homespun wool and, pipe in mouth, held the following dialogue:

"Miss Jackson, these shoes are a sight too big for me. I wear fours."

"That's so, Miss Jacocks. Fours is my number, too. And I hev worn threes."

Of my ninety-four recipients ninety-four signed with a mark; and in my subsequent issues I found that this was the usual proportion.

CALLS FOR CORN

And now the public talk was of corn. The crop of 1866, both of cereals and other productions, had been a short one for various reasons. Capital, working stock, and even seed had been scarce; a new system of labor had operated, of course, bunglingly; finally, there had been a severe drought. During the autumn and early winter I was called upon to arrange a hundred or two of disputes between planters and their hands as to the division of the pittance which nature had returned them for their outlay and industry.[4] The white, feeling that he ought to have a living out of his land and fearing lest he should not get enough "to go upon" until the next harvest, held firmly to the terms of his contract and demanded severe justice—in some cases more than justice. The Negro could not understand how the advances which had been made to him during the summer should swallow up his half or third of the "crap."

Honesty bids me declare that, in my opinion, no more advantage was taken of the freedmen than a similarly ignorant

4. De Forest's problem here was not a local one, for the crop failure of 1866 had made the management of labor contracts more difficult than ever throughout South Carolina. Webster, "Freedmen's Bureau in South Carolina," pp. 115-117.

class would be subjected to in any other region where poverty should be pinching and the danger of starvation imminent. So far as my observation goes, the Southerner was not hostile toward the Negro as a Negro, but only as a possible office-holder, as a juror, as a voter, as a political and social equal. He might cuff him, as he would his dog, into what he calls "his place"; but he was not vindictive toward him for being free, and he was willing to give him a chance in life.

On the other hand, the black was not the vicious and totally irrational creature described in reactionary journals. He was very ignorant, somewhat improvident, not yet aware of the necessity of persistent industry, and in short a grown-up child. I venture these statements after fifteen months of intercourse with the most unfair and discontented of both parties. The great majority of planters and laborers either did not dispute over their harvest of poverty or came to an arrangement about it without appealing to me.

The ignorance of the freedmen was sometimes amusing and sometimes provoking. When Captain Britton, of the Sixth Infantry, acted as Bureau officer in a South Carolina district, a farmer and Negro came before him to settle the terms of their contract, the former offering one third of the crop, and the latter demanding one sixth. It was only by the aid of six bits of paper, added and subtracted upon a table, that the captain succeeded in shaking the faith of the darkey in his calculation.

"Well, Boss," he answered doubtfully, "ef you say one third is the most, I reckon it's so. But I allowed one sixth was the most."

I passed nearly an entire forenoon in vainly endeavoring to convince an old freedman that his employer had not cheated him. I read to him, out of the planter's admirably kept books, every item of debit and credit: so much meal, bacon, and tobacco furnished, with the dates of each delivery of the same; so many bushels of corn and peas and bunches of "fodder" harvested. He admitted every item, admitted the prices affixed; and then, puzzled, incredulous, stubborn, denied the totals. His fat, old wife, trembling with indignant suspicion, looked on grimly or broke out in fits of passion.

"Don' you give down to it, Peter," she exhorted. "It ain't no how ris'ible that we should 'a' worked all the year and git nothin' to go upon."

The trouble with this man was that he had several small grandchildren to support, and that he had undertaken to do it upon a worn-out plantation. I could only assure him that he had "nothing coming" and advise him to throw himself upon the generosity of his employer. As the latter was himself woefully poor, and as it was my duty to set even-handed justice on its legs, any exaction in favor of the laborer beyond the terms of the contract was out of the question.

There were hundreds of cases like this; and there were the old, the widows, and the orphans. Although my district was a grain country, corn rose to two dollars a bushel, and bacon to forty cents a pound. In the lowlands of South Carolina the destitution was still more pinching and prices still higher. Governor Orr published a moving appeal for aid, composed mainly of letters showing a widespread want nearly approaching starvation. Evidently the hour was coming upon me when I should be obliged to make an issue of provisions.

CATALOGUING MISERY

Early in the spring of 1867 a circular from the Commissioner at Washington directed each Bureau officer to furnish a return of the blind, the deaf and dumb, and the naturally deformed among the freedpeople of his sub-district.[5] Will the reader please to consider what was exacted of me by this order? In my satrapy of at least two thousand square miles I was alone, without a clerk or a soldier; and yet I was called upon to furnish information which a corps of census-takers could not have collected in three months. Seeing that I should be obliged to have recourse to the civil authorities, I resolved to lump the born unfortunate in one job with the indigent and obtain lists of both.

As I have already stated, South Carolina has no townships. But each of my districts was divided into two "regiments," and each regiment into eight or ten "companies," otherwise known as "beats." The organization was formerly military as well as

5. For the statistics thus compiled, see *Report of the Secretary of War*, 40th Cong., 2d Sess., I, 637.

civil; each beat had its captain as well as its magistrate; each regiment sent a battalion to the Confederate army. It will be seen that I had under me between thirty and forty civil officers, properly disseminated, and each having his own domain. This machinery I set in motion. Stretching my powers to perhaps their utmost, I issued through the local papers a circular [6] to the Greenville and Pickens magistrates, calling on them to send me lists of their blind, dumb, and deformed Negroes, and their indigent of both races. I furnished a model table, ruled in columns, showing name, age, color, number of children under fourteen years of age, nature of deformity, and cause of poverty.

My circular, as I guessed from the first and saw fully afterward by experience, was directed to the right quarters. Every farmer in the region knows everybody within ten miles of him; and a "Square" who lacks in this species of information is considered unfit for his office. Moreover, the magistrates were as willing as able; they did their work with zeal, thoroughness, and generally with promptitude; they surprised me by their good will, for I had expected some unreconstructed sulkiness and some human laziness.

It was months, to be sure, before I gathered the full fruits of my circular; but that was the fault of circumstances rather than of my civilian adjutants. In springtime the roads of that region are quagmires, and at all times the mails go, as the Arabs say, when God pleases. If I wrote to the magistrate of Jones's Beat, Pickens District, some twenty miles distant from Greenville, the letter must go down to Anderson, thence up to Pendleton, and thence across the country to its destination, by a carrier who performed the journey once a week. A return document must meander its way about the country in the same leisurely fashion. Thus I was separated from Jones's Beat by an interval of from a fortnight to a month. Moreover, if a messenger came from thence and found my office door shut, he would, as likely as not, go home again without trying the knob,

6. This appeal is printed in the Greenville *Southern Enterprise*, April 18, 1867. It asked for lists of the destitute, the naturally unfortunate, the blind, the deaf and dumb, the insane, the imbecile and idiotic, the clubfooted, or those otherwise deformed. The appeal stated that, "In view of the ignorance of the majority of the colored population, it is desired that special pains be taken to obtain a full list of their destitute." File of the *Southern Enterprise* in Charleston Library Society, Charleston, S. C.

for it is the fashion in the South to keep all doors open, and the closing of one is considered a sure sign of absence, if not of death.

My circular brought upon me a prodigious correspondence. Men not accustomed to drawing up ruled forms and making official reports easily bungle at such labor and produce documents which can not be understood without correction or explanation. Some of the beats being without magistrates, I was obliged to learn the names of residents who were capable of making out the required lists, to issue orders appointing these gentlemen "distributors," and to forward them manuscript instructions. Private individuals all over the district wrote to me, urging the claims of indigent families of their acquaintance; and to these I had to reply, explaining my proposed method of distribution and referring them to their magistrates; or, having already received the official list, I added the new names thereto. It required steady determination and some little savageness of demeanor to prevent the system from centralizing. The general disposition was to rush to Greenville and see the Major. The pauper classes, snuffing corn in the wind, made for me like pigs for an oak tree in autumn. Forty times a day my office was the scene of dialogues like the following:

"Mornin', stranger. Got anythin' for the lone wimmin?"

"Where do you belong?"

"I b'long up on Saludy."

"Who is the magistrate of your beat?"

"Square Runnols."

"Go to him and offer your name for his list."

"But he's an old Reb, an' he won't take no names but Reb names."

"Have you tried him?"

"No, I ha'n't."

"Well, try him. If he refuses your name, let me know, and I will inquire into it."

Low-downer waits another half hour and then goes off disgusted. Had expected corn on the spot; wanted, perhaps, to trade it off in the village; had doubts, possibly, that her character would not pass with the magistrate. Meanwhile the next has spoken:

"Got anythin' for poor folks?"

"What beat do you live in?"

"I dun'no."

"You must go back and find out."

"I dun'no how to find out."

"Ask some of your intelligent neighbors what beat you live in and who your magistrate is. Then give your name to him.".

"Wal, 'pears like I never should git no corn. Of all the drawin's that's been here I never got not the first dust of a thing. 'Pears like thar an't nothin' for poor folks. Them that don't want can git. That's allays the way."

"Find out your magistrate and give him your name."

Had I once commenced taking names from the farming regions I should have been overwhelmed, and two thousand people would have traveled an average of fifteen miles apiece without a particle of benefit. Moreover, aside from my general supervision and the routine duties of my office, I had taken upon myself a special labor which was more than enough for one man. The two magistrates of the incorporation of Greenville being lawyers and abundantly occupied with their own affairs, and the two neighboring beats known as Reed's and Piney Mountain being without magistrates, I made out the lists for those four precincts myself, aided by the clerk of the district court. This involved not only a large amount of writing, but conversations, not to say quarrels, with at least five hundred eager applicants, some of them ignorant and unreasonable beyond belief.

"Mrs. Cooper, you must tell me what beat you live in," I said to one hard-featured, persevering woman of fifty. "I will not take your name until I know on what list to put it. Go to the clerk of the court, tell him precisely where you live, and ask him what your beat is."

Across the street rushes Mrs. Cooper and returns after an absence of five minutes.

"Well, Madame, which is your beat—Reed's or Piney Mountain?"

"Wal, I forget what place he said it was; but he allowed I was poor enough. He said if anybody oughter draw, I oughter."

"Here, take this note to him; it asks for the name of your beat; when he has written it, bring it back."

Mrs. Cooper, suspicious that she is somehow being juggled out of her corn, dashes off desperately and seeks out an officer of the court, called the Ordinary, who knows her family. The Ordinary has lost one leg at Bull Run, but at the call of distress he stumps over to my office.

"My dear fellow, I am sorry that you have been put to this trouble," I apologize, giving him a chair. "But I can't find out where this person lives."

"Oh, I don't know her present residence myself. I only know that the family has always been poor. I can't give the name of her beat."

"Mrs. Cooper," I implore, "why *won't* you go to the clerk of the court and learn the name of your beat? That is all I want to know."

Here Mrs. Cooper, conceiving herself to be humbugged and bullied, loses heart and bursts into tears. The Ordinary takes her in charge, carries her before the clerk, has her describe the locality of her "settlement," and sends her back with the word "Reed's" written on her paper.

"Ah, Reed's!" I say. "Do you know Mr. Thomas Turner?"

"Yes. He lives next neighbor to us; about a mile this side."

"Well, go to Mr. Turner and state your case to him. When the corn comes—it has not arrived yet—go to him for it. Don't come here. You will get nothing except from Mr. Turner."

This conversation, it must be understood, has been carried on parenthetically between similar dialogues with the other half dozen or so of applicants who crowd the office.

"I should think you would go crazy," said a citizen to me. "This kind of thing would drive me mad in a day."

After the lists were made out, it was necessary to sift them. I was determined that the notoriously idle, the habitual beggars, the thieves and prostitutes should only have corn in case there should be too much of it for worthier applicants. After cataloguing some two hundred and fifty paupers from the two beats of the incorporation, I reduced the number to about one hundred and seventy-five, copied it out in alphabetical order, with age, race, cause of poverty, and number of children, and handed the paper to the Poor Commissioners for a further revision. They called in three influential freedmen, elders of the colored people, and held solemn session, striking out some twenty names and adding as many more. To my delight—for misery loves company—the meeting was invaded and pestered by "lone women," etc., the mendicant public having by this time become amazingly alert and knowing.

The list was now alphabetized a second time; a column was added showing the allowance due each family, based on the official monthly ration of one bushel of corn and eight pounds of bacon for adults, and half the same for children under fourteen; and the document was ready for delivery to the distributors. The Reed's and Piney Mountain lists were alphabetized and the rations figured out in the same manner. Most of this writing I was obliged to do, for the clerk of the court had his own duties. My position in those days was so far from being a sinecure that I worked pretty regularly till midnight.

All this trouble was necessary to make an intelligent issue. Numberless vagrants attempted to impose upon me with tales of hardships which they had not suffered or which they had fully deserved by steady, hard-working vice and laziness. Families "sot in to rovin' round," in order to get their names on the lists of several beats. "Lone women" bewailed the loss of fictitious husbands and claimed my pity for children who had never been born. As far as I could compare the two races, able-bodied Negroes were much less apt to apply for rations than able-bodied "low-downers." When I complained of these impositions to Mr. Alexander, a worthy old gentleman who has aided many a poverty-stricken wretch out of his own small income, he smiled and said: "They don't call it cheating, Major; they call it tryin' to git."

For the correctness of the lists from the farming precincts I had to trust to the magistrates. I had warned them to take only the names of persons who were in danger of starvation, and I believe that they followed my instructions as accurately as men could do under the circumstances. They, as well as myself, were pestered with applicants, and their credulity tried with false tales of distress. Several of them informed me that poor people had turned up in their precincts of whom they had never before had any knowledge. They often came to Greenville, riding from ten to thirty miles, to consult with me. They did their work most zealously, most conscientiously, most honorably, without a prospect of remuneration, and frequently to the neglect of their private interests. In order to show the nature of their labor I will introduce one of the three or four successive lists sent me by an aged magistrate in Pickens District.

List of Destitute in ⸺ Comp beat No. ⸺ 5th Regiment Pickens District, S. C. Taken down by the under Signed Magistrate

Names	Age	Coler	No under 14	
Elizabeth Wilson wid	36	white	3	has no provisions and no money & will Suffer
Mary Ann Jeffris	75	do	0	Verry infirm not able to work & is Suffering
Jinney Glenn w^d	31	Colered	3	left arm disabled and in want
Rarry Sexton	80	white	0	Verry infirm and greatly in need of help
David Lesley	56	do	9	infirm & wife Very Sickly, has only ½ bushel Corn & no meat and his Labor is not Sufficient to Support his famley no money & no means to by any thing
Susan Chertain, wid	65	Colered		thinks She must Suffer without help
Tilda Burgess do	50	do	7	and Verry hard Run to git bred
J. C. Fortner male	60	white	5	him Self not able to work much and his wife Sickly and now in want.
J. C. Heaton male	42	white	5	has no Corn or meat & is unable to support his famly
Salley Turner w^d	32	do	1	Rather Ediot & nearly naked nothin to Eat
Mary Phillips	45	do	2	has Some Corn no meat—no money
Edy Turner wid	51	do	3	no provisions nothing to by with & will Suffer
Cayty Aytes	48	do	2	no provisions Says She is Suffering
Sarah Gowan wid	80	Colered	0	Very feeble has Sore leg & Cant work no provisions
Learer McCoy	48	do	5	has no provision nor not able to work much

List of Destitute in ——— Comp beat No. ——— 5th Regiment
  Pickens District, S. C. Taken down by the under Signed
  Magistrate

Rosa Corban	36	white	2	hasen had any meat in 4 months & litle bred
Milly Hendruks	24	do	2	has no provisions nor Cant git for her work

(Signed) _____

Magistrate

To Magr J. W. De Forrest & *S. A. Comr Bureau of District Greenville, S. C.*

The reader may have drawn from the above a somewhat exaggerated inference as to the meagreness of what one of my Greenville friends called the "spelling crap" in South Carolina. It must be understood that the jurisdiction of a magistrate is limited to cases below twenty dollars, and that consequently the office is scorned by such country gentlemen of position and education as have leanings toward public life. The "Square" is usually a butcher, miller, or small farmer. A few of the lists sent to me were correctly written; the majority were better than the above specimen; one or two were worse, like the following:

PICKENS DIST s. c.

the destutes persons of ——— Beet

Dick Hunt Freedman age about......................... 75
Wife of Dick Hunt Freedwoman........................ 76
Jane ponder Freed woman age......................... 35
2 childearn in Sain
Eda Hunt Freedwoman age............................. 65
Sarey Mancill Freedwoman age........................ 65
Lucia Hester Weder about a White.................... 35
& 5 childearn all under............................. 14
Kin Looper Freedman age............................. 62
& his Wife Freedwoman age........................... 70
Selnartan Vandervear white Widear age.............. 70
Nancy pensean a Widear white age................... 47
& 2 childearn dautars one with Tumaer on her
    Neck and has spasames

This is Tru List of the Destutes of ——— Beat as fair as I have Knowlege at this time

(Signed) ——— _____

M. P. D.
J. B. T.

Mr J. W. De Forist
You Will pleas Let Wm Holden have the Rasheans for theas pearsons & oblege Yours &c
(Signed) ——————— ————————.
M. P. D.
J. B. T.
P.S. Pleas take those names off of Esq. Reid's List that I gave you the other day as I have them on this and oblige
(Signed) ——————— ————————
M. P. D.

AN ISSUE OF CORN

On the 30th of March, 1867, an Act of Congress appropriated one million of dollars for the relief of the destitute of the South, to be distributed under the supervision of the Commissioner of the Freedmen's Bureau. On the 15th of May I received notice that five hundred bushels of corn had been consigned to me by the Assistant Commissioner at Charleston. At the same time Governor Orr forwarded, as a gift from the state of Maryland, 250 bushels to W. K. Easely, Esq., for Pickens, and 200 bushels and one hogshead of bacon to Mr. J. M. David for Greenville. As I now had my machinery of distribution nearly completed I volunteered to take charge of the entire issue, and the offer was accepted.

The first thing to be done was to foot up my lists and assign a pro-rata allowance to each beat. The result of my calculation amazed and dismayed me. From a population of perhaps forty-five thousand persons I had received lists to the amount of about one thousand adult destitute and about eighteen hundred children under fourteen,[7] enough to draw, as one month's ration, nineteen hundred bushels of corn and seven thousand two

7. These figures are, for some reason, at variance with those which De Forest included in his monthly report for May, 1867. The following table summarizes the lists of destitute certified by the magistrates:

Greenville District

	Adults	Children	Total
Colored	367	611	978
White	474	837	1311

Pickens District

	Adults	Children	Total
Colored	126	224	350
White	387	780	1167

hundred pounds of bacon. To meet this demand I had nine hundred and fifty bushels of corn and one thousand pounds of bacon. Fortunately it soon appeared that other stores had been sent to persons in Walhalla and Pickens Court House for the relief of the western regiment of Pickens. Thus I was only obliged to supply thirty beats, containing about twenty-three hundred destitute.

Stretching my authority to its utmost once more, I issued another circular, assigning a certain quantity to each "company," and ordering the magistrates to distribute it. They were to send wagons to Greenville for the corn; raise subscriptions in their several neighborhoods to cover the expense of transportation; issue the rations on their retained copies of their lists; then forward me a statement of issues. It was laying a heavy burden on them; most of them were farmers and busy just now with their crops; many of them hardly knew how they could live until the next harvest; it was a heavy burden, but it was lifted manfully. I shall feel to the end of my life that I abused those men and that they deserve my respect and praise.

The subscription idea proved a failure, for the Southerners are not accustomed to organized benefaction. Moreover, some hard-hearted wretches, such as exist in all communities, did not want to aid in the issue, for the reason that it reduced the market value of the contents of their cribs. But the corn was all sent for, and all, as I believe, honestly issued. One distributor, an elderly man in impoverished circumstances, ground the allowance for his beat in his own mill in order to perfect the charity. Another, who told me that he did not know whether he should be able to feed his family till the next harvest, came thirty miles with his own team to get the allowance for his beat. The following letter (one of dozens), from one of the worthiest of these worthy men, will show (together with some eccentricities of spelling) the good will of the writer and the difficulties under which he labored.

——— Beat, Greenville Dist. S. C.
May 21st, 1867.

Maj. J W De Forest
Dear Sir
You will pleas let Mr ——— have a load of the supplys which you have for Distribution amongst the Destitute persons in my Beat & he will hawl

it up & deliver it to me. but I shall have to pay him for hawling this first months Rashions out of the Corn as I have failed so far to make out a sufficient subscription from the Citizens to defray this expence—but I will try to do so by the time of drawing comes round again if I posibly can, but I think it doubtful. I find it a vary hard matter to git a team & Wagon at this vary busy season but we must do the best we can & try to releave as far as posible the starving people of the Country. this is a gloomy day with the people of S C indeed & it seems that starvation with many is inevitable. I would like to see you personally & I hope I will be able by next sail day to come down.

        I am sir with Respect

              your obedient Servant

              (Signed) —————— ——————————

                                    M. G. D.

Paying the wagoner out of the rations was all wrong; it was contrary to the "army accountability system"; it was blasphemy against the Commissary-General and the Third Auditor. But with my plan of distribution, what could I do but wink at the enormity? The destitute got one fifth or one sixth less corn thereby; but, on the other hand, they did not walk ten miles after what they did get; and as most of them were old or sickly or young children, the walking was a serious consideration. I put it this way: that they paid the carter for his trouble; only they paid him in advance and *en masse*. Defying the Third Auditor and taking the risk of having my pay stopped and being reprimanded or even tried by court-martial, I got a good deal of my transportation done in this manner, allowing the teamster one fifth or one sixth of his load, according to the distance.

One resource had already failed me. When my two hundred and fifty sacks of corn were invoiced to me I noticed that I was called upon to receipt for the corn alone, and I had said to myself, "The sacks shall pay for the cartage." A few days later came an order to return the worthless tow receptacles to the Assistant Commissioner. Was there ever anything so irrational or provoking? Supposing that the sacks had been given outright, I had already paid out fifty of them as the niggardly price of transportation; and some were scattered thirty miles away, behind the mountains of the Dark Corner; and some were twenty-five miles in another direction, amidst the wilds of Pickens. In fear of unimaginable punishments I·wrote a dozen letters to reclaim my bags, knowing that nothing but those very bits of tow would appease that ogre, the Commissary-General. People who have not been in the army can not easily imagine the terrorizing influence of the "accountability system." The result was that I only lost about two dozen sacks, and that I was graciously spared court-martial, or even a reprimand.

ACCOUNTING FOR CORN

This brings me to the mode of accounting for the corn itself. For this object a new system of papers had been devised, more complicated and laborious than anything that I had ever yet seen, even in the War Department. To give an idea of it I exhibit a copy of "Voucher No. 75" for my Provision Return of June, 1867:

CERTIFICATE OF APPLICANT

GREENVILLE DIST. S. C. June 7, 1867

We, *Elizabeth Stone, Joseph Reed, Benjamin Bowen, Elsie Sandlin, Margaret Hawkins & Elizabeth Sizemore,* heads of families consisting of *8 adults & 16 children under 14 years,* of *Greenville, Dist.* of *Greenville,* and State of So. Ca., do hereby solemnly declare and upon *our* word of honor certify that *we* are in absolute need of food "to prevent starvation and extreme want," rendered so by the following circumstances: *Elizabeth Stone, widow, 2 children; Joseph Reed, old, 2 grandchildren & old wife; Benjamin Bowen, 66 years, 2 small children, old wife; Elsie Sandlin, widow, 5 children; Margaret Hawkins, deformed hand, 1 child; Elizabeth Sizemore, widow, 4 children.*

(Signed by all the applicants)

her
Elizabeth + *Stone*
mark
his
Joseph + *Reed*
mark
his
Benjamin + *Bowen*
mark
her
Elsie + *Sandlin*
mark
her
Margaret + *Hawkins*
mark
her
Elizabeth + *Sizemore*
mark

RECEIPT

Received of *Bvt. Maj. J. W. De Forest,* in the service of the United States of America, *896* pounds of Corn, issued under authority of Joint Resolution of Congress, approved March 30, 1867, "to prevent starvation," &c.

(Signed)

her
Elizabeth + *Stone*
mark

his
Joseph + *Reed*
mark

his
Benjamin + *Bowen*
mark

her
Elsie + *Sandlin*
mark

her
Margaret + *Hawkins*
mark

her
Elizabeth + *Sizemore*
mark

Witness of Issue
  Alexander McBee, jr

The manuscript portions of the voucher have been designated by italics. As it was made out in duplicate, it will be observed that I had to write the names of each batch of recipients eight times, and the causes of their indigence twice. These receipts were consolidated monthly into an Abstract of Issue, showing the dates of the several issues, number of men, number of women, number of children, and number of pounds of corn. The abstracts were then combined into a Return of Provisions, exhibiting the same footings, also the number of whites and freedpeople, total amount issued, balance on hand, etc.

The entire monstrosity would have pieced together into sufficient nether garments for that Dutchman who bought the island of Manhattan by covering it with his breeches.[8] As I scribbled over these acres of vouchers and footed up number of men, number of women, number of children, etc., etc., I decided that the Romans conquered the world because they had

8. See Washington Irving's *A History of New York by Diedrich Knickerbocker,* Book II, chapter vii.

no paper, and I wished that we had one of them at the head of the War Department. It must be observed that while making my returns for one month, I had to go on with my issues for the next, rearranging supplementary lists from the magistrates [9] and listening to the babble of suffering or humbugging applicants. The result personally was a loss of fifteen pounds and a fit of illness.

Now why did General Howard, a benevolent man and admirable officer, overwhelm his subordinates with such an exaggerated amount of labor and cause such delay in the transmission of food to persons who were supposed to be on the verge of starvation? The answer is that the general himself was terrorized by the accountability system; he wanted to show his superiors that he had not speculated on his corn and that the proper persons had received it. It is my belief that every military officer who is permanently responsible for government stores has his life shortened a year or two thereby.

RESULTS

My grand total of issue was 1,325 bushels of corn and 1,000 pounds of bacon, distributed among 1,666 poor persons, of whom 813 were white and 853 colored, including 193 men, 411 women, and 1,062 children.[10] A far larger result could have been attained but for the superfluous minuteness of the accounting papers. As things were, it was a matter of pride to me that I had done so much without a clerk or soldier, and with only the willing aid of citizens. The manual distribution of the rations

9. Though De Forest prepared revised lists of the indigent in the district, no further issues of corn and bacon are mentioned in his monthly reports.

10. In the first year and a half after the war the Bureau distributed rations on a vast scale, the total number up to September 1, 1866 (a month before De Forest took office), amounting to 1,111,847 (a ration consisted of one bushel of corn and eight pounds of pork per month for an adult, and half of these amounts for a child). Then, by means of his Circular No. 10 Commissioner Howard attempted to reduce this form of relief. Tornadoes, crop failures, and other factors, however, created such distress that Congress passed the relief bill which De Forest mentions on p. 83, and the Bureau resumed the issue of rations. In South Carolina, between September 1, 1866, and September 1, 1867, 242,643 rations were issued to refugees and 810,309 to freedmen. De Forest's issue, it would appear therefore, was proportionately very small. For full discussion, see Webster, *op. cit.*, pp. 119–124. Correspondence by De Forest in relation to this issue may be found in his book of Letters Sent, June 5–June 27, and in his monthly reports, April–July, 1867. National Archives.

for Greenville Court House, a worrying job of three days' dura-
tion, was performed by a merchant of the village, assisted by a
volunteer clerk or two from other establishments. The clerk
of the freight agent at the railroad station gave out over two
hundred sacks of corn to persons presenting my orders.

So far as I know I was the only Bureau agent who tried this
method of issue. Other officers collected no lists of destitute
and sent no loads to the farming precincts, but sat in their offices and, aided by a clerk and a soldier or two, gave out corn to
the struggling crowds which came for it, filling up applications
and taking receipts as they made the deliveries. They fed the
strong and impudent vagrants who could march twenty miles,
and I fed the old, weakly, and infantile, whose destitution was
guaranteed by respectable neighbors. Theirs was the official
method, and mine was not. Every time that I think of my humane and effective corn distribution I wonder that I was not
fined or reprimanded or court-martialed, and I rejoice with
tears in my eyes over my escape from the Commissary-General
and the Third Auditor.

I found that whenever I undertook to issue without the
guidance of citizens I was pretty sure to be imposed upon. For
instance, three "low-down" fellows from Pickens District obtained eighteen bushels of corn on the score of having starving
families, handed it over to a distiller for whisky, and went on a
three weeks' bender. I could do no more than report the still to
the United States revenue officer and have the proprietor (a
woman) fined for carrying on her business without a license.

Even the magistrates confessed to me that they were sometimes deceived. Yet they were scrupulously careful; some of
them scarcely gave out a full ration to a single applicant; to
doubtful cases they issued by the half-bushel and the peck. One
man made eighty bushels answer for eighty-one adults and one
hundred and thirty-six children, when a full month's ration
would have been one hundred and forty-seven bushels. Even
in reporting the destitute to me the magistrates were particular
to designate such persons as had dubious claims to charity. I
remember crossing out one Negro who was described as "fond
of his gun," and various women whose characters were spoken
of as not fit for close inspection.

My summary of the distribution of 1867 is that it did good and harm in equal proportions. It alleviated a considerable amount of suffering, prevented possibly a few cases of starvation, seduced many thousands of people from work, and fostered a spirit of idleness and beggary. Except under the pressure of mortal famine, it will not do to run the risk of letting corn fall into the hands of a large class who "never did a lick of work" and of another large class who only "try to git, seein' it's a-gwine."

CHAPTER V

THE MAN AND BROTHER [1]

T O begin modestly with the Negro, to show how ignorant and simple and childish he can be, I will state

A REMARKABLE COMPLAINT

One morning, as my predecessor in office, Brevet Colonel Niles, emerged from his hotel, he was confronted by a venerable trio.

There stood a paralytic old Negress, leading by the hand a blind old Negro, to whom was attached by a string a sore-eyed, limping and otherwise decrepit bulldog. The aunty asserted that the dog sucked her hens' eggs and wanted him killed; the uncle denied the animal's guilt and insisted on prolonging his days; and the trio had walked eight miles "to leave it out to de Burow."

"Ef she kin prove it agin him, let him be hung right up yere," said the uncle excitedly. "But she can't prove no sech thing; no she can't."

The colonel had been pestered during his term of office with many absurd complaints, and he was annoyed now by the grinning and chaffing of several unreconstructed village jokers. Instead of issuing an order that a hen should lay an egg, and that the same should be set before the dog to test his proclivities in the matter of suction, he broke out impatiently:

"Go away with your stupid quarrel. Go home and settle it between yourselves. Pretty business to bring before a United States officer!"

1. Originally published in *The Atlantic Monthly*, XXII (September, 1868), 337–348. The chapter title has its origin in the inscription "Am I not a man and brother?" which appeared on a medallion, struck in 1787 by Josiah Wedgwood; on it was figured a Negro in chains, kneeling and raising his arms toward heaven. This representation and motto later was adopted as a seal by the Anti-Slavery Society of London.

A "NIGGER" GRAVEYARD

That the freedmen should be ignorant and unintelligent does not appear strange when it is considered that they were brought to us, not so very long ago, in the condition of savages, and that since they have been among us they have been kept down as bondsmen or cast out as pariahs. Walking in a wood a mile or so from the village where I held sway, I came upon a Negro cemetery of the times of slavery. A headstone of coarse white marble, five or six of brick, and forty or fifty wooden slabs, all grimed and mouldering with the dampness of the forest, constituted the sordid sepulchral pomps of the "nameless people." On the marble monument I read the following inscription:

"This stone is placed here by James M. Burden, in memory of his wife, Viney, who died Dec. 21, 1860, Aged 29 years.—A good wife & faithful servant."

Painted in black letters on the white ground of a wooden headpiece was the following:

"to the memory of Claraca M. Ceth died on the 25 September 1850. Blessed are the dead who die in the Lord for they rest from their labors."

It is a wonder that the word "servant" and the word "labors" were not put in italics. How much knowledge or activity of brain or high moral feeling can be fairly claimed of a race which has been followed into the grave's mouth with reminders that its life was one of bondage and travail?

UNCLE DUDLEY

Nevertheless, I brought away from the South some fine reminiscences of the Negro. Among the elders of the colored people at my station—one of the persons to whom I trusted for information concerning the character of applicants for official favor—was a short, square-built, jet-black, decently dressed, well-mannered, industrious, worthy man of sixty-five or seventy, named Dudley Talley, commonly known as Uncle Dudley. Between him and Professor Charles Hopkins, the colored schoolteacher, I was pretty sure to learn whether a Negro who asked for rations was a proper object of charity, or whether another who brought a complaint was worthy of credence.

"Did you ever hear of Uncle Dudley's misfortunes in business?" asked a white citizen of me. "Poor Dudley! He bought the freedom of a son, and the son died; then he bought another boy's freedom, and the boy was emancipated. Dudley will tell you that he has had heavy licks in his time."

Yes, Dudley had sunk three thousand dollars in emancipating himself, his child, and another youth, only to see death and President Lincoln render his labors nugatory, leaving him dependent for his living upon a poor mule and cart and scarcely able to pay his taxes. The story of his own manumission is a fine instance of the kindly relations which often existed between white and black during the days of slavery. Long ago, when his old master, Dr. Long, was living, Dudley was a pet servant. Hired out at the Goodlett House, he had charge of the stables and was, moreover, allowed to keep his own bar—a demijohn of corn whisky, whereat to quench the thirst of such tavern-haunters as might not, on account of their color, get drunk like gentlemen in the hotel. Those were his days of ignorance, at which we must do some charitable winking.

From this Elysian existence, in a healthy mountain district, surrounded by friends who had grown up beside him, he was awakened by the death of his master, the sale of the estate under letters of administration, and the appearance of Negro-traders from Arkansas and Louisiana. It was rumored that Dudley was an object of especial desire to these gentlemen and that his remaining days in the land of his birth were numbered. Terrified at the thought of separation from home and family, he looked about for some citizen of the village to buy him. His choice fell upon a gentleman whom he had always known, a lawyer by profession, Colonel Towns.

"Dudley, I don't like it," said the colonel. "I never have bought a slave, and I have a sentiment against it."

"But won't you save me from being carried off, Colonel?" implored Dudley.

"I don't like the idea of owning you," was the answer; then, after some reflection, "but I will manage it so that you shall own yourself. I will bid you off; you shall repay me, principal and interest, at your convenience; and, when the money is refunded, you shall be free. The law will not let me emancipate you; but you shall not be my property, nor that of my heirs. We will call it an investment, Dudley."

The purchase was made; the agreement between the two was drawn up and signed; the Anglo-Saxon waited, and the African worked. This bond between an honorable gentleman and an honorable slave was kept to the end. Every payment which Dudley made was indorsed upon the note, and, when the debt was extinguished, he received a quittance in full. From that time, although nominally and by law the property of Colonel Towns, he was practically his own master and did what he pleased with his earnings. It was truly unfortunate for him that he should have invested them so as to be ruined precisely in the same manner as if he had been a slaveholding Rebel.

If all freedmen had the persevering industry of Dudley Talley, the race would have no cause to fear for its existence under the crucial test of free labor. But myriads of women who once earned their own living now have aspirations to be like white ladies and, instead of using the hoe, pass the days in dawdling over their trivial housework, or gossiping among their neighbors. In scores of instances I discovered that my complaining constituents were going astern simply because the men alone were laboring to support the families. When I told them that they must make their wives and daughters work, they looked as hopeless as would Mr. Potiphar,[2] should any one give him the same wholesome counsel. Of course, I do not mean that all the women were thus idle; the larger proportion were still laboring afield, as of old; rigid necessity held them up to it. But this evil of female loaferism was growing among the Negroes as it has grown, and is growing, among us white men and brethren.

COX, LYNCH, AND COMPANY

Another cause of trouble for the freedpeople was their disposition to seek the irregular employment and small, bartering

2. The indulgent husband of a socially ambitious woman in *The Potiphar Papers* (1853) by G. W. Curtis.

ways of the city and the village. Now and then one established himself as a drayman, or did a flourishing business as a barber or shopkeeper; but what kind of success they generally attained in the towns may be pretty fairly inferred from the history of Cox, Lynch, and Company.

Edward Cox, an elderly mulatto who boasted F. F. V. blood, and Thomas Lynch, a square-headed, thoroughbred Negro, formed a mercantile partnership with two other freedmen. The "store" was a single room in a deserted hotel, and the entire stock in trade might have been worth forty dollars. On this chance of business four families proposed to live. By the time the United States license of twenty dollars, the town license of five dollars, and certain other opening expenses had been paid, the liabilities of the firm were nearly sufficient to cover its assets. In a week or so the community were startled by a report that Cox, Lynch, and Company were in difficulties. The two minor partners sold out for nothing, and two others were taken in. Unfortunately, our merchant princes were ignorant of the revenue law, and, instead of continuing the old partnership, they formed a new one, thus exposing themselves to another tax for a fresh license. This mistake was fatal, and Cox, Lynch, and Company went to pieces.

Tom Lynch had meanwhile been studying at the freedmen's school and had acquired an intermittent power of writing his name. Sometimes he could lay it fairly out on paper, and sometimes it would obstinately curl up into an ampersand. He occasionally called on me to write letters for him—mainly, as I believe, to show that he could sign them; and I had become somewhat restive under these demands, holding that I could employ my time more profitably and agreeably. When the firm went down, however, and when Tom wanted me to indite an epistle for him to his late partner, Edward Cox, concerning certain articles in dispute between them, I reflected that such opportunities do not present themselves twice in a man's life, and I consented to the labor.

It appears that Tom had borrowed a table, a balance, and a set of weights wherewith to commence the business; and that, when the crisis came, Edward had impounded these articles and sold them for his own profit, leaving partners and creditors and lender to whistle. Such, at least, was the case which Tom stated to me and which I wrote out in the letter. The day after the sending of the epistle Tom reappeared with it, explaining that he had forwarded it to Edward by a messenger, and that Edward, having had it read to him, had put it in a clean envelope and returned it without note or comment.

"I should like to know what he means?" observed the puzzled Thomas.

"So should I," said I, much amused at this method of managing a dunning letter.

"It's mighty cur'ous conduct," persisted Thomas. " 'Pears to me I'd like to get you to write another letter to him for me."

"Suppose he should send that back in a fresh envelope?" I suggested, not fancying the job. "I think you had better see him and ask him what it means."

What it did mean I never learned. But Edward Cox, to whom I subsequently spoke on the general subject of justice in regard to those weights and balances, assured me that Tom Lynch was a liar and rascal. In short, the history of Cox, Lynch, and Company remained as much of a muddle as if the firm had failed for a million, under the management of first-class Wall Street financiers.

LACK OF PRACTICAL ARITHMETIC

One great trouble with the Negroes was lack of arithmetic. Accustomed to have life figured out for them, they were unable to enter into that practical calculation which squares means with necessities. Cox, Lynch, and Company, for instance, had not the slightest idea how large a business would be required to support four families. As farm laborers the freedmen failed to realize the fact that it was needful to work entirely through spring, summer, and fall, in order to obtain a crop. They did admirably in the planting season and were apt to sow too much ground; then came a reaction, and they would indulge in a succession of day huntings and night frolics; and the consequence was a larger crop of weeds than of corn. If the planters were forehanded enough to pay their people day wages and discharge a man as soon as he turned lazy, things would go better.

But the general custom, dictated by habit and by lack of capital, was to allow the Negro a share of the crop; and as he thus became a partner in the year's business, he was disposed to believe that he had a right to manage it after his own pleasure.

It was enough to make one both laugh and cry to go out to Colonel Irvine's fine plantation and look at the result of his farming for 1867, on land which could produce, without manure, an average of thirty bushels of corn to the acre. A gang of Negroes, counting thirteen field hands, had taken a large part of his farm; and, as the produce of one field of thirty-five acres, they had to show about a hundred bushels of wretched "nubbins"; the weeds meanwhile standing four feet high among the cornstalks.

"They neglected it during the hoeing season," said the colonel, "and they never could recover their ground afterwards. It was of no use to order or scold; they were disobedient, sulky, and insolent. As for frolicking, why, Sir, from fifty to seventy darkies pass my house every night, going into the village. The next day they are, of course, fit for nothing."

And, after the land had been used for naught, these Negroes did not want to repay the advances of rations upon which they had lived during the summer; they were determined to take their third of the crop from the fields and leave the colonel to sue or whistle, as he pleased, for what was due him in the way of corn, bacon, molasses, and tobacco. Fortunately for him, I had an order from the Assistant Commissioner to the effect that all crops should be stored, and accounts for the expense of raising the same satisfactorily settled, before the parties should come to a division. When I read this to the assembled Negroes, they looked blasphemies at the Freedmen's Bureau.

It must not be understood, however, that all freedmen were indolent and dishonest. A large number of them did their work faithfully and with satisfactory results. But with these I seldom came in contact; they had no complaints to make and seldom suffered injustice. My duties very naturally led me to know the evil and the unlucky among both blacks and whites.

To show the simple notions of this untaught race as to what constitutes wealth or, at least, a sufficiency of worldly goods, I will relate a single incident. A gaunt Negress, named Aunt

Judy, called on me with a complaint that Mrs. F—, an impoverished old white lady, owed her a dollar and would not pay it.

"Come, aunty, you must not be hard on Mrs. F—," I said. "You must give her time. She is very poor."

"Oh, *she* ain't poor—don't you believe that," responded the aunty. "No longer'n two months ago my sons paid her eight dollars for rent. Oh, go 'way, *she* ain't poor; *she's* got money."

Still convinced, in spite of this startling fact to the contrary, that Mrs. F—was not wealthy, I continued to plead that she might not be pressed, until Aunt Judy was graciously pleased to say:

"Wal, I won't be hard on her. I'se a square nigger, I is. I don't want to do no hardness."

The actual state of the case was this. Aunt Judy had hired, for five dollars a month, a cabin attached to Mrs. F—'s tumbledown house and had paid up two months' rent, but at this very time owed for half a month. Having, however, done washing and "toting" for her landlady to the value of a dollar, she wanted to collect the money at once, instead of letting it go on the account.

Five months later I found that this "square nigger" had not settled for the rent since the payment made by her sons, and was in debt twenty-four dollars to poor old Mrs. F—, who meanwhile had nearly reached the point of starvation. I was obliged to threaten Aunt Judy with instant eviction, before I could induce her to put her mark to a due-bill for the amount of her arrears and enter into an arrangement by which the wages of a son-in-law became guaranty for regular liquidations in future.

It would probably be unfair to suppose that this "square nigger" seriously meant to be lopsided in her morals. But she had two or three small children; the washing business was not very brisk nor very remunerative; she had benevolently taken in, and was nursing, a sick woman of her own race; and, finally, it was so much easier not to pay than to pay! My impression is that she was a pious woman and disposed to be "square" when not too inconvenient. I should not have interfered to bring her to terms, had it not been a case of life and death with the venerable lady who let her the cabin, and had not, moreover, this evasion of rent-dues been a very common sin among the Negroes. Indeed, I aided her to the amount of a dollar and a half, which was desirable for some small matter, conscious that I owed her at least that amount for the amusement which I had derived from her statement that Mrs. F— "had money."

The thoughtless charity of this penniless Negress in receiving another poverty-stricken creature under her roof was characteristic of the freedmen. However selfish, and even dishonest, they might be, they were extravagant in giving. The man who at the end of autumn had a hundred or two bushels of corn on hand would suffer a horde of lazy relatives and friends to settle upon him and devour him before the end of the winter, leaving him in the spring at the mercy of such planters as chose to drive a hard bargain. Among the freedmen, as among the whites of the South, the industrious were too much given to supporting the thriftless.

TOO MUCH AMUSEMENT

As I have already hinted, the Negroes wasted much of their time in amusement. What with trapping rabbits by day and treeing 'possums by night, dances which lasted till morning, and prayer-meetings which were little better than frolics, they contrived to be happier than they had "any call to be," considering their chances of starving to death. It was not entirely without foundation that the planters and the reactionary journals complained that the Loyal Leagues were an injury to both whites and blacks.[3] As an officer, I wanted to see reconstruction furthered, and as a Republican I desired that the great party which had saved the Union should prosper; but, believing that my first duty was to prevent famine in my district, I felt it necessary to discourage the zeal of the freedmen for political gatherings. I found that they were traveling ten and twenty miles to League meetings and, what with coming and going, making

3. Loyal Leagues or Union Leagues had originally formed during the war to promote the cause of union among Southern whites. After hostilities ended, and especially after Congressional Reconstruction began to develop, these Leagues became primarily Negro in membership. Using the attractions of oaths, secrecy, and ritual, they became, in effect, organizations to train freedmen for political activity and to bind them to the Republican party.

a three days' job of it, leaving the weeds to take care of the corn. The village was an attraction; and, moreover, there was the Bureau schoolhouse for a place of convocation; there, too, were the great men and eloquent orators of the party and the secret insignia of the League. I remonstrated strenuously against the abuse and reduced the number of meetings in the schoolhouse to one a week.

"Go home, and get up your own League," I exhorted a gang who had come fifteen miles from a neighboring district for initiation. "Let your patriotism come to a head in your own neighborhood. Do you suppose the government means to feed you, while you do nothing but tramp about and hurrah?"

My belief is that nearly all my brother officers pursued the same policy, and that there was little or no foundation for the charge that the Bureau was prostituted to political uses. On the whole, no great harm resulted from the Leagues, so far as my observation extended. The planters in my neighborhood made few complaints, and my district raised more than enough corn "to do it."

NATIVE OPINIONS OF "NIGGERS"

On the way from Charleston to my station I was amused at a conversation which went on behind me between a rough, corpulent, jolly old planter of the middle class and a meek-looking young Northerner, apparently a "drummer" from New York. The old fellow talked incessantly, sending his healthy, ringing voice clean through the car and denouncing with a delightful fervor the whole "breed, seed, and generation of niggers."

"They're the meanest, triflingest creeturs a-goin'," said he. "Thar ain't no good side to 'em. You can't find a white streak in 'em, if you turn 'em wrong side outwards and back again."

The six or eight Southerners in the car seemed mightily taken with the old man and laughed heartily over his phillipic. Addressing one who sat in front of me, a tall, powerful, sunburnt young fellow, with a revolver peeping out from beneath his homespun coat, I said:

"Do you consider that a fair judgment?"

"Well, middlin' fair," he answered; "it ain't no gret out of the way, I reckon."

"I tell you the nigger is a no-account creetur," went on the old planter. "All the men are thieves, and all the women are prostitutes. It's their natur' to be that way, and they never'll be no other way. They ain't worth the land they cover. They ought to be improved off the face of the earth."

Here the New Yorker spoke for the first time in an hour.

"You are improving 'em off pretty fast," he said meekly. "Got some of 'em 'most white already."

So unfair is the human mind that nobody but myself laughed at this retort. The planter turned the conversation on crops, and the audience looked out of the windows.

During the same journey I fell into conversation with an elderly Carolinian, a doctor by profession and planter by occupation, who, it seems, resided in the village to which I was ordered, and whom I afterwards learned to respect for his kindly and worthy qualities. We talked of the practice of whipping slaves, and he assured me that the report of it had been much exaggerated.

"Multitudes of planters never had a Negro whipped," he said. "I have owned twenty or thirty, and I never punished but one. I'll tell you the whole story, and I believe you'll allow that I did right. It was a girl named Julia, who was brought up in our house, a regular pet of the family. Finally she went wrong somehow and had a mulatto child; they would do that, you know, no matter what pains you took with them. After that I noticed that Julia didn't have no more children; wouldn't have nothing to say to her own color; wouldn't take a husband. At last I thought I ought to talk to her, and says I, 'Julia, what does this mean?' Says she, 'Doctor, I've had one white man's child, and I'm never going to have no black man's child.' Says I, 'Julia, that's wrong, and you ought to know it.' Says she, 'Well, Doctor, wrong or not, I feel that way, and I'm bound to stick to it.' Now, I knew she was wrong, you see, and I couldn't let the thing go on so. I felt in duty bound to get such ideas out of her head. I whipped her. I took her out, and I give her one right good switching with a hickory. I thought I ought to do it, and I did it."

Whether the hickory reformed Julia of her wicked and unfruitful pride, so deleterious to the growth of the doctor's planting population, I was too fastidious to inquire. Whether Julia's morals would have been in better hands than the doctor's, had her forefathers remained in Africa, is a question more important to my present purpose, and which must probably be decided in the negative.

CHASTITY AND TEMPERANCE

First savages, and then slaves, it is evident that the Negroes had little chance to keep all the Commandments. They were in 1867 precisely what might be expected, considering their history. Illegitimate offspring were less common than formerly, but still disastrously abundant. A large proportion of the colored applicants for Bureau rations were young women with three or four children, and without the pretense of a husband, —this, although bigamy was fearfully frequent; although the average woman was apt to marry again if her "old man" went off for a year; although the average man might take a wife in every place where he stayed for six months. If I exaggerate in this matter, it is because, like most officers of justice, I saw chiefly the evil side of my public—all the deserted ones coming to me for the redress of their grievances or for help in their poverty.

An emigration agent, named Passmore, who collected a large gang of Negroes in my sub-district for work in Louisiana, told me that one of his recruits had asked him to write a letter for him to "his Cousin Jane." The man went on dictating, "Give howdy to little Cousin Abel and little Cousin Jimmy and little Cousin Dinah." Suddenly Passmore looked up:

"You rascal, those are your children; aren't they your children?"

After some stammering, the man confessed it.

"Then why didn't you say your *wife,* instead of your *cousin?*"

"Bekase I didn't want the ole woman *yere* to git to know about it."

General Howard distributed a large number of ruled forms for temperance pledges to his officers, with instructions that they should endeavor to found total-abstinence societies among the freedmen. I soon discovered that if I wanted to raise a "snicker," ending, when out of doors, in a hearty guffaw, I had only to exhibit one of these documents and explain its purpose to a party of my constituents. The blacks were unquestionably less addicted to ardent spirits than the Southern whites; but I suspect that it was mainly because, up to the emancipation, they were kept from it in a measure by police regulations, and because they were as yet too poor to purchase much of it. Like all uncultured peoples, they had a keen relish for the sense of freedom and grandeur which it gives to man, and already many of them had learned "to destroy a power of whisky." Of General Howard's temperance pledges they certainly thought very small beer. I never got a signature; nothing but snickers and guffaws —irrepressible anti-temperance laughter.

HONESTY

In the matter of honesty the freedmen were doing as well as could be expected, considering their untoward education, first as savages and then as slaves. Stealing, although more common among them than even among the low-down whites, was far less known than when they held, not without reason, that it was no harm "to put massa's chicken into massa's nigger." Freedom had developed a sense of self-respect which made the prison more terrible than was the whip or the paddle. Planters still complained that their hogs and hens disappeared; and, during my official term of fifteen months, I procured the liberation of, perhaps, twenty Negro thieves from jail, on condition that they should take contracts to go to Florida or Louisiana; while at least as many more were sentenced by the courts for various forms and grades of dishonesty. But, except where the population had been pinched by famine, this vice had diminished steadily and rapidly since the emancipation.

As for driving sharp bargains and downright swindling, I am reminded of the story of Dick Ross and Caroline Gantt. Caroline's husband died toward the close of 1866, but not until he had harvested, and left to his widow, fifty-five bushels of corn. Dick Ross, a jet-black, shiny-faced fellow of twenty, saw a chance of providing himself with "something to go upon" and went to Caroline with a specious story that he was about to set up a store, that he had several boxes of goods on the way from Charleston, and that he could do well by her if she would put her corn into his business. The widow was led away by his smooth talk and soon found that she had made a permanent investment. Dick wagoned the corn to the village, sold it, and bought himself some "store close." Patient waiting and inquiry developed the facts, that no goods had arrived for him by railroad and that he had hired no stand for business.

Then Caroline came to me for redress. I sent for Dick and bullied him until he refunded five dollars. As he had no property beyond what was on his back, nothing more could be collected; and, as imprisonment for debt had been done away with by order of General Sickles,[4] he could not be punished. Caroline, however, sued him, obtained judgment against him for sixty-five dollars, and, when I left, had got two dollars and a half more, which had gone to pay her lawyer.

In short, I found that the Negroes not only swindled the whites quite as much as they were swindled by them, but that they cheated each other. The same man who would spend his whole substance in feeding a host of relatives and friends would circumvent whatsoever simple brother or sister darkey might fall in his way. I was more edified than astonished by the discovery of this seeming clash of virtues and vices, for I had seen the same mixture of thoughtless generosity and dishonest cupidity among the Syrians and other semi-civilized races. The explanation of the riddle is an imperfect moral education as to the distinction between *meum* and *tuum:* the Negro learned slowly that he had a full right to his own property, that his neighbor had a full right to his.

LYING

As for lying, I learned not to put faith in any complaint until I had heard both sides and examined into the proofs. But this is a good general rule; I recommend it to all officers of justice; I presume that every lawyer has arrived at the same judgment. The human plaintiff, whether black or white, sees his

4. See Introduction, p. x.

trouble from his own point of view and does not mean that you shall see it from any other. If he varies at all from the exact truth, it will surely be to exaggerate his griefs.

So fluent and brazen-faced in falsehood were many of my constituents that it was generally impossible to decide by personal appearances between the blameless and the guilty. A girl of eighteen, charged with obtaining goods on false pretenses, displayed such a virtuous front and denied her identity with the criminal with such an air of veracity, that I confidently pronounced her innocent; yet, by dint of keeping her for an hour in a lawyer's office, putting the charge to her persistently, and threatening her with prosecution, she was brought to own her knavery and point out the spot where she had secreted her plunder.

Another day I was kept in a ferment of uncertainty for a couple of hours by two boys of about twelve—a black and a mulatto, one or the other of whom had stolen a valuable pocket-knife from a little white boy. The plundered youth and his father, a farmer, agreed in stating that the black boy had borrowed the knife "to look at it" and had never returned it.

"Yas, so I did borry it," admitted the accused, a shiny-faced youngster, glib, loud-tongued, and gesturing wildly in his excitement. "But I didn't steal it. Yere's a good knife of my own, an' why should I steal another knife? I jes borry'd it to see it, cos it had so many blades. Then, this yere yaller boy asked me to let him take it to cut a watermillion. So I handed it over to him, and that's the last I see of it. That's so, jes as suah as you's bohn."

The mulatto, a handsome, dignified little fellow, faced this accusation in the calmness of innocence. A citizen whispered to me, "The black boy is the thief," and I also felt pretty sure of it. I had both the youngsters searched, but without result. Then, finding that the property had disappeared near the farmer's wagon, I told him to take the accused back there to search for it and, if they did not find it, to bring them to me again, to be sent to jail. In ten minutes the party returned without the knife. The mulatto still wore his calm front of innocence, while the Negro was now quite wild with excitement.

"I shall have to confine you both for trial," I said, "if you don't give up the knife."

" 'Fore God, I dun'no whar 't is," exclaimed the darkey. "I'd lose a hundred knives 'fore I'd go to jail. *He* don't care 'bout jail, he's been thar so often."

"Oho!" said I, turning to the mulatto. "You have been in jail,—have you? Then you are the thief. If you don't find that knife in ten minutes, I will have you severely punished."

There was another search; the criminal was still obdurate, but his mother arrived on the scene of action and "got after him" with a broomstick; and the result was that he pointed out the missing article amidst a pile of straw where he had contrived to secrete it. Yet so blameless had been his countenance during the whole transaction, that probably not one person in ten would have selected him as the guilty party.

NEGRO TESTIMONY

On the other hand, there were Negroes as truthful as the sunlight—Negroes who would bear honest testimony in a matter, though against their interest—Negroes whose word passed for as much as that of a white man. I have often heard Southerners say, "I would much sooner believe a decent nigger than one of these low-down white fellows." As witnesses before the courts, the freedmen astonished their friends, as well as their detractors, by the honesty and intelligence with which they gave their testimony. They felt that they were put upon honor by the privilege, and they were anxious to show themselves worthy of it. Great was the wonder and amusement of the community in which I was stationed at the superiority which Aunt Chloe, the first Negro ever placed upon the stand there, exhibited over her former master and present employer, a wealthy old planter, whom we will call McCracken.

Mr. McCracken had brought suit against a so-called Union man, named Bishop, for plundering his house after the proclamation of peace. The indictment was for theft; the case was tried before the Court of Common Pleas; the counsel for defense was the well-known Governor Perry. Mr. McCracken, a sanguine, voluble old gentleman, who had held such public trusts as magistrate, foreman of a jury, and commissioner of the poor, was called and sworn as the first witness.

"Well, Mr. McCracken, what do you know about this case?" inquired the solicitor.

"I know all about it," answered McCracken, smiling in his confident style. He then stated that he was away from home when the theft happened, but that on his return he missed two hams and some bunches of yarn and was told that Mr. Bishop had taken them.

"But did you see Mr. Bishop take them?" demanded the counsel for the defense.

"No, sir."

"Did you see Mr. Bishop at your house that day?"

"No, sir."

"Did you ever see those hams and bunches of yarn in his possession?"

"No, sir."

"Then, Mr. McCracken, it appears that you don't know anything about this case."

McCracken fidgeted and made no reply.

"Mr. McCracken, you may come down," was the next remark. "Sheriff, call Chloe McCracken."

Amidst suppressed tittering from the audience, Aunt Chloe took her place on the witness stand. She gave a straightforward, simple story—told what she had seen, and no more—said nothing which was not to the point. When she came down, there was a gentle buzz of admiration and wonder, and the question of believing Negro testimony was no longer a mooted one in that community. Surely we may hope something for a race which, in spite of its great disadvantages of moral education, has already shown that it appreciates the solemnity of an oath. We could not fairly have expected this much virtue and intelligence from manumitted slaves under half a century of freedom and exercise of civil rights.

Of course, such new acquaintance as the Negro and law do not always agree. Wat Thompson, when called on to testify against a brother freedman who was charged with assault and battery upon a white man, refused to say anything at all, holding that he was not bound "to swear agin a friend." The judge dissented from this opinion and sent Wat to jail for contempt of court. Lame Ben, a black busybody who had put Wat up to his blunder, took exceptions to this mode of treating it and wanted me to interfere. I advised Lame Ben that he would make a reputation for better sense by minding his own business. Another freedman, a spectator in this same case, came to me in great indignation, complaining that the jury had believed the evidence of the prosecutor and not that of the defendant; and that the court had sentenced the latter to jail and done nothing at all to the former. I was obliged to explain that the prosecutor had not been on trial and that the jury had a right to decide what testimony seemed most credible.

OUTRAGES AGAINST WHITES

As chief of a sub-district I made a monthly report headed "Outrages of Whites against Freedmen"; and another headed "Outrages of Freedmen against Whites." The first generally, and the second almost invariably, had a line in red ink drawn diagonally across it, showing that there were no outrages to report. After three small gangs of white robbers, numbering altogether ten or twelve persons, had been broken up by the civil and military authorities, few acts of serious violence were committed by either race against the other. The "high-toned gentlemen," a sufficiently fiery and pugnacious race, were either afraid of the garrisons or scorned to come to blows with their inferiors. The "low-downers" and small farmers, equally pugnacious, far less intelligent, and living on cheek-by-jowl terms with the Negroes, were the persons who generally committed what were called outrages. They would strike with whatever came handy; perhaps they would run for their guns, cock them, and swear to shoot; but there was no murder. There had been shootings, and there had been concerted and formal whippings; but that was during the confusion which followed the close of the war; that was mainly before my time. Such things were still known in other districts, but mine was an exceptionally quiet one.

The Negroes themselves were not disposed to violence. They

were a peaceable, good-tempered set, and, except when drunk, no more likely to pick a fight than so many Chinamen. Whether it is a virtue to be pacific I cannot say. Anglo-Saxons are the most belligerent race, either as individuals or as peoples, that the world now contains; and yet they have been of far greater service in advancing the interests of humanity than Negroes or Chinamen; at least they will tell you so, and whip you into admitting it. But if peaceableness is a virtue and has any promise of good in it, the Negro is so far admirable and gives hopes.

Now and then there was a bad boy of this stock in my district. There was one such called Wallace, a bright, restless mulatto of seventeen or eighteen, who stole hens, overcoats, etc., and occasionally fought. Tom Turner, a low-down white man, getting jocosely drunk one day, thought it a fine thing to slap this youth in the face with a meal bag. Wallace collected a party of his comrades, chased Turner nearly half a mile, dragged him from his wagon, stabbed him in the shoulder with a jack-knife, and was hardly prevented from killing him. All the parties in the scuffle, including the white man, were arrested, fined, and sentenced to various terms of imprisonment.[5] Wallace became a convert to the Baptist Church and was let out of jail one Sunday to undergo immersion.

"Well, have you got the wickedness all out of you?" I heard an unbelieving citizen say to him. "I reckon *you* ought to have hot water."

"Oh, yes! all out this time," returned Wallace, with a confidence which I thought foreshadowed a speedy falling from grace.

Whether many Wallaces will arise among the Negroes, whether the stock will develop aggressive qualities as it outgrows the timidity of long servitude is not only an interesting, but a very important question. If so, then there will be many riots and rencontres between them and their old masters; for the latter are as bellicose as Irishmen, and far more disposed than Irish-

5. An account of the incident is included in De Forest's monthly report of outrages for August, 1867. In the October report De Forest indicates that Wallace Williams was sentenced to six months in the penitentiary.

men to draw the lifeblood. It is desirable, in my opinion, that the freedmen may be moderate in their claims and grow up with some meekness into their dignity of citizens.

OUTRAGES AGAINST FREEDMEN

Meanwhile most Negroes were overfearful as to what the whites might do to them. A freedman from St. George's Creek, Pickens District, shut himself up with me in my office and related in a timorous murmur, and with trembling lips, how he had been abused by two low-down fellows, named Bill and Jim Stigall.[6]

"I never done nothin' to 'em," said he. "They jes come on me yesterday for nothin'. I'd finished my day's job on my lan', an' was gone in to git my supper—for I lives alone, ye see—when I heerd a yell, an' they come along. Bill Stigall rode his mewl right squar inter the house. Then Jim come in, an' they tole me to git 'em some supper, an' take care of the mewl. While I was out takin' care of the mewl, they eat their supper, an' then begun to thrash roun' and break things. I stayed outside when I heerd that. But my brother Bob come down that day to visit me, an' walked inter the house; an' then they got kinder skrimmagen with him, an' wanted to put him out. But when Bob pulled out his pistil, they clar'd out, an' as they were gwine away they threatened me. Says they, 'You leave this settlement, or we'll shoot your brother an' you too.' An' sence then, they's been hangin' roun' my place, an' I'm afeard to stay thar."

"Have they done anything to you?" I asked, doubtful whether the affair was more than a rough frolic.

"Yes. They sont word to me sence, how they was gwine ter shoot me ef I didn't leave the settlement."

"But they haven't shot?"

"No. But I'm afeard of 'em. An' some of the folks thar tole me to come over yere an' name it to the Bureau."

Thinking that some harm might come if I did not interfere, I wrote a note to the magistrate at St. George's Creek, requesting

6. De Forest's monthly report of outrages, August, 1867, includes a statement that Henry and Patrick Stigall beat and scratched one, Berry Blasingame, and later took refuge in the swamps.

him to examine into the complaint and if it seemed important, to bind the Stigalls over to keep the peace. The Negro went off with it, evidently disappointed that I had not used the military force against his persecutors and fearful of venturing back into their "settlement." Three days later the magistrate called and stated that these Stigalls were a nuisance to his neighborhood; that they had persecuted whites as well as blacks with their rowdyism; that he had issued a warrant for their apprehension; and that they had taken refuge in the swamps. In a day or two more the Negro reappeared in a state of great terror.

"Well, what is the news?" I asked.

"I took your ticket to the square," he said; "but he don't seem to do nothin'."

"But he tells me that he has done all he can. The fellows have run away, haven't they?"

"Yes," he admitted sheepishly; "not to say run clear away. They's thar somewhar, lyin' out, an' waitin' roun'. Las' night I heerd a gun fired in the woods back o' my house."

"Come, you are too much of a coward," I protested. "You want more protection than there is to give. Do you suppose that I can send a guard of soldiers to watch over you?"

He probably had supposed that I could and would do it. Very unwillingly and fearfully he retraced his steps to St. George's Creek, and I heard no more of Jim and Bill Stigall.

CHAPTER VI

MORE MAN AND BROTHER [1]

IALOGUES similar in nature to the following were quite frequent in the office of the Bureau Major and will give a fair idea of the Negro's

DOMESTIC AFFECTIONS

"I wants to know ef I can't hev my little gal," explains a ragged freedwoman of an uncertain age.

"I suppose you can, if you can prove that she is yours and if you have not bound her out as an apprentice."

"I ha'n't bound her out. I let Mr. Jack Bascom, up to Walhalla, have her to stay with him awhile, an' now I wants her back, an' I sont to Mr. Bascom more'n a month ago to fotch her back, an' 'pears like he ain't gwine to fotch her."

"Perhaps she is very well off with Mr. Bascom; I understand that he is a man of property. What do you want her back for?"

"I wants to see her. She's my little gal, an' I has a right to hev her, an' I wants her."

Here a citizen who was lounging in the office took part in the conversation:

"Look here, aunty, you had better leave your girl with Mr. Bascom; he is a very kind, honorable man. Besides, he made twenty-five hundred bushels of corn this last season, and it stands to reason that she won't suffer there, while you, probably, don't know whether you'll have enough to go upon through the winter. It's going to be a hard winter for poor folks, aunty, and you'd better take as light a load into it as you can."

"I don't keer for all that," persists the short-sighted, affectionate creature. "Yes, I does keer. But I can't go without seein' my little gal any longer. I ha'n't sot eyes on her for nigh

1. Originally published as the second installment of "The Man and Brother," in *The Atlantic Monthly*, XXII (October, 1868), 414-425.

four months, an' I can't stan' it no longer. 'Pears like I don't know how she's gettin' on."

"But you must have faith," I said, attacking her on the religious side, always an open one with the Negroes. However sinful their lives may chance to be in practice, they feel bound to admit the authority of certain doctrines. "It's your duty to have faith," I repeat. "If you have put your child into the hands of a decent man, well off in this world's goods, if you have done by her to the best of your intelligence, you must trust that God will do the rest. You are bound to believe that He will take just as good care of her as if you were there and saw it all."

"Yes, that's so; that's true preachin'," responded the woman, nonplussed at discovering that preaching could be made so practical as to apply to Bureau business. "But I don't keer for all that. Yes, I does keer, but I wants to see my little gal."

"Suppose you should move up to Walhalla yourself? Then your child could keep her good place, and still you could see her."

"No, no, I can't do that," she affirmed, shaking her head with energy.

"Ah, aunty! I see through you now," said I. "You have a lot of old cronies here; you love to gossip and smoke pipes with them; you care more for them than for your girl. All you want of her is to wait on you while you sit and tattle. You just want her to go for water and to put a chunk of fire on your pipe."

"No, no, no!" denied the aunty, but she looked dreadfully guilty, as though my charge were at least half true. The result was that, by dint of ridicule, coaxing, and arguing, I prevailed upon her to leave her child with Mr. Jack Bascom, in whose care the pickaninny was of course far better off than she could have been with her poverty-stricken parent.

Other women wanted their children, male and female, big and little, brought back from Florida, Louisiana, Tennessee, and Arkansas. It was useless to say, "They have but just gone; they have not fulfilled a quarter of their year's contract; besides, they are earning far more than they can here."

A combination of affection, stupidity, and selfishness easily responded, "I don't keer for all that, an' I wants to see 'em."

The only effective opposition which the Bureau Major could

raise consisted in declaring with official firmness and coldness, "I have no transportation for such purposes."

A middle-aged freedwoman came to me with a complaint that her son-in-law would do nothing for the support of his wife and children.

"He's down on the railroad twenty-five miles below yere, an' he's git'n good wages, an' I can't keep 'em no longer."

"Won't he have them with him?" I inquired.

"Yes, he's sont for 'em once or twice; but I ain't gwine to let 'em go so fur off. Ef he wants my da'ter, he's got to live with her, and she's got to live with me."

"Very well; then you may continue to support her," was of course my decision.

Another granny pestered me by the hour for a week together to induce me to save her youngest son, Andy, from being deported. Andy had stolen a pig, and as a result he was in jail, awaiting trial; but the sheriff was willing to release him on condition that he would take a contract out of the state; and consequently a planter who was going to Florida had hired him, paid his jail fees, and secured his liberation.

"He must go," said I. "If he breaks his bargain, I'll have him shut up again."

"Oh, I wouldn't keer for that," whimpered the old creature. " 'Pears like I'd rather hev him in jail all his life than go away from me."

Andy did break his bargain, lurked in the neighborhood a few days, and then, being pursued by the sheriff, absconded to parts unknown.

These aged freedwomen, and many also of the aged freedmen, had the bump of locality like old cats. No place in the world would answer for them except the very place where they had been brought up and had formed their little circle of now venerable gossips. If all their sons and grandsons went to Florida or Louisiana, they would stay with the ancients with whom they were accustomed to smoke and tattle.

And yet the Negroes have a great love for children; it is one of the most marked characteristics of the race. Allowing for their desire to have somebody to wait on them and somebody at hand over whom they can exercise authority; allowing also for their prejudice against everything which in any manner recalls their ancient burden of slavery—they must still be credited with a large amount of natural affection.

One of the strongest objections to the apprenticing of colored children lay in the fact that the relatives soon sickened of their bargain and wanted to regain possession of the youngsters. If the father and mother were not alive to worry in the matter, it would be taken up by grandparents, aunts, and cousins. They coaxed the pickaninny to run away, and they brought horrible stories of cruel treatment to the Bureau officer. Finding, in every case which I investigated, that these tales were falsifications, I invariably refused to break the bond of apprenticeship and instructed the applicants that their only resource was a trial for the possession of the orphan before the judge of the district court. I did this partly from a sense of justice to the master, partly because he was always better able to care for the apprentice than the relatives, and partly because I considered it my duty to aid in setting the civil law on its legs and preparing the community to dispense with military government. As an application for a writ of *habeas corpus* costs money, I never knew mother, grandmother, aunt, or cousin to make it.

One might think that apprentices thus furiously sought for would be gladly let go by their masters; but the Southern whites are themselves noticeably fond of children, and even of Negro children. I have known two small farmers to carry on a long war, involving fights, drawing of knives, suits for assault and battery, and writs of *habeas corpus,* for the possession of a jet black girl only seven years of age and almost valueless except as a plaything. I have known a worthy old gentleman of the higher class to worry away time and money in endeavoring to recover a pet little octoroon from her relatives.

If the Negro younglings were well loved, they were also well whipped; the parents had no idea of sparing the rod and spoiling the child; and when they did flog, it was in a passion and with a will. Passing a cabin, I heard a long-drawn yell of anguish from within and then saw a little freedman rush out, rubbing his rear violently with both hands, his mouth wide open to emit a scream of the largest calibre and the longest range. In the language of a spectator, he looked "powerful glad to git out o' do'."

One of the teachers of the Bureau school at my station having dismissed a girl for bad behavior, the mother appeared to remonstrate. "What you turn her out for?" she demanded. "Ef she's naughty, why don' you whip her?"

"I don't approve of whipping children," was the reply. "It is a punishment that I don't wish to inflict."

"It's your business," screamed the mother,—"it's your business to whip 'em. That's what you's sont here for."

DESIRE FOR EDUCATION [2]

The most hopeful sign in the Negro was his anxiety to have his children educated. The two or three hundred boys and girls whom I used to see around the Bureau schoolhouse—attired with a decency which had strained to the utmost the slender parental purse, ill spared from the hard labor necessary to support their families, gleeful and noisy over their luncheons of cold roasted sweet potato—were proofs that the race has a chance in the future. Many a sorely pinched woman, a widow

2. For a background discussion of the educational work conducted in South Carolina by the Freedmen's Bureau and the philanthropic American Freedmen's Union Commission, see Webster, "Freedmen's Bureau in South Carolina," pp. 128–138. The Bureau's state superintendent of education, whom De Forest mentions on p. 119, was Reuben Tomlinson of Philadelphia. Tomlinson's administration was regarded as remarkably successful, and the Bureau, aided by benevolent societies and by an eager response from the Negroes, made rapid advances. An incomplete Bureau report in 1867 enumerated, for the state, 69 schools (with 7,912 pupils) on which data had been filed, and 40 more on which there were no data; but the inadequacy of this count is suggested by the fact that the Freedmen's Union Commission alone reported 103 schools which its branches were supporting. Free public schools were not established until the 'seventies. De Forest's comment upon the zeal of the Negroes, the budgetary peculiarities of Bureau policy, the use of white teachers from the North, and the aid of Northern philanthropy are all paralleled by evidence in Webster, but there is one aspect in which Greenville appears to have been distinctive: though the whites apparently opposed Negro education in most other places, they supported the endeavor in this sub-district. In March, 1867, for instance, De Forest reported to his superiors that Dr. Lardner Gibbon intended to build a schoolhouse for freedpeople in a neighborhood six miles from Greenville; and also that another planter, Mr. Samuel E. Mays, was encouraging the Negroes of his district to build themselves a schoolhouse. National Archives.

or deserted by her husband, would not let her boy go out to service, "bekase I wants him to have some schoolin'."

One of the elder girls, a remarkably handsome octoroon with Grecian features and chestnut hair, attended recitations in the morning and worked at her trade of dressmaking in the afternoon. There were some grown men who came in the evening to wrestle, rather hopelessly than otherwise, with the depravities of our English spelling. One of them, a gray-headed person in circular spectacles, bent on qualifying himself for the ministry, was very amusing with his stereotyped remark, when corrected of a mistake, "I specs likely you may be right, mum."

It is a mooted point whether colored children are as quick at learning as white children. I should say not; certainly those whom I saw could not compare with the Caucasian youngster of ten or twelve, who is "tackling" French, German, and Latin; they were inferior to him, not only in knowledge, but in the facility of acquisition. In their favor it must be remembered that they lacked the forcing elements of highly educated competition and of a refined home influence. A white lad gets much bookishness and many advanced ideas from the daily converse of his family. Moreover, ancestral intelligence, trained through generations of study, must tell, even though the rival thinking machines may be naturally of the same calibre. I am convinced that the Negro as he is, no matter how educated, is not the mental equal of the European. Whether he is not a man, but merely, as "Ariel" and Dr. Cartwright [3] would have us believe, "a living creature," is quite another question and of so little practical importance that no wonder Governor Perry wrote a political letter about it. Human or not, there he is in our midst, millions strong; and if he is not educated mentally and morally, he will make us trouble.

3. Both "Ariel" and Dr. Cartwright sought to demonstrate the biological inferiority of the Negro. "Ariel" was the pseudonym of Buckner H. Payne who had published in 1867 a pamphlet entitled *The Negro, What Is His Ethnological Status? Is He the Progeny of Ham? Is He a Descendant of Adam and Eve? Has He a Soul? Or Is He a Beast in God's Nomenclature? What Is His Status as Fixed by God in Creation? What Is His Relation to the White Race?* (Cincinnati, 1867). Dr. Samuel Cartwright was a New Orleans physician whose essay, "Slavery in the Light of Ethnology," was first published in the *New Orleans Medical and Surgical Journal,* and was later reprinted in E. N. Elliot, editor, *Cotton Is King, and Pro-Slavery Arguments* (Augusta, 1860).

By way of interesting the adherents of the "living creature" hypothesis, I offer the following letter, which I received from a Negro "pundit," probably to be forwarded to his relatives:

Pittsburg, Pennsylvania,
the 14 March 1867

To the freedmen Bureau in Green ville S. C.

Dear freinds the deep crants of rivous ceprate ous but i hope in God for hours prasous agine and injoying the same injoyment That we did before the war begun and i am tolbile know but much trubbel in mind and i hope my truble Will not Be all Ways this Ways for which enlist the roused up energies of nation and Which Would Be followed by the most disastrous consequences but for these master spirits That reign over the scene of their troubled birth thare are no tampests in a tranquil atmosphere no maountain Waves upon a great sea no cataracts in an even stream and rarely does a man of pereminent po Wars burst upon our admiration in the ever undisturbed flow of human affairs those men Who rise to sway the opinions or control the energies of a nation to move the great master springs of human action are developed By events of infinite moment they appear in those conflicts Where pollical or religious faith of nation is agitated and Where the temporal and eternal Welfare of millions is at issue if on please to inquire for Caline then inquire for marther live at Jane Ransom and Harriett that live at doctor Gant and if you heir from tham let me know if you Plese soon Writ to Pittsburg Pa to Carpenters No 28

Robard Rosemon that lived in Andison Destrect my farther and Carline my mother i remien your refactorate son

SAM ROSEMON.

It will be observed that Sam has tackled some large subjects, if he has not satisfactorily thrown them. I recommend to him the "living creature" hypothesis, as being perhaps worthy of his attention.

A NEGRO PHILANTHROPIST

I took much pride in the Greenville colored school, for I had aided to establish it. Its real founder, the person who can boast that without him it would not have existed, was Charles Hopkins, a full-blooded black from the low country, for many years a voluntary exhorter among his people and eventually an ordained preacher of the Methodist Church. His education, gathered in the chance opportunities of a bondage of fifty years, was sufficient to enable him to instruct in the lower English branches. He was a meek, amiable, judicious, virtuous, godly man, zealous for the good of the freedmen, yet so thoroughly trusted by the whites that he was able to raise a subscription of two hundred and sixty dollars among the impoverished citizens of Greenville.

During the summer of 1866 Hopkins obtained a room in a deserted hotel which had been seized by the government and, aided by two others of his race, gave spelling and reading lessons to sixty or seventy scholars. For this labor he eventually received a modest remuneration from the New York Freedmen's Union Association. When I assumed command of the sub-district the school had closed for the autumn, the hotel had been restored to its owners, and a schoolroom was needed. The officer whom I relieved had much to say concerning plans of rent or purchase and earnestly recommended Hopkins to my consideration. It was at this time that the enthusiastic old man raised his subscription. Meanwhile I wrote to the Bureau Superintendent of Education and received assurances of help in case a school was established.

His private purse reduced to a few dollars, his remaining means pledged for the support of his assistants, Hopkins purchased a storehouse belonging to the defunct state arsenal works and took a three years' lease of a lot of ground in the outskirts of the village. A mass meeting of freedmen tore the building to pieces, moved it nearly two miles, and set it up on the new site. Then came much labor of carpenters, masons, and plasterers, and much expense for new materials. By the time the schoolhouse was completed it had cost, together with the rent of the land, five hundred and sixty dollars, or more than twice the amount of the subscription. Hopkins was substantially bankrupt, and, moreover, he was drawing no salary.

It must be understood that the Bureau had no funds for the payment of teachers; by the act of Congress it was limited in the matter of education to the renting and repairing of schoolhouses. Teachers were supported by generous individuals or by benevolent societies at the North, which converged into various larger organizations, and these into the Bureau. For instance, a sewing circle in Lockport might raise five hundred dollars for the blacks, or a wealthy gentleman in Albany might give the same sum from his private purse, and both forward their contributions to the Freedmen's Union Association in New York City. But each of these subscribers naturally desired to know by whom the money would be used, or had in view a worthy person who deserved a mission of some small profit and much usefulness. The consequence was that the Freedmen's Union and the Bureau received few unappropriated contributions and were not able to do much toward the payment of Negro teachers.

Application on application was forwarded, but Hopkins was grievously bullied by his creditors before he received a penny of salary. For his two colored assistants I could obtain nothing, and they left, after two months of unrequited labor, indebted to Hopkins and others for their support. The spirit of the Freedmen's Union was willing, but its purse was weak. The Bureau supplies, on the other hand, were easily obtained, the cost of land and building slipping nicely into the appropriation for "rent and repairs," and the money arriving promptly enough to save Hopkins from falling into the hands of the sheriff. Eventually, too, he secured payment for all his services at the rate of twenty-five dollars a month; and when I last saw him he was as nearly square with the world as the majority of his white fellow citizens.

Meantime he had received ordination from the Charleston missionary branch of the Methodist Church North. With a commission as "Professor" from the Freedmen's Union Association, with the title of clergyman from one of the great branches of the Christian Church, with the consciousness of having founded the Greenville Elementary Freedmen's School, he was a gratified man and worthy of his happiness.

It must not be supposed that he was rolling in pelf. As the school kept open only eight months in the year, as the Methodist missionary society was short of funds and had never paid him the promised annual salary of one hundred dollars, and as the voluntary contributions of his congregation amounted to perhaps seven dollars a quarter, his income was less than he could get by superintending a plantation.

Two white teachers joined the school toward the close of

1866;[4] and the force before I left had been gradually increased to five; Hopkins remaining in charge of the lower classes. The number of scholars on the rolls was something like three hundred. The higher classes were in geography, arithmetic, English grammar and written exercises, and declamation. Class books of the latest issue were gratuitously supplied by a leading New York publishing house. The discipline was admirable; the monotony of study was relieved by gleesome singing; there was a cheerful zeal, near akin to hilarity; it was a charming spectacle. Most of the leading scholars were from one family, a dozen or so of brothers, sisters, and cousins—all of mixed blood and mostly handsome. When I first saw those hazel or blue eyes, chestnut or flaxen heads, and clear complexions, I took it for granted that some of the white children of the village had seized this chance for a gratuitous education. I had met the same persons before in the streets, without suspecting that they were of other than pure Anglo-Saxon race.

The superior scholarship of these octoroons, by the way, is not entirely owing to their greater natural quickness of intellect, but also to the fact that before the emancipation they were petted and encouraged by the family to which they belonged. A man's chances go very far toward making up the actual man.

SOCIAL STATUS

What is the Negro's social status, and what is it to be? I was amused one Sunday morning by a little tableau which presented itself at the front door of my hotel. The Bureau Superintendent of Education having arrived on an inspecting tour, my venerable friend Hopkins had called to take him to church and was waiting in his meek fashion under the portico, not choosing to intrude upon the august interior of the establishment. Having

4. De Forest's reports show that in November, for example, the enrollment was 106 Negroes, and the average attendance was 96. Though none of the pupils paid tuition, they brought in wood and goods to the value of $6.75. The numbers of students in various subjects were as follows: alphabet and primer, 25; reading, in first, second, third, fourth, and fifth readers, respectively, 40, 20, 4, 0, 0; mental and written arithmetic, respectively, 36 and 18; second arithmetic series, 12; third arithmetic series, 6; geography, 36; second geography series, 24; third geography series, 12; grammar, 10; writing on slates, 40; writing in books, 20. National Archives.

lately been ordained and conceiving himself entitled to the insignia of his profession, he had put on a white neckcloth, which of course contrasted brilliantly with his black face and clothing. In the doorway stood a citizen, a respectable and kindly man, excellently well reconstructed too, and with as few of the Southern prejudices as one could have in Greenville. But he was lost in wonder at this novel spectacle; he had a smile of mingled curiosity and amusement on his face to which I can not do justice; he seemed to be admitting that here was indeed a new and most comical era in human history. A "nigger" in regular clerical raiment was evidently a phenomenon which his imagination never could have depicted and which, fact alone —so much stranger than fiction—could have brought home to him as a possibility. Whether he believes to this day that he actually did see Hopkins in a black coat and white cravat is more than doubtful.

Not for generations will the respectable whites of the South, any more than those of the North, accept the Negroes as their social equals. That pride of race which has marked all distinguished peoples, which caused the Greeks to style even the wealthy Persians and Egyptians barbarians, which made the Romans refuse for ages the boon of citizenship to other Italians, which led the Semitic Jew to scorn the Hamitic Canaanite, and leads the Aryan to scorn the Jew—that sentiment which more than anything else has created nationality and patriotism, has among us retreated to the family, but it guards this last stronghold with jealous care. Whether the applicant for admission be the Chinaman of California or the African of Carolina, he will for long be repulsed. The acceptance of the Negro as the social equal of the white in our country dates so far into the future that, practically speaking, we may consider it as never to be, and so cease concerning ourselves about it. Barring the dregs of our population, as, for instance, the poor-white trash of the South, the question interests no one now alive.

MIXED BLOODS

I had not been long in Greenville before I was invited to what Mr. Hopkins styled "a concert." Repairing in the evening

to the Bureau schoolhouse and seating myself amid an audience
of freedpeople, I found that the "concert" consisted not of singing or other music, but of *tableaux-vivans.* At one end of the
room there was a stage of chestnut boards, with a curtain of
calico and an inner curtain of white gauze to assist the illusion.
Presently the calico was withdrawn, and I beheld a handsome
Pocahontas, her face reddened to the true Indian color as seen
in colored woodcuts, a wealth of long black hair falling down
her back, saving the life of a Captain John Smith with Grecian
features and Caucasian complexion. Powhatan and his war-
riors were painted up to a proper ferocity and attired with a
respectable regard to the artistic demands of savageness. The
scene was hardly uncovered before it was hidden again. I whispered to Hopkins that the spectators were not allowed a fair
chance, and the consequence was a repetition. This time the
curtain was kept open so long that Pocahontas, unable to bear
the lengthened publicity, gave a nervous start which amazingly
tickled the beholders.

Then came the Goddess of Liberty, a charming girl of seventeen, with wavy chestnut hair, rosy cheeks, and laughing eyes,
quite imposingly draped in stars and stripes. Next followed
a French family scene: one black face here as servant, and one
or two mulatto ones as old folks; but the grandeur and grace of
the scene represented by blue eyes, auburn hair, and blond complexions. I was puzzled by this free mingling of the African and
Caucasian races and repaired to Hopkins for an explanation.
He informed me that the "concert" had been got up by
the octoroon family which I have heretofore mentioned,
and that its members had furnished nearly all of the perform-
ers.

Great is color, and patrician is race. I have heard a mulatto
candidate for the Convention declare to an assemblage of Negroes: "I never ought to have been a slave, for my father was a
gentleman." I have heard him declaim: "If ever there is a
nigger government—an unmixed nigger government—established in South Carolina, I shall move."

It may well be supposed that the pure blacks do not listen to
such assumptions with satisfaction. Although this speaker was
the most notable colored man in his district, although he was

(for his opportunities) a person of remarkable intellect, information, and high character, he ran behind all the white candidates on his ticket.

In Greenville there was deep and increasing jealousy between the blacks and mulattoes. To some extent they formed distinct cliques of society and crystallized into separate churches. When the mulattoes arranged a series of *tableaux-vivans* for the benefit of their religious establishment, the far more numerous blacks kept at a distance and made the show a pecuniary failure. When the mulattoes asked that they might hold a fair in the Bureau schoolhouse, for the above-mentioned purpose, some of the blacks intrigued against the request and were annoyed at my granting it.

This fair, by the way, was a pleasing sight. As Bureau officer and guardian of the freedmen, I of course went; so did all the dignitaries of the United States District Court then sitting in Greenville; so also did three or four of the wiser and kindlier white citizens. The room was crowded, for the blacks had been unable to resist the temptations of a spectacle and had forgotten temporarily their jealousy of the mixed race.

As usual on such occasions, the handsomest and brightest girls sat behind the counters and were extortionate in their prices. Wishing to make a gay present to my friend Hopkins, I was a little astonished at being called upon to pay five dollars for a frosted cake and at learning that another, of extra size and grandeur, had been sold for twelve dollars. There were ice creams and oysters and solider viands; there were fans, perfumeries, and jim-crackeries for the ladies; there were candies and toys for the children, slippers for the lords of creation. What the proceeds of the entertainment were I do not know; but the treasurer of the occasion had a roll of greenbacks which excited my wonder.

One incident was comical in its results. Standing with the Hon. Mr. Blank, a benevolent and liberal-minded Southerner, near one of the prettiest of the octoroon sisters, I called his attention to her Greek purity of profile. He replied that the circumstance was noways singular and that one of the most notedly beautiful women in the state had been of that mixed race. A little colored tailor, who was at our elbows, half understood this statement, applied it to the girl behind the counter, and reported through the assemblage that the Hon. Mr. Blank had called Jenny W——the handsomest girl in South Carolina. A certain wicked young gentleman got hold of the story and spread it all over town in the following outrageous fashion. Whatsoever belle of the Anglo-Saxon race he might encounter, he would say to her, "Well—hum—you are very pretty—but you are not as pretty as Miss Jenny W——."

"Who is Miss Jenny W——?" would be the benighted and curious response.

Then would this intolerable young gentleman maliciously tell his tale and go on his way laughing. The result was high excitement among the belles of the Anglo-Saxon race, and much feminine chaffing of the Hon. Mr. Blank. What made the matter worse was that on the day of the fair he had accepted an invitation to a young ladies' reading society and then had withdrawn it, because of the invitation from the humble race which held festivity at the Bureau schoolhouse.

"What! going to disappoint us for those people!" a fair patrician had said to him. "We ought to cut your acquaintance."

"My dear, I can't disappoint *them,*" he had replied, very wisely and nobly. "When people whom God has placed so far beneath me ask for my presence, I must give it. It is like an invitation from the queen. It is a command."

That had been comprehended and pardoned; but to call Jenny W—— handsomer than them all! The Hon. Mr. Blank was bullied into making explanations.

But this gossip was matter of laughter, without a shade of serious umbrage or jealousy, so secure is the Anglo-Saxon race in its social pre-eminence. Between the mulattoes and Negroes the question is far different; the former are already anxious to distinguish themselves from the pure Africans; the latter are already sore under the superiority thus asserted. Were the two breeds more equally divided in numbers, there would be such hostility between them as has been known in Hayti and Jamaica. The mixed race in our country is, however, so small, and its power of self-perpetuation so slight, that it will probably be absorbed in the other. Meantime it holds more than its share of intelligence and of those qualities which go to the acquisition of property.

POLITICAL QUALIFICATIONS

With a Bureau officer who was stationed in the lowlands of South Carolina, I compared impressions as to the political qualifications and future of the Negro. "In my district," he said, "the election[5] was a farce. Very few of the freedmen had any idea of what they were doing or even of how they ought to do it. They would vote into the post office or any hole they could find. Some of them carried home their ballots, greatly smitten with the red lettering and the head of Lincoln or supposing that they could use them as warrants for land. Others would give them to the first white man who offered to take care of them. One old fellow said to me, 'Lord, mars'r! do for Lord's sake tell me what dis yere's all about.'

"I explained to him that the election was to put the state back into the Union and make it stay there in peace.

" 'Lord bless you, mars'r! I'se might' glad to un'erstan' it,' he answered. 'I'se the only nigger in this yere districk now that knows what he's up ter.' "

In my own district things were better. A region of small farmers mainly, the Negroes had lived nearer to the whites than on the great plantations of the low country and were proportionately intelligent. The election in Greenville was at least the soberest and most orderly that had ever been known there. Obedient to the instructions of their judicious managers, the freedmen voted quietly and went immediately home, without the reproach of a fight or a drunkard and without even a hurrah of triumph. Their little band of music turned out in the evening to serenade a favorite candidate; but a word from him sent them bedward with silent trumpets, and the night was remarkable for tranquillity. Even the youngsters who sometimes rowdied in the streets seemed to be sensible of the propriety of unusual peace, and vanished early. Judging from what I saw that day, I should have halcyon hopes for the political future of the Negro.

5. For this election of 1867, see Introduction, p. x.

My impression is, although I can not make decisive averment in the matter, that a majority of the Greenville freedmen had a sufficiently intelligent sense of the purport of the election. The stupidest of them understood that he was acting "agin de Rebs," and "for de freedom." None of them voted into the post office or into hollow trees.

A NEGRO REVOLUTION

There was a tragedy in my satrapy during the autumn of 1867. A meeting of Union Leaguers,[6] composed chiefly of Negroes, but presided over by a white man, was held one evening in an inconsiderable hamlet near the southern border of Pickens District. According to an absurd and illegal fashion too common with such convocations, armed sentinels were posted around the building, with orders to prevent the approach of uninitiated persons. In a schoolhouse not far distant the whites of the neighborhood had met in a debating society.

A low-down white named Smith approached the League rendezvous—as the sentinels declared, with threats of forcing an entrance; as he stated, by mistake. Either by him or by one of the Negroes a pistol was fired; and then arose a cry that a "Reb" was coming to break up the meeting. A voice within, said by some to be that of the president, Bryce, ordered, "Bring that man a prisoner, dead or alive."

The Negroes rushed out; Smith fled, hotly pursued, to the schoolhouse; the members of the debating club broke up in a panic and endeavored to escape; a second pistol was fired, and a boy of fourteen, named Hunnicutt, the son of a respectable citizen, fell dead. The ball entered the back of his head, showing that, when it struck him, he was flying.

Then ensued an extraordinary drama. The Negroes, unaware apparently that they had done anything wrong, believing, on the contrary, that they were re-establishing public order and enforcing justice, commenced patrolling the neighborhood, entering every house, and arresting numbers of citizens. They marched in double file, pistol in belt and gun at the shoulder,

6. The term Union League was used interchangeably with Loyal League. See p. 99 n.

keeping step to the "hup, hup!" of a fellow called Lame Sam,
who acted as drill sergeant and commander. By noon of the
next day they had the country for miles around in their power,
and a majority of the male whites under guard. What they
meant to do is uncertain; probably they did not know themselves. Their subsequent statement was that they wanted to
find the disturber of their meeting, Smith, and also the murderer of Hunnicutt, whom they asserted to be a "Reb."

On the arrival of a detachment from the United States garrison at Anderson the whites were liberated, and the freedmen
handed over to the civil authorities for trial before the next
district court. The Leaguers exhibited such a misguided loyalty
to their order and each other, that it was impossible to fix a
charge for murder on any one person or to establish grounds
for an indictment of any sort against Bryce. Eighteen were
found guilty of riot, and sentenced to imprisonment; eight of
homicide in the first degree, and sentenced to death.

Still no confessions; the convicted men would not believe
that they would be punished; they were sure that the Yankees
would save them or that the Leaguers would rescue them; they
refused to point out either the instigator or the perpetrator of
the murder. It was not until the United States marshal of South
Carolina assured them of the fallacy of their hopes that they
dismissed them. Admissions were then made; nearly all coin-
cided in fixing the fatal pistol shot upon one; and that one was
hung.[7]

This affair was mainly important as showing how easily the
Negroes could be led into folly and crime. Themselves a peaceful race, not disposed to rioting and murder, they were brought
without trouble to both by the counsels of the ignorant and pugnacious whites who became their leaders in the Loyal Leagues.

Not three days after the Hunnicutt tragedy, a farmer from
Pickens District called on me to obtain a permit for an armed
meeting of Union men and seemed quite dumbfounded when I
not only refused the permit, but assured him that, if he at-

7. This incident is included in De Forest's monthly report of outrages for October,
1867. It later became the subject of an extensive government investigation and was
apparently regarded as a case of major importance, since the evidence is fully recorded in the *Annual Report of the Secretary of War*, 40th Cong., 3d Sess., I, 370–
467.

tempted to hold such a meeting, I would have him arrested. In justice to the Union men and the Negroes, however, it must be remembered that they had been governed by the mailed hand; and that, in seeking to enforce their political ideas by steel and gunpowder, they were but following the example of the high-toned gentlemen who formerly swayed the South. On the whole, we must admit that, although they committed more follies and crimes than were at all desirable, they committed fewer than might reasonably have been expected, considering the nature of their political education.

HIGH TAXES AND LOW WAGES

At least one of the political privileges of the Negroes soon became a heavy burden to them. Every day or two some ragged fellow stepped into my office with the inquiry, "I wants to know ef I've got to pay my taxes."

"Certainly," I was bound to reply, for the general commanding had declared that the civil laws were in force, and moreover I knew that the state was tottering for lack of money.

"But the sheriff, he's put it up to eight dollars now, an' when he first named it to me he said it was three, an' when I went to see him about it arterward he said it was five. 'Pears like I can't git at the rights of the thing nohow, an' they's jes tryin' to leave me without anything to go upon."

"My dear fellow, you should have paid up when you were first warned. The additions since then are charges for collection. The longer you put it off, the more it will cost you. You had better settle with the sheriff without any further delay, or you may be sold out."

"Wal, 'pears like it's mighty hard on us, an' we jes a-startin'. I was turned off year befo' las' without a grain o' corn, an' no lan'. Boss, is they comin' on us every year for these yere taxes?"

"I suppose so. How else are the laws to be kept up and the poor old Negroes to be supported?"

Exit freedman in a state of profound discouragement, looking as if he wished there were no laws and no poor old Negroes.

The taxes were indeed heavy on labor, especially as compared with wages. Eight dollars a month, with rations and lodging, was all that the best field hand could earn in Greenville District; and those freedmen who took land on shares generally managed, by dint of unintelligent cultivation and of laziness, to obtain even less. I knew of able-bodied women who were working for nothing but their shelter, food, and two suits of cheap cotton clothing per annum.

MIGRATION [8]

As a result of this wretched remuneration there was an exodus. During the fall of 1866 probably a thousand freedpeople left my two districts of Pickens and Greenville to settle in Florida, Louisiana, Arkansas, and Tennessee. Only a few had the enterprise or capital to go by themselves; the great majority were carried off by planters and emigration agents. Those who went to Florida contracted for twelve dollars a month, a cabin, a garden patch, fuel, and weekly rations consisting of one peck of meal, two pounds of bacon, and one pint of molasses; but on reaching their destination and seeing the richness of the land, they sometimes flew from their bargains and secured a new one, giving them one third of the crop in place of wages and increasing the quantity and quality of their rations. The emigrants to Louisiana and Arkansas went on the basis of fifteen dollars a month, lodgings, patch, fuel, and food; and then kept their contracts if they pleased, or violated them under the temptation of thirty, forty, and even fifty dollars a month. The Negroes, having never been taught the value of

8. Migration of Negroes from the Southeastern states was a widespread trend during 1866. A few philanthropic societies established employment agencies in the North and encouraged migration thither. Several hundred Negroes went to Liberia, but the majority of emigrants went to Florida or, in response to higher wage levels, to the Southwest. Many, disappointed in their hope for "forty acres and a mule" in South Carolina, were attracted by the prospect of free land under the Homestead Act of June 21, 1866, with the government furnishing them transportation and six months' rations. There is no accurate estimate of how many thousands migrated. F. B. Simkins and R. H. Woody, *South Carolina during Reconstruction* (Chapel Hill, 1932), pp. 233–234; Webster, *op. cit.*, pp. 140–141. De Forest commented on this emigration in his monthly reports for October, November, December, 1866, and January, 1867; and on July 3, 1867, he wrote to state headquarters about certain Negroes under contract to be transported by W. P. Passmore who was, he suspected, "an emigration speculator." National Archives.

honesty by experience, nor much of its beauty by precept, were frequently slippery. The planters, pressingly in need of labor, were generally obliged to accede to their demands.

On the other hand, the emigration agents were accused of some sharp practice and particularly of leaving their emigrants at points whither they had not agreed to go. A freedman who had contracted to work at Memphis might be landed at Franklin in Louisiana without knowing the difference. In short, the matter went on more or less smoothly, with some good results and some evil. Labor was transferred in considerable masses from where it was not wanted to where it was. The beneficent effects of the migration were of course much diminished by the accidental circumstances of overflows in Louisiana, and a fall in the value of the cotton crop everywhere. Moreover, these Negroes of the mountains suffered nearly as much from lowland fevers as if they were white men from our Northern frontiers.

PROSPECTS OF THE RACE

Will the freedmen acquire property and assume position among the managers of our national industry? The low-down Negro will of course follow the low-down white into sure and deserved oblivion. His more virtuous and vital brother will struggle longer with the law of natural selection; and he may eventually hold a portion of this continent against the vigorous and terrible Caucasian race; that portion being probably those lowlands where the white can not or will not labor. Meantime the Negro's acquisition of property, and of those qualities which command the industry of others, will be slow. What better could be expected of a serf so lately manumitted?

When I first took post in Greenville, I used to tell the citizens that soon their finest houses would be in possession of blacks; but long before I left there I had changed my opinion. Although land in profusion was knocked down for a song on every monthly sale day, not more than three freedmen had purchased any, and they not more than an acre apiece. What little money they earned they seemed to be incapable of applying to solid and lasting purpose; they spent it for new clothes and other luxuries or in supporting each other's idleness; they remained penniless where an Irishman or German would thrive. Encumbered with debt as were many of the whites of Greenville, deficient as they might be in business faculty and industry, they needed not to fear that black faces would smile out of their parlor windows. The barbarian and serf does not so easily rise to be the employer and landlord of his late master.

What is to become of the African in our country as a race? Will he commingle with the Caucasian, and so disappear? It is true that there are a few marriages, and a few cases of illegal cohabitation, between Negro men and the lowest class of white women. For example, a full-blooded black walked twenty miles to ask me if he could have a white wife, assuring me that there was a girl down in his "settlement" who was "a-teasin' every day about it."

He had opened his business with hesitation, and he talked of it in a tremulous undertone, glancing around for fear of listeners. I might have told him that, as it was not leap year, the woman had no right to propose to him; but I treated the matter seriously. Bearing in mind that she must be a disreputable creature, who would make him a wretched helpmeet, I first informed him that the marriage would be legal and that the civil and military authorities would be bound to protect him in it, and then advised him against it, on the ground that it would expose him to a series of underhanded persecutions which could not easily be prevented. He went away evidently but half convinced, and I presume that his Delilah had her will with him, although I heard no more of this odd love affair.

Miscegenation between white men and Negresses diminished under the new order of things. Emancipation broke up the close family contact in which slavery held the two races, and, moreover, young gentlemen did not want mulatto children sworn to them at a cost of three hundred dollars apiece. In short, the new relations of the two stocks tended to separation rather than to fusion. There will be no amalgamation, no merging and disappearance of the black in the white, except at a period so distant that it is not worth while now to speculate upon it. So far as we and our children and grandchildren are concerned, the Negro will remain a Negro and must be prophesied about as a Negro.

But will he remain a Negro, and not rather become a ghost? It is almost ludicrous to find the "woman question" intruding itself into the future of a being whom we have been accustomed to hear of as a "nigger," and whom a ponderous wise man of the East always persisted in abusing as "Quashee." [9] There was a growing disinclination to marriage among the young freedmen, because the girls were learning to shirk out-of-door work, to demand nice dresses and furniture, and, in short, to be fine ladies. The youths had, of course, no objection to the adornment itself; indeed, they were, like white beaux, disposed to follow the game which wears the finest feathers; but they were getting clever enough to know that such game is expensive and to content themselves with looking at it. Where the prettiest colored girls in Greenville were to find husbands was more than I could imagine.

There are other reasons why the blacks may not increase as rapidly as before the emancipation. The young men have more amusements and a more varied life than formerly. Instead of being shut up on the plantation, they can spend the nights in frolicking about the streets or at drinking-places; instead of the monotony of a single neighborhood, they can wander from village to village and from South Carolina to Texas. The master is no longer there to urge matrimony and perhaps other methods of increasing population. Negroes, as well as whites, can now be forced by law to support their illegitimate offspring and are consequently more cautious than formerly how they have such offspring.

In short, the higher civilization of the Caucasian is gripping the race in many ways and bringing it to sharp trial before its time. This new, varied, costly life of freedom, this struggle to be at once like a race which has passed through a two-thousand-years' growth in civilization, will probably diminish the pro-

9. The "wise man" was Thomas Carlyle, who, in his "Occasional Discourse on the Nigger Question" in *Fraser's Magazine,* December, 1849, repeatedly spoke of the Negro as "Quashee." An earlier use of the term was by Michael Scott, in 1836, in his *Tom Cringle's Log.*

ductiveness of the Negro and will terribly test his vitality.

It is doubtless well for his chances of existence that his color keeps him a plebeian, so that, like the European peasant held down by caste, he is less tempted to destroy himself in the struggle to become a patrician.

What judgment shall we pass upon abrupt emancipation, considered merely with reference to the Negro? It was a mighty experiment, fraught with as much menace as hope.

To the white race alone it was a certain and precious boon.

CHAPTER VII

THE LOW-DOWN PEOPLE [1]

ALTHOUGH, as an officer of the Bureau of Refugees, Freedmen, and Abandoned Lands, I was chiefly concerned with the affairs of Negroes and Unionists, I was occasionally obliged to deal with other classes of our Southern population and especially with that wretched caste commonly spoken of as the "mean whites" or the "poor-white folksy," but in my district as the "low-down people." I have strung together, on as brief a thread as the subject will admit, a few gems from the character of this variety of our much-boasted Anglo-Saxon race.

MORALITY

The 4th of April, 1867, was made memorable to the Bureau Major by the strangest case that was ever presented for his consideration.

As he sat in his little vaulted office in the lower story of the old courthouse of Greenville, there entered two women from the mountains of the Dark Corner, the one thirty-five years of age and the other forty, their faces haggard and their arms sinewy with long endurance of hardness of life, if not of pinching

---

1. Published originally in *Putnam's Magazine*, I, n.s. (June, 1868), 704-716. Upon the general subject of the poor-whites of the South, the best account, both literary and historical, is Shields McIlwain, *The Southern Poor-White from Lubberland to Tobacco Road* (Norman, 1939). McIlwain, by the way, appears to be the only modern writer who is aware of the existence and the value of De Forest's observations on Southern society. He characterizes this essay and the one on "Drawing Bureau Rations" as being "not only the finest glimpses we have of the poor-whites in Reconstruction, but also the keenest and most complete comment upon them." In his opinion, De Forest's "expertness of description and dialogue . . . equals that of any author preceding him" and had the literary importance of "keeping the idiom and manner of the poor-white before the public" until modern writers like William Faulkner could begin to use the type. In a subsequent novel, *Kate Beaumont* (1872), and in the story, "An Independent Ku-Klux" (*Galaxy*, April, 1872), De Forest himself portrayed further the class of people he describes in this chapter.

poverty, and their lean shapes attired in scant, soiled gowns of coarse homespun, cut without form or comeliness and falling as straight from their hips as if the Empress Eugenie had never tasked her mighty brain to put hoops in fashion.

The elder, Mrs. Jones, was evidently of the original "mean-white" breed, yet her visage was not without some woeful remnant of former seemliness; and she led by the hand a black-eyed, rosy-cheeked daughter of ten or eleven, who was passably pretty. The younger, Mrs. Singleton, had been in good circumstances and had a smart, brusque, and not unattractive bearing. Although it was only ten o'clock in the morning, they had walked fourteen miles since "sun-up," and they had come an equal distance since noon of the day before. Their clogged shoes and draggled skirts showed the condition of the traveling.

"My man has run me off," abruptly commenced Mrs. Jones, in that dull, sour, dogged tone of complaint which seems to be the natural utterance of the low-down people.

"Do you mean your husband?" inquired the Bureau Major.

"No; he wasn't my husband."

Awkward silence, which continues until it is broken by the clear, brisk voice of Mrs. Singleton:

"You see, this woman has been living in adultery with this man. That's his child. Now he's run her off and took up with another man's wife."

MRS. JONES. "Though he warn't married to me, he was bound. He'd taken me up for ninety-nine years. It was proved in court."

THE MAJOR (*with bewilderment*). "Proved in court?"

MRS. JONES. "Yes, thar was the paper, signed an' swore to. He couldn't marry me because he had a wife. But he made a contrack to keep me; else I wouldn't go to him."

THE MAJOR (*nearly speechless*). "Is this a common case? Did you ever hear of such another?"

MRS. SINGLETON (*calmly*). "No, I never did."

MRS. JONES. "Wal, he contracked to keep me ninety-nine years; an' it was proved in court when his brother tried to break it; an' now he's druv me off, to take up another woman; an' I think he ought to be fo'ced to take me back."

MRS. SINGLETON (*sympathetically*). "Can't you make him take her back?"

THE MAJOR. "No, I don't think she has any legal rights over him; and if she has, it is not my business to enforce them. I have no authority except in matters pertaining to Negroes and refugees—that is, Union people."

MRS. JONES. "Wal, I was always agin the war."

THE MAJOR. "Still, the affair does not come within my jurisdiction. You had better see a lawyer."

Mrs. Singleton then complained that one of her neighbors had interfered with her right of way to the public road, and was also recommended to seek redress at the hands of the civil authorities.

The case of Mrs. Jones, although unparalleled even in the eyes of Mrs. Singleton, did nevertheless indicate pretty faithfully the state of morals among the low-down people. Dissolute when they came from England as convicts or as stupid farm-laborers, dissolute through all those many years in which slavery condemned them to idleness and consequent poverty, they were in 1867 more debauched than ever, because the war had left so many wives without husbands and so many girls without the chance of marriage. The state swarmed with widows and girls who migrated after the garrisons and led a life like that of the "wrens of the Curragh." [2] Our soldiers easily provided themselves with a new set of brides or sweethearts in every village. A soldier's marriage, be it understood, was frequently but a temporary contract, much like that by which a sailor secures himself a home in every port, and by no means so permanent as the bargain entered into by the Mrs. Jones above mentioned. Occasionally a female of decent connections espoused a bluecoat; and presently found herself with a child on her hands, a woman of the town or, at the best, an applicant for government rations; while her husband, perhaps in Alaska, offers his inexhaustible affections to an Esquimaux. In no part of the Christian world did I ever see a village no larger than Greenville which contained so many women who were known to be Cyprians. It is true that I am not familiar with many Southern villages.

2. Prostitutes who frequented the military camp at Curragh near Dublin.

But although morals were worse than formerly among the low-down people, they were never nice. A citizen of Greenville told me a story which fairly illustrates their notions of delicacy and self-respect. In former times, when the public whipping post was still a vigorous institution, he saw a crowd coming from behind the courthouse and heard that a Negro had been flogged by the sheriff. Amid the crowd was Uncle Joe, a simple old fellow of the thoroughbred mean-white stock, a little drunk in honor of the occasion, and vociferating cheerfully, "I got that nigger paid off, I reckon."

"What was the row, Uncle Joe?" inquired my informant. "What had the fellow been doing?"

"I ketched him a-sweeteartin' with one of my da'ters," returned the venerable "white trash" indignantly, "an' I don't allow no nigger to do that."

In a community where there has been no sentimental talk concerning Negro equality and where, on the contrary, the prejudice of race has been cultivated by every possible appeal, only the extremest degradation could lead a white woman to listen to overtures of love from a "nigger." Yet, among the low-down females of Greenville, I knew of two who had mulatto children, others who were maintained by Negroes, and one who had a Negro husband. For the most part, however, these were widows or orphans whom the war had robbed of their natural protectors. There was no fastidious Uncle Joe to save or to avenge.[3]

For mothers to connive at the illicit *liaisons* of their daughters and even to endeavor to bring about such arrangements, was by no means uncommon among the low-down people. Partly, no doubt, in consequence of the destruction of men during the war a large proportion, if not the majority, of the

3. Cf. the statement by Stephen Powers, *Afoot and Alone* (Hartford, 1872), p. 41, on this subject. Powers made a walking tour of the South in 1868, and, having conducted "diligent inquiry" about miscegenation, he declared: "I never found but . . . one instance . . . in respectable life. In those districts of South Carolina where the black population was densest and the poor whites most degraded, these unnatural unions were more frequent than anywhere else. In every case, without exception, it was a woman of the lowest class, generally a sandhiller, who, having lost in the war her only supporter, 'took up with a likely nigger' to save her children from absolute famine. In South Carolina, I found six cases of such marriages, but never more than one in any other state."

children born among them were illegitimate. Infanticide was unknown, for the reason that shame was unknown. The unmarried mother proudly dressed her infant in what finery she could obtain and took it about among her friends, or paraded it in the nearest village as a new claim on human charity. Why should she be humbled over it, when it was as decently born as herself?

DRUNKENNESS

Drunkenness was not very common among these abject creatures. They had no sentimental or moral objections to it; they probably never heard of a temperance society, or could conceive of such a thing unaided; but they were so lazy that they would rather go without liquor than work for it. In the good old times before the flood, when South Carolina gloried in her militia, and muster-days were enlivened by the colonel's gratuitous whisky, when politics was the business of a gentleman, and candidates refreshed their adherents by the barrelful, the low-downer enjoyed his periodical benders without expense. After the war the colonel, the "high-toned" Congressman, and the public pails of strong drink became things of the past. If our vagrant friend could not become the humble retainer of a distillery, taking pay in kind for his services and consuming himself off the face of the earth with rotgut, he generally limited his enjoyments to hog, hominy, and laziness. Moreover, he had perhaps vanished; his body was lying in some ditch around Richmond or Atlanta; and he was represented in the world by his widow and orphans. Women of this class were for some reason sober; at least, I never saw one of them intoxicated; they drink, but in moderation.

IDLENESS AND IMPROVIDENCE

"I wish you c'u'd holp us to buy a coew," petitioned a mean-white family to which I had furnished rations.

"How much would it cost?"

"We kin git it for fifteen dollars. The woman said she'd take part pay now an' wait for the rest. She's a powerful good coew; she gives a gallon an' a half o' milk a day. That would be mighty nigh enough to feed us; if we had that, we wouldn't want much bread an' bacon."

"But you have no land to pasture her."

"Oh, thar's the woods an' the old fields. She c'u'd pick up enough for herself."

"Yes, and when winter comes, you would let her starve to death, and then you would be just where you are now."

"Ef we only had her, 'pears like we might git along somehow."

This dialogue exhibits the idleness and improvidence of the low-down people. The family in question consisted of a grown-up youth, three women, and a stout boy of twelve; yet they only wanted the cow to save themselves from working for pork and cornmeal; and they had not a plan to propose whereby the animal could be kept through the winter.

Another woman got herself "holped" to buy a loom on the plea that, if she had that, she could support herself and her two small children. Three months later I learned from one of her neighbors that she had "never set it up." In short, so far as my observation and experience went, it seemed useless to encourage the low-down people to industry and forethought. What they got by begging, they spent for clothing, provisions, and tobacco, and then lay down in their "rotten laziness" until routed out of it by hunger. No exertion was welcome to them except that of gossiping from cabin to cabin, or visiting some village to stare at the shops and learn the news. If ever the household obtained an unusual supply of corn or a little money, whisky was bought, the neighbors were invited, a Negro fiddler was perhaps hired, and there was a dance. I exceedingly regret that I never attended one of these festivities.

BEGGARY

It used to seem to me, at Greenville, that the main subsistence of the low-down people was derived from beggary. I had far more applications for food and money from this class than from my proper constituents, the freedmen. Whenever my office was invaded by a woman in threadbare homespun or torn calico, her black or brown or gray stockings of coarse wool grimed with mud, her down-at-the-heel shoes foxy with long wear and perhaps tied with tow strings, on her arm a bag or basket, and in her mouth a pipe with a reed stem and a clay bowl, I was pretty sure to hear, "Anythin' to git?" or, "Got anythin' for the lone women?" or, "When is the next draw day?"

Accustomed to beg of the planters while these were wealthy, and to receive rations from the Confederate government during its brief existence, they promptly brought claims against the United States. One would suppose that, in conquering the South, we had inherited some everlasting debt to the low-downers.

One thing which they wanted was land. They nourished an absurd belief that, if they had farms, they would cultivate them. But instead of working, laying up their wages, and so buying land while it was only a dollar or two an acre, they proposed that it should be given them, no matter at whose expense. The idea of confiscation was received with more favor by this caste than by the Negroes. A lean, sallow, lank-haired inhabitant of Spartanburg District suspended his chaffering with a neighboring planter for the hire of a plot of ground and walked twenty-three miles to ask me what were the prospects "for a dividin'." A loyal "mean-white" from the mountains of the Dark Corner, who visited Greenville to attend a League convocation, improved the occasion by marking out and in his own mind pre-empting a hundred acres or so of Colonel Irvine's richest bottoms. Over and over have dirty, ragged, stupid creatures slyly inquired of me, "When is our folks a-gwine to git the lan'?"

Not that they were Union people; not that they had a spite against the planters as Rebels: their longing for confiscation was but a part of their scheme of life; it was sheer, bald beggary. If they had their forty acres apiece, the moneyed classes would recover all in twenty years, leaving the low-downers as poor as now, and as anxious for a new division. To give them land would be just as useless as it is to give them corn and bacon. In general, what a man does not work for is of no permanent value to him.

VAGRANCY

One morning my office was entered by two women, a mother and daughter. The former, perhaps forty years of age and perhaps sixty—it was impossible to guess which from her appearance—was a gaunt, crouching creature with a pinched visage and a hungry eagerness of aspect, indicative of years of want and beggary. The daughter, twenty years old, had regular and delicate features, a complexion which, though sunburnt, was of a fine blonde, and long golden hair which would have been beautiful but for neglect. On the other hand, her feet were bare, her lips stained with tobacco juice, and her expression as wild as that of a mustang. Both wore dirty dresses of the coarsest cotton homespun, falling straight from the hips, and without the slightest trimming or adornment.

"*Be* you the man we've been a-lookin' for?" said the mother. "We come nigh upon twenty-two miles yesterday to see you. We went to your place, and they said you was out to walk. We come here this mornin' at sun-up, and we've been settin' around ever sence. We want help. I tell you, stranger, that ef ever anybody wanted help, we want it."

Then they told me their story. The father of the family had died long since. The daughter's husband and brother had been shot by the Confederates: the former was killed at home while trying to escape a conscription detail; the latter was dragged into the army, deserted, was retaken, and executed at Petersburg.

"Ef I could git hold of them that killed my old man," the girl declared grimly, "I wouldn't show 'em no mercy, stranger."

Robbed of all the men of their family, and without land, they were in dire poverty. Their cabin let in the wind and snow through the unchinked logs and had no flooring but the earth.

"Ef you could see it, stranger," said the mother, "you mought think it was a place for hogs, but not for human creeturs. In the hard rains, one half the floor is covered with water."

The daughter had not had a pair of shoes since her husband was killed, two years before.

"Ef I had shoes, I reckon I couldn't wear 'em," she observed;

"my feet is so swelled and bursted with walkin' on the snow and the frozen ground."

They wanted clothes, corn, or "whatever there mout be to give out," and they also wanted protection. Since the war they had been persecuted by a gang of young roughs whom they stigmatized as "Rebs," who in the first place ousted them from the neighborhood of Marietta by pulling down their cabin and, now that they had migrated to Pickens District, were in the habit of stoning them and driving them into the woods whenever there was a convenient opportunity for that amusement.

"John De Launey Morgan is the one that plagues us most," said the daughter. "He never passes our house but what he gits off his critter and stones us and calls us all the names he can think of. And we are so scared of him that, when we hear of his comin' our way, we always run into the woods and hide till he gits by."

"And what it's all for, we don't know no more'n the dead," asseverated the mother with emphasis. "We never did a thing to him. It's jest because our men went agin the war, stranger; that's it."

Little versed, as yet, in Bureau business, I supposed that Mrs. Taylor had given me a correct explanation of her troubles and that I had before me a family of persecuted Unionists. I accordingly wrote a letter to the magistrate at Marietta, directing him to protect the women in case they chose to return thither, and to bring John De Launey Morgan and his confederates to justice. While I was thus occupied the mother begged for a smoke from my pipe, and, although averse to the concession, I could not but grant it.

"I've been a-lookin' at it myself," said the daughter with a laugh, "but I was afeared to ask for it."

I subsequently learned that these women were in various ways low characters. On that account, and because they had no men to protect them, rather than for their supposed loyal sentiments, they were persecuted by John De Launey Morgan and his contemptible fellow roughs.

"The annoyances are illegal, of course, whatever may be the character of the women," said the magistrate to me on his next visit to Greenville. "I will institute any suit that these people may choose. They can have Morgan bound over to keep the peace, or they can bring a case for damages. But it is not a political matter and is not worthy of your attention."

The men of the family had been as worthless as the women; they had evaded service in the Confederate army, as they would have evaded service in any army; their loyalty just extended to the point of wanting to stay at home and do nothing. There are intelligent and zealous loyalists in the mountains of the Dark Corner, but they are of a type somewhat different from the son and son-in-law of Mrs. Taylor.

The story of this family exhibits one cause of the vagrancy of the low whites. Without property, mere squatters on the land of others, destitute of character to inspire respect, prostitutes, beggars, and perhaps thieves, they are chased from neighborhood to neighborhood, the sport of rowdies little better than themselves.

Another family which came upon me for help consisted of a man, his wife, two sisters, a sister-in-law, and three small children, all as healthy as need be. The man was a farm-laborer in the mountains, but he had fallen into the toils of a low-down woman of evil character, and his wife, despairing of otherwise keeping her husband, dragged him down to the village. The enchantress followed them to their refuge, and the wife applied to me for an order to make her leave town. Moreover, they wanted lodging, food, and clothing, for the husband could find no work, and they were utterly destitute. For a while they lived with other low whites and a set of equally low Negroes, in a deserted hotel; then, the nest having been cleaned out by the civil authorities, they hired a room; but presently they were back again in their mountains. I could not discover that these four women did any work or had a desire to do any. The man, as I was credibly informed, made an effort to earn a living by offering to take other men to visit his wife's sister.

Thus, from one cause or another, the poor-whites wandered up and down on the earth, rarely staying many years in one neighborhood. Usually, however, their migrations were short flights; they went from Greenville District to Spartanburg, and thence perhaps to Laurens; then, presently, they were back in Greenville. Usually, also, they did not tend to settle in towns.

Unlike the gregarious and jolly Negroes, they were solitary in their dispositions, and, if they alighted near a village, it was not so much for society as for convenience in begging.

SOCIAL DEGRADATION

Two women from Pickens District, an aunt of about thirty and a niece of about twenty, called on me with the complaint that the lover of the former would not support his illegitimate child. The aggrieved woman handed me a dirty scrap of wrapping paper, on which were some scribblings so crabbed and illegible that I could not make out two successive words.

"I cannot read this," I said. "Where did you get it, and what is it about?"

"*She* wrote it," answered the aunt with a paralytic stutter. "It's my complaint."

The niece looked ashamed, either for me or for herself or for her aunt. I was sorry that I had not been able to read the girl's writing; she had undoubtedly learned what little she knew under great disadvantages; she deserved something in the way of a compliment. The case was then stated to me in vocal English, and I referred the complainant to a magistrate. During the conversation I discovered that these women were living in the same cabin with a black family, the Negroes occupying one end of the building and the Anglo-Saxons the other—this, in a country where land could be bought at from one to ten dollars an acre, where a cabin could be built for forty or fifty dollars, and where the pride of race is fiercer than in any other part of the world!

A woman of another family asked me, "Can anybody say anythin', stranger, ef I hire out to hoe for one of the black 'uns?"

It is, at first sight, a singular thing that the debased types of humanity seldom incline to suicide. The easy explanation is that the low-downer has but a low ideal of success in life and is consequently exposed to no harrowing disappointment over its failures. Furnished with the necessities of hog and hominy and with the luxuries of tobacco and laziness, he is, in the main, content and "has no use for pizen."

I could not discover that he had any religion or even any superstitions. This fleshly, unspiritual creature did not seem even to believe in ghosts.

In justice to my district I ought to state, in passing, that its low-down class was by no means so degraded or so numerous as are the "sand-hillers" who inhabit the waste places of regions nearer the seacoast, or the "beechers" and other wild paupers of North Carolina, or the "crackers" of Georgia and Alabama. An ordinary traveler might not discover much evidence of the breed; and, indeed, there seemed to be a belief that it did not exist in this portion of South Carolina. A visitor from Charleston said to me, "You will find few people here who cannot read and write."

The receipt rolls on which I issued clothing told a different story; not one white recipient out of thirty made any other signature than a mark; and the experience of the United States marshal, in paying witnesses, was not very dissimilar. Any one who doubted that there were mean whites in abundance around Greenville could be cured of his delusion by going thither and giving notice of a public distribution of charity. Still, degraded misery was less prominent here than in many other districts, and much of what existed was the result of the war.

PUGNACITY

"I'm one of the Fox family, and you can't tread on my toes," screamed a girl of seventeen, who was carrying on a scolding-match with a young man just outside of my office. Every week some low-down woman came to me or to my neighbors, the magistrates, to complain that some other low-down woman had beaten her or attempted to pull down her cabin or perpetrated some other manual outrage. In general, these aggrieved females had defended themselves right heartily, scratching, pulling hair, tearing homespun, striking with "chunks of brush," and throwing "rocks." We officials seldom investigated these cases; and, if we did, we discovered that they had been fair fights, one party being about as much to blame as the other.

Accordingly, when Mrs. Dunkin, a tall and rather handsome

young savage, appeared and stated that she had been obliged to slap Mrs. Ambler's daughter for charging her with being too intimate with Negroes, and to demand that some punishment should be meted out to the Amblers for their slanderous tongues, I, inferring that sufficient justice had already been accomplished, advised the lovely plaintiff to let the matter rest where it was, if it could. Nor was I much astonished when she reappeared, an hour later, with the story that the Amblers had taken advantage of her absence to charge upon her cabin and drive her mother, younger sister, and little boy into the woods with a shower of brickbats. I sent her to a magistrate, and he, with my full approval, refused to entertain the case, on the ground that she could not give security to prosecute it. The result was that the Amblers, frightened by their own victory and perseveringly threatened with a "lawing," migrated to another district. Before departing, they begged a dollar of me, and various dollars of other persons, to pay their traveling expenses.

These pugnacities diversified and adorned the intercourse of relatives. The Tonys and Fosters, who were sisters and cousins inhabiting the same cabin, had a battle royal which resulted in the Fosters' being expelled and forced to seek another residence, where Mrs. F. soon had a fight with her landlord.

"Mother is perfec'ly redic'lous," I heard a young girl say. "She allowed she'd switch me if I didn't go home, and she picked up a bit of brush. I up with another and told her to come on."

In fact, these women were not only as bellicose as men, but as proud of their martial qualities. I was amused at the grim hatred with which a feeble old woman named Moward talked of a Negro neighbor whom she wished me to take in hand for a multitude of alleged offenses. He had, if she might be credited, starved his own children nearly to death, cut down and sold his landlord's timber for firewood, attempted to set fire to her house, "rocked" her cow, and threatened to murder her family. Her exaggerations, her repetitions, her dour and deliberate drawl, her settled bitterness of visage, and her old-fashioned dialect were all exceedingly curious.

"He swore that kill my son he would," was one of her expressions. The emphatic title by which she addressed me was, "My dear, blessèd stranger." Having complained that the "black 'un" had sought to burn her "roughness," I asked what she meant by the word and found that it represented shucks, or corn husks.

"Where is your husband?" I asked, knowing that she had one.

"Whar is my husband?" she repeated in her bitter drawl. "Well, I'll tell you whar he is: he's up in the mountains. That's whar he is. He can't live here; thar's nothin' to live on. He's up in the mountains, livin' with his own kin. That's whar my husband is."

Meeting the Negro and charging him with his innumerable misdoings, he denied them all and asserted that the Mowards belied him in order to get him out of his cabin and put in another black whom they favored. Finding that both families were living, rent-free, on the land and in the cabins of a charitable citizen, I referred the quarrel to him, telling him that it was his duty and in his power to evict the tenant who was most to blame. But he was too soft-hearted to send either of them adrift, nor would he so much as indicate to me which party he considered accountable for the uproar; so that the feud between the Mowards and Balus Russel lasted while I remained in Greenville. The daughter of the old woman attempted to bully me into an interference. "I shall hold you responsible," she said, shaking one finger at me; "if that nigger does murder, I shall hold you responsible for it."

It was difficult to settle any dispute peaceably between antagonists of this pugnacious class; and even among the class of small farmers a difference was pretty sure to run into blows or, at the mildest, into "lawing." I was both provoked and amused over a quarrel between the Willimans and Parkmans on one side, and on the other a wild Irishman named Johnny O'Neill, who had gone wilder than his Hibernian wont in South Carolina. Mrs. Williman, a portly person of forty-five, with piercing, dark eyes, called on me with her daughter, Mrs. Parkman, a delicate-looking brunette of eighteen, with the most classic of faces, the low, broad Greek forehead, rippling black hair, clear, sparkling black eyes, and the sunniest of smiles. They complained that Johnny O'Neill had seduced away, with promises of biscuit and honey, a little black girl of seven years old, who was Mrs. Parkman's only pet and servant.

"My daughter is sickly and has no children of her own," explained the mother. "She's powerful fond of this little nigger, and we want an order to git her back."

"Has the child no relatives to decide where she shall live?" I asked.

"No; we don't know who her father is, and her mother's dead; her mother wanted us to keep her."

Finding that they lived eight miles distant and thinking it not worth while to order all the parties to come to me, I wrote a letter to Mr. O'Neill, to the effect that the child should be taken before the nearest magistrate or before some respectable citizen and, in the presence of both claimants, should select her employer. This decision, I added, should hold good until further orders from me, unless the blood-relations of the girl chose to claim her by process of civil law.

Scarcely had the two ladies been gone an hour, when Johnny O'Neill arrived on his spavined "chunk of a pony." One of the reddest of Irishmen, with shining corkscrew ringlets of red hair, sharp features, and snapping green eyes, lean, leathery, crouching, and springy, he so danced about my office in the excitement of telling his story that it seemed as if he might at any moment run up the wall like a lizard or spider. The Parkmans had treated the little girl shamefully, he said; they had half starved her, kept her in rags, and beaten her so that she was a sight to behold; and she had of her own accord sought refuge with him from a cruelty which would soon have cost her life.

Accustomed to hear two sides of a story and believe very little of either, I gave Mr. O'Neill an order similar to the one which I had given the Parkmans. Hearing that they had been to see me and had set out on their return, he started in great haste to overtake them. "Was the ould man with 'um?" he asked, as he opened the door.

"No," said I, "there was no man with them. But don't let us have any fighting in this matter. Settle it before a neighbor, precisely as I have directed."

"Oh, it's not me that 'ud go a-blatherin' and fightin'," declared Mr. O'Neill. "I'm as paceable a man as there is in these parts."

The men of these parts being as much like gamecocks as they well could be without feathers, this was a very feeble certificate of Quakerism, but the O'Neill did not know it and honestly meant to praise himself.

Next morning he reappeared, flew all about my office like a cat in a fit, and told a terrible tale concerning the violence and ferocity of the Parkmans.

"Would ye belave it?" said he. "Thim two women went to me house and broke in the door. As soon as the little gal saw 'um, she dodged undher the bed to keep from goin' wid 'um. Thin the ould 'un knocked me wife down, an' the young 'un thrampled on her so that I'm despairin' of her life. Thin they grabs up the little gal an' goes off wid her in spite of her scrames. Whin I got home an' found how things were, I follys 'um down to ould Williman's, for I reckoned they'd be dodgin' in there to hide. Whin I got there, they was makin' down the crossroad for Parkman's. The young 'un was runnin' one way—to desave me, ye see—an' the ould 'un was runnin' the other, a-draggin' the little neegur. I afther the ould woman an' come up wid her jist before she got to the house. She thried to git over the fence, an' I thried to stop her—jist to give her the letther, ye see. 'Here's a letther from the Major,' says I, a-houldin' it out in me hand. Oh, I'm as paceable a man as there is, Major; I'm not for fightin', when talkin' u'll do. Well, whin she mounted the fence, she fell on the other side, an' I fell over her; that's jist the way it happened; an' she set up a hullabaloo that I'd sthruck her. Sorra a bit."

"Who got the child?" I asked.

"Well, they come out o' the house an' dhragged her in—she a-scramin'. Thin Parkman an' his wife come at me. 'Here's a letther from the Major,' says I, but divil a one of thim would take it; an' Parkman he out with his knife, an' his wife up with a stick: 'I'll knock your brains out, ye son of a b—h!' says she. 'So,' says I, 'let's be paceable about it,' says I, an' I came away, afther seein' that they wouldn't listen to me; an' that's the end to it."

"That's a pretty end to it," I commented. "Here I wanted

you to settle it quietly by arbitration, and you have been knocking each other down and raising the Old Harry!"

"Oh, ye can't do anythin' with those onraisonable crathurs," responded Mr. O'Neill. "Sich tempers as they've got! Wouldn't so much as take your letther out of me hands. An' now the ould woman is goin' to prosecute me, because she says I thrampled on her. I can prove, on me Bible-oath, that all I did was to fall over her as I was thryin' to hand her the letther. They've been to the square about it already."

"Well, you had better see the squire yourself and tell him what your defense will be. When he hears both sides, he may advise the Parkmans not to push the case. It is best to avoid the law, if possible."

"Thrue for you, Major. I'll do that same, an' let the square know what me defense is. An' I'll prosecute thim, too, for knockin' down me ould woman an' breakin' into me house."

It was not long after the departure of the O'Neill before Mr. Williman, Mrs. Parkman, and her husband arrived in a pouring rain, bringing the little black cause of all this turmoil. I saw at once that the child was nicely dressed in clean homespun and had been evidently well treated. As she had spent only one day with Johnny O'Neill, this prosperity could not be due to his bounty, and I felt at once inclined to take the Parkman side of the question.

"Where is your mother?" I asked the young woman.

"She is at home, a-bed. Mr. O'Neill knocked her down and trampled on her, so that she is in great pain."

"You had some difficulty in getting the girl, I understand."

"No; she ran to us as soon as she saw us. O'Neill's wife scolded a great deal, but we didn't mind her; we didn't want no quarrel. Then he come after us and knocked my mother down as she was climbing the fence to get away from him."

I could not help laughing over this tissue of contradictions.

"I will tell you what Mr. O'Neill says," I added. "He declares that your mother knocked his wife down and that your husband drew a knife on him."

"Oh!" exclaimed the little beauty, as if much shocked; and her husband muttered some equivocal denial.

"Well, such matters must be settled by the civil law," I said.

"Only I should advise you all to keep out of it and, if possible, let bygones be bygones."

Then, turning to the little Negress, I asked her, "Whom do you want to live with?"

"With these yere people."

"Do they give you enough to eat?"

"Yes."

"What made you run away from them?"

No answer from the child, but Parkman told how O'Neill had promised biscuit and honey.

"Did he promise you biscuit and honey?" I asked.

"Yes."

The result of the examination was that I gave the pickaninny a sharp lecture on the sin of running away, and sent her back to live with her present employers. I hoped that here the difficulty would end, but such was not the purpose of the O'Neill; and when I last heard of him, he was "lawing" it with the Parkmans, apropos of assault and battery and of cruelty to the "neegur."

Quarrelsome as the cracker is, he has no self-respect and no moral courage. As in former days he was submissive to the planter, so he became subservient to the Yankee; exhibiting not a spark of animosity because of his wooden leg or cracked skull or burned cabin; obeying the behest of every man in uniform, even though he were a drunken deserter; and always ready to declare himself an original Unionist. Indifferent to law, he revered power like an Oriental and put his mouth in the dust before whomsoever represented it. It is my belief that he sincerely admired and venerated his Northern conqueror.

FEROCITY

The pugnacity of the low-down people included indifference to human life. After the great nocturnal fight of the Tonys and Fosters, when the former expelled the latter from their common domicil, Mrs. Foster hung about the battlefield for an hour, cursing by herself and meditating projects of vengeance. The male Tony, a sallow youth of eighteen, hearing some noise in the neighboring darkness, got down an old musket on which he prided himself and blazed away at a venture, sending the bullet through a post not a yard from his aunt. His sister, a year younger, informed me of this feat, probably with a view to forestall a complaint from their respected relative.

"Your brother mustn't do that sort of thing," I said. "He has no business to fire about the country at random, especially by night."

"Wal, folks needn't be hangin' 'round folks' houses after dark," she replied. "What else could they look for but to git shot at?"

The next time Mrs. Foster applied for rations, I questioned her concerning the adventure.

"Come mighty nigh hittin' me, Jim did," she answered coolly, and by no means angrily.

"What did you do?"

"Do? I did jest what other folks would 'a' done. I hadn't no gun to fire back, an' I put out. If I'd had a gun, though, I'd 'a' given 'em one."

One of the most extraordinary murders that I ever heard of was committed by a boy named Langston, only fourteen years old. He and a Negro had applied simultaneously for the loan of a fishing net; the Negro was the favored claimant, and the boy walked home inflamed with rage and envy. Loading an old musket, he went down to the river, stretched himself on the bank, rested his weapon on a stone, and shot the Negro dead in the water.

The affrays in which the low-down whites butcher each other seldom receive much notice from the Southern papers and are, I believe, not always taken up by the courts. Whenever such an affair ends fatally, the respectable portion of the community, if it is interested at all, thanks God and takes courage. A series of rencontres in Anderson District, which cost the life of one black and two whites, was quietly ignored by the neighboring magistrate until his attention was called to it by the commandant of the post. My impression is that most of the murders of the Negroes in the South are committed by the poor-whites, who do not mean any harm to the "black 'uns" because they are black, but simply kill them in the exercise of their ordinary pugnacity. They could not shoot slaves in the good old times without coming in conflict with the slaveowner and getting the worst of it. Now, the Negro is no better than they are, and they pay him the compliment of fighting him as an equal.

HISTORY OF A FAMILY [4]

Partly from glimpses of history, partly from the reminiscences of old citizens, and partly from my own observations, I have constructed the record of a low-down family. Serfs to Saxons in the days of Alfred, serfs to Normans in the days of Richard the Lion-Hearted, indigent, ignorant, stupid, and vicious farm-laborers during succeeding centuries, the Simminses (as they pronounce a name which they cannot spell) finally crossed the ocean in the person of Bill Simmins, transported for poaching.

A convict-apprentice on the tobacco lands of James River, then a refugee, bushwhacker, and squatter on the extreme verge of colonization, Bill married a London courtesan, who, like himself, had been deported and run wild, and gave birth to a tribe which then had no specific name, but which now obtains recognition under the titles of crackers, sand-hillers, mean whites, and low-down people. During the colonial period the Simminses fought for their scalps against Indians and sharpened their Anglo-Saxon pugnacity to ferocity. In the Revolution

---

4. In describing the ancestry of the Simminses De Forest accepted the contemporary assumption that Southern poor-whites were uniformly descended from indentured servants and convicts. As early as 1724 Hugh Jones, in *The Present State of Virginia,* declared that, "for the generality, the Servants and Inferior Sort of People who have been sent over to Virginia or have transported themselves thither, have been and are the poorest, idlest, and worst of Mankind, the *Refuse of Great Britain* and *Ireland,* and the *Outcast of the People*" (p. 114). Later, as the "descent" theory was given credence, these people were described as the progenitors of the poor-whites: e. g., see William Meade's *Old Churches, Ministers, and Families of Virginia* (Philadelphia, 1857) I, 366, where it is stated that "the lower order of persons in Virginia, in a great measure, sprang from these apprenticed servants, and from poor, exiled culprits. It is not wonderful that there should have been much debasement of character among the poorest population." Since De Forest's time, however, revisionist studies, such as Thomas J. Wertenbaker's *Patrician and Plebeian in Virginia* (Charlottesville, 1910), have basically modified historical opinion as to the character and standing of the indentured servant class and, accordingly, as to the ancestry of the poor-whites. See also "The Tradition of 'Poor-Whites'" by A. N. J. Den Hollander, in W. T. Couch, editor, *Culture in the South* (Chapel Hill, 1935), pp. 403–431.

they were Tories, not because they loved the king, or knew anything about him, but because the landed gentry, whom they wished to plunder, were Whigs. Forced at last into the Continental Militia and having no heart in the cause, they threw down their guns at sight of the British bayonets and left Greene's Regulars [5] to fight the battle alone.

From their first arrival in America they had "sot in to rovin' 'round," partly because their lawless natures could not bear the restraints of a settled community, partly because stable society elbowed them out of its way as nuisances, and partly because their aversion to regular work obliged them to seek wild land and abundant game. They were nomads and squatters; their only service was to drive off the still more worthless Indian; where they turned up the soil, they exhausted rather than improved it. Outstripped and surrounded at last by the current of civilization, they changed from hunters and backwoodsmen to cultivators, but still preserved a tendency to wandering. The Simminses have moved from one district to another, or from one state to another, at least once in every generation. The only exception to this rule is where hordes of such families have been shut up in some great stretch of pine barrens or mountain sterilities or sea beaches, into which the wealthy landholder has not cared to intrude, and from which there was no escape except by a long migration.

In general, the Simminses have been the parasites and, so to speak, the feudatories of some great planter. The "high-toned gentleman" settled quarrels with persons of his own caste by his own hand; but if he wanted a "free nigger" run off or a Yankee "emissary" mobbed, he winked to his humble and ferocious adherent. In return, he put up with Bill's petty pilferings, poachings, mendicities, and illicit dickerings with Negroes.

Thus the Simminses remained vicious and lazy. The father hunted 'possums, cultivated a little patch of corn, and did an occasional "lick of work" for some well-to-do neighbor, taking

5. General Nathanael Greene had occasion to be disappointed in the local militia at a number of engagements during his Southern campaign, but the most famous instance of their unreliability was their precipitate flight from the battlefield of Camden in 1780 when Horatio Gates was in command of the Continental forces in the South.

his pay in bacon. The women spun and wove an hour or so a day; the rest of the time they smoked, tramped, and gossiped. The most productive part of the family industry consisted in procuring whisky and various worthless gimcracks and exchanging them with the Negroes for chickens, shoats, and corn, a portion of which was stolen from the slaveowner. Simmins lived off the neighboring plantations as much as did their proprietors. He was one of the incidental expenses of slavery.

Now and then an enterprising specimen of the breed set up a "crossroads grocery" and prosecuted his nocturnal trade with the blacks on a large scale. A citizen gave me instances of low-down men who had accumulated handsome fortunes from such a start; one whom he named had become proprietor of eighty Negroes and four thousand acres of land; yet, to the day of his death, he had kept up his illicit dealings with slaves. But, in general, the race remained miserably poor, as well as ignorant and vicious.

During the late war the Simminses did their share of the fighting; for, if a good many of them evaded the conscription or deserted, none of them had influence to get "bomb-proof" places and keep in the rear. They volunteered promptly while they believed that service simply meant plunder, and, after that pleasant delusion had vanished, they were "fo'ced in" by armed details. The women and children lived for a while on the neighboring planters; then, as the resources of the latter diminished, they reached the verge of starvation; then they were fed by monthly issues of rations from local authorities or the Confederate government. When Bill effected his final desertion from Lee or Johnston and reached home at the close of the war, he found his family the same lazy paupers that he had always known them, but without a source of charity from which to draw food; no more rich planters to beg from, and no more sleek slaves to deal with.

His own character had in some respects improved: under the discipline of the army he had learned to do what he did not like; he had learned that it is possible for him to work. Thus drilled and, moreover, driven by gaunt necessity, he hired a plot of poor land and contracted with one or two shiftless Negroes. But his native laziness soon regained its empire; he left hoeing to his "black 'uns" and spent much time at groceries; and the consequence was a crop of two bushels to the acre. At the end of the year he "run his niggers off" to keep from paying them. This brought him before the Bureau officer, with whom he endeavored to make interest by declaring that he was always opposed to the war, etc.; but the case being referred to a civil court, the jurymen, who are respectable landholders and detest the Simminses, decided it against him; and Bill was left without a cent to pay his lawyer. The consequence was a new migration or a piteous appeal for government rations.

FUTURE POSSIBILITIES

In general, the low-downers have been even less fortunate than is supposed in the above history. I think that I do not exaggerate when I declare that two thirds of the men of this class had fallen in the war or were cripples, leaving their wives and children to stark beggary in an impoverished community. They would not work, and they did not know how to work, and nobody would set them to work. Such a thing as a "poor-white" girl going out to domestic service was absolutely unknown; not merely because she was as ignorant of civilized housewifery as a Comanche squaw, but also because she was untamed, quarrelsome, perhaps dishonest, perhaps immoral; and finally, because she was too proud to do what she called "niggers' business." She might go into a factory and could be taught to perform tolerable work there, subject to fits of nomadism and pugnacity. The chiefest benefactors of the crackers will be those who shall introduce into the South manufactures, with their natural sequences of villages and public schools. Before the era of factories, the wandering, shiftless, low-down breed was known in New England.

I do not wish to be understood as saying that the cracker has never risen above his birth, even under the discouragements of the system of slavery. Some families now respectable, some men who have stood high in Southern politics, originated in the strata of the Simminses. So far as I have known these last, however, they were fortunate enough to become orphans in early years and so learn industry in a workhouse, or acquire the rudiments of education in an asylum. Their birth was a barrier to success, but not an impassable one. The crackers are not a caste, but only the dregs of society.

With time enough and under the stimulus of the free-labor system, the low-downer may acquire settled habits, industry, and civilization. But will the immigration from the North and from Europe, which must ere long descend upon the South, give him time? [6] And when it reaches him, will it absorb and thus elevate him; or will it push him into wilds and fastnesses, there to die out like any other savage? It did not seem to me that there was much vitality in the creature.

I cheerfully leave him to the operation of the great law of natural selection.

In other words, "The devil take the hindmost."

6. De Forest's expectation of immigration into the South probably resulted from the activity of South Carolina at this time in attempting to attract immigrants. In 1865 the legislature had created the office of Commissioner of Immigration. This official wrote a pamphlet, *South Carolina, a Home for the Industrious Immigrant* (1867), which was translated into German and the Scandinavian languages. Agents were sent to these countries, and immigration societies were organized at various places in South Carolina. On November 28, 1867, a German vessel arrived at Charleston with 152 immigrants on board. Ultimately, this effort to attract settlers from abroad produced almost negligible results. For further detail see Simkins and Woody, *South Carolina during Reconstruction*, pp. 243–247.

CHAPTER VIII

SEMI-CHIVALROUS SOUTHRONS [1]

I CLASS the loyalists of my district under the head of "semi-chivalrous Southrons," because, being seldom large planters or even slaveholders, they do not exhibit all the characteristics of the "high-toned" population. They are mostly small farmers, inhabiting the mountains of Pickens and of a certain portion of Greenville known as the Dark Corner. I did not always find it easy to distinguish them from Rebels. One gaunt old female laid claim to Bureau rations on the double ground that she was a good Union woman and that she had lost two sons in the Confederate army. This story was so contradictory that I believed it; remembering first that truth is often much more improbable than falsehood; and second that many loyal families saw their children carried off by Rebel press gangs.

These poor, uncultured, and, in some cases, half-wild people have always been true to the United States Government. In the days of Nullification and in other subsequent disunion excitements, when Governor Perry (or, as they called him, Ben Perry) fought a good fight against Calhounism,[2] they were his firmest supporters and regarded him with something like adoration. As a Greenvilleite said to me, "They believed they would go to him when they died."

1. Published originally as part of the second installment of "Chivalrous and Semi-Chivalrous Southrons" in *Harper's New Monthly Magazine*, XXXVIII (February, 1869), 341–346. The expression "Southron," referring originally to an Englishman as distinguished from a Scotsman, appeared in the novels of Sir Walter Scott, and the Southerners in the United States quickly and proudly applied the term to themselves. Later, outsiders occasionally used the appellation derisively.

2. During the Nullification contest Perry had conducted a dramatic and memorable campaign as leader of the Union forces in the up-country. As editor of the Greenville *Mountaineer* he vigorously opposed the Nullificationists, and when they forced him into a duel, he killed his adversary. He headed the Union ticket which was triumphantly elected, and thus he was sent as a delegate to the Nullification Convention, where he, Joel Poinsett, and James L. Petigru were the foremost spokesmen for the minority. Kibler, *Benjamin F. Perry*, pp. 92–158.

"But now," in the words of one of their patriarchs, "Ben Perry has fallen from the faith"; and consequently the mountaineers deserted him in a body and stigmatized him as "the biggest Reb a-going." One of the prime staples of the Republican speeches which I heard in that region was the showing up of the apostasy of this distinguished "central monkey." [3]

THE MOUNTAINEERS

It is a striking instance of the reliability of history that I never learned to my satisfaction the date or manner of the famous advance of the mountaineers upon Greenville during the war. One informant assured me that it took place before Bull Run; that the loyal men of the Dark Corner and vicinity mustered six hundred strong; that they marched toward the low country with the intention of forcing South Carolina back into the Union; that Greenville, unable to meet such a host in the field, sent forth Governer Perry to dissipate it by the breath of his eloquence. This dramatic informant, rising from his chair and extending his arm, proceeded to deliver with flashing eye and thunderous tongue a fragment of the governor's oration:

"Men of Greenville," he represented him as saying, "the government under which you were born no longer exists; and that loyalty which you formerly owed it and which you rendered so nobly is now due to the Confederate States." Whereupon the invaders separated into two bodies, one of which went back to its mountains in wrath and discouragement, while the other formed two companies for the Rebel army and fought heroically at Bull Run.

The other version of this affair is that it took place late in the struggle; that there was no advance upon the low country, but only a general marauding of deserters and other desperadoes; that the Confederate authorities offered them pardon in case

---

3. In the original magazine article "central monkey" was an allusion to "an old traveler's story" which De Forest had mentioned in the previous installment. Because he changed the order of the various sections when he prepared the book-length manuscript, the clue to the meaning of the term is now on p. 194.

they would surrender and agree to lead peaceful lives; that sixty or seventy of them were got together, and that Governor Perry was induced to make them a pacificatory speech; the result being that the majority of them laid down their bush-whacking rifles and resumed the ways of peace. As I had both these tales from good local authority the reader will be justified in believing them both. My own opinion inclines to accept the latter of the two as the most probable.[4]

It is certain that the majority of the able-bodied men of the mountains were eventually bullied or dragged by main force into the Rebel army. They sought to remain loyal; there is no reasonable doubt of that; but the conscription details were too much for them. Long lines of videttes were run clear through the mountains, and the distances between the lines were traversed by relentless patrols. Men who fled on being summoned to surrender were shot at once; they were massacred in their own dooryards in the presence of their families. It must be understood that by the Conscription Act every male Southerner was placed on the rolls of the Confederate army and thus was constituted a deserter in case he failed to repair to the depot of the regiment to which he had been assigned. It was nominally as deserters, and not as Unionists, that these victims were murdered.

The Rebel authorities even used bloodhounds to aid their troops in scouring the refractory mountains. "But that didn't amount to much," said a stalwart old mountaineer to me with a chuckle. "The dawgs would run ahead yelping, and the boys would take a crack or two at 'em with a rifle, and that would be the end of the dawgs."

It took at least two lowlanders to catch one highlander, and when caught, he was very nearly worthless as a soldier. He sel-

4. Perry's personal scrapbook contains an account of a speech delivered by him on May 20, 1861, to a group of several hundred Unionist men at a militia muster in the upper part of Greenville District. He assured these men that he himself had shared their Unionist convictions, but he urged them to accept the decision of the people of the state and to offer their services as soldiers. His speech influenced them so deeply that they, thereupon, formed two volunteer companies. There is nothing in the scrapbook to indicate that there was, at any time, an advance upon Greenville by hostile Unionists. Kibler, *op. cit.,* p. 351.

dom fired a gun at the Yankees; if there was a chance to desert he improved it; if he got back to his native rocks he was a bigger pest than ever. Nearly all the youth of the Dark Corner were at one time or another chased into the Rebel army, without doing it a particle of benefit.

Meantime, the elders of the mountains harbored such of our men as escaped to them from Columbia or Andersonville [5] and acted as guides in running them through the Rebel lines to eastern Tennessee. Several of them showed certificates to this effect from Union officers whom they had thus befriended.

"I tell you this paper was a mighty big scare to me as long as the war lasted," said a stooping, meagre farmer in a threadbare suit of yellowish homespun. "If it had been found on me it would have cost me my life. I walked five miles and back for an auger to bore a hiding hole. I bored the hole in one of the inside beams of my house, put the certificate into it, and then drove a wooden hat-pin on top of it. The very next day thar was a Reb detail along to sarch me for signs of Yankees. They looked me all through, but they didn't find nothin'. The captain hung his cloak up on that very hat-pin. When I see that, stranger, I could hardly help a-smilin'."

Solomon Jones, the Union patriarch of the mountains, a tall, robust, florid, hale man of over sixty, as alert and healthy as humanity can be at thirty, a kindly, generous, fair-minded, honorable though uncultured spirit, was persecuted during the war as the upright are persecuted in evil times. He was hunted from his house; he lay out for weeks in the forests, fed in secret by his family and friends; caught at last, he was thrown into Greenville jail with felons. His sole crime consisted in speaking against a rebel government, and for the government of his country. To the honor of Mr. Perry it must be mentioned that he procured the liberation of this martyr and that he declared with his accustomed courage, "If Jones deserves prison I deserve it, for he has said no more than I." To the bank credit of the governor it must be added that he charged and collected a hundred dollars for the service. However, there were few men in the South who would have had the will or the fearlessness to do that service at any price.

5. Two war-prison towns, in South Carolina and in Georgia, respectively.

A UNION SOLDIER OF THE MOUNTAINS

One drizzly autumn morning Solomon Jones brought into my office a man of about twenty, a lean, leathery, wild-looking youth, with a curiously stealthy and springy gait like that of a panther, whom he introduced to me as John M'Lean.

"He's in trouble," said the patriarch in his quick, jerky style of speaking. "Some of these Rebs have got after him with the law. He's been a soldier in your army. He's your brother. See if you can help him."

My pantherish brother proceeded to state that he had been arrested on a charge of horse-stealing, at the suit of a "Reb" neighbor, and that his case was to come off before the district court then in session.

"You know what the penalty for horse-stealing is, I s'pose?" he said with a wild grimace, at the same time pointing to his left ear in token of hanging.

His discharge from the army was perfectly regular in form and showed that he had been private in a loyal North Carolina regiment.

"Yes, I run the lines and joined our folks in East Tennessee," loudly declaimed John, whom I now discovered to be under the influence of liquor. "Then I enlisted with a heap more of our mountain folks; and they put us into the North Carolina regiments. And we did heaps of fighting, Major, I can tell you. We took to it. I say, Uncle Sol, can't the mountain men fight?"

"Yes, they can fight," returned Jones. "Go on with your story; show the Major your other paper."

The other paper turned out to be a permit from the chief of some hospital in the West, giving John M'Lean leave of absence for four days. The date was important; it was very nearly the date of the alleged theft; if genuine, the paper proved an alibi. Documents in hand, I conducted John M'Lean to the private room of the solicitor and stated the case.

"I shall drop the prosecution," said the solicitor. "These papers seem to be genuine and to the point. Moreover, the prosecutor has failed to bring his witnesses. John M'Lean can go home."

"And how about my witnesses?" respectfully whispered John, as two long, lean North Carolinians, his former comrades in arms, presented themselves at the door.

"They can all go," said the legal official. "I sha'n't want them."

"I want to discourage these suits," observed the solicitor to me in private. "They are mostly vindictive results of the war. They tend to keep up bad blood, and I am anxious to escape them."

Shortly after my return to my office John M'Lean appeared, drunker than ever.

"I say, Major, you've got to take something for this," he insisted loudly. "Come down on me for anything I've got. That's what I want. Just come down on me."

When I refused pay, presents, and drinks, he rushed to his wagon, picked out a dozen superb apples and persisted in leaving them on my table.

During the day I saw him staggering about among numerous other staggerers. There was the usual crowd in attendance on court, and it had drunk its lawful allowance of whisky.

Next morning John was again on hand, sick and sorry by this time, with a bend toward the maudlin. Twisting his face into the pucker of an aggrieved child, he let fall a couple of manly, mountain tears and whimpered, "Major, I wish I had my me—wl."

"What has become of your mule?"

"Major, a nigger has got him. He says I swapped a horse for him. God Almighty knows I wouldn't swap away my mewl for sech a horse."

So I went out anew to investigate the troubles of John M'Lean. I found that he had swapped his mule for a horse with a white man, who had immediately turned the animal over to a Negro by means of another swap.

"Well, John," I said in substance, "you made your bed when you were drunk, and you must lie upon it now that you are sober."

Puckering his face up to a ludicrous whimper, he sobbed out, "Major, I wish I was in Nor—th Carliny."

"I wish to Heaven you were!" was my impatient answer.

Eventually all the bargaining parties reversed their barters, and John M'Lean drove off with his mewl to North Carliny.

A PLANTER-UNIONIST

He was not a mountaineer, but lived a few miles from the base of the hills, where he owned thousands of acres of fat bottom and fair upland. He was a man, I suppose, of fifty, but in some respects he did not seem over forty. His beard of a day's growth showed grizzly, but his long, dark brown hair had scarcely a trace of silver. Unlike the majority of the lengthy-limbed population of the Allegheny slopes, he was short and broadly built. His face was very red, and his eyes a little bloodshot. He bore unmistakable signs of being a regular and by no means stingy drinker of his own excellent white whisky. But he was an honest, worthy, generous, hospitable, honorable nature. I had heard of him, and of his tribe and set, as determined Unionists. Loopers and Durhams. "Gualandi con Sismondi e Lanfranchi." [6] Yet, stubborn as they were, the Confederacy had known how to make them bend.

"My son went into their army," he said to me. "It was go in or be shot. I never went in. I furnished a substitute and did everything under God's heaven to escape it. Yet they were always after me. I was open-mouthed. Everybody knew what Looper thought.

"They took every cow that I had, curse me if they didn't! One day a party of twenty came, with a lieutenant at their head. I saw them at my barn and went out to meet them. Said they, 'Have you any claims on these cattle?' Says I, 'By ———, they are mine.' Says they, 'We are going to take them for the government to help carry on the war. What are your opinions of the war?' Says I, 'It's a dam' wicked war, and you are a dam' set of fools for trying it.' Says the lieutenant, 'You say another word, and we'll hang you to the next tree.' 'By ———, you may hang me,' says I; 'but as long as I live you can't shut my mouth.' I tell you I cursed them as long as they stayed. If you

---

6. The line in Dante's *Divina Commedia*, Inf. XXXIII, 32, reads as follows: "Gualandi con Sismondi e con Lanfranchi." These families formed an alliance of Pisan Ghibellines and, in 1288, drove the Tuscan Guelfs from their city.

doubt what sort of a man I am ask anybody in Pickens District. Everybody knows me. Everybody knows what Looper is.

"Ah, those dam' scoundrels have robbed me cruelly! Every one of my cattle, and every horse except an old broken-down critter! But it can't be helped now. My son never went into your army, but he has done service for your side; he has helped your runaways through the lines. There was Adjutant Johnson; write to him if you don't believe it. Write to Captain Bray; he knows us.

"And now they've got my son, just for killing a dam' Rebel named Miller, who was passing himself off for the bushwhacker Largent and insulting our women and children—just for shooting that dam' scoundrel they've got him shut up in the penitentiary, curse me if they haven't! Why, Sir, that Miller had been threatening to plunder me and kill me for harboring your men. He knew about my ways; everybody knows Looper. My door had been broken in by the bushwhackers two nights before. I suppose I came near being shot. That was a way they had: make a noise at your door, perhaps call you to it; then if you opened it, fire! Off rides the bushwhacker in the dark, and nobody ever knows who he is. More than a dozen men in our district had been killed that way.

"I've got up a petition for my son's release. He ought not to be shut up there with thieves and rascals. He's as amiable and good and gentlemanly a boy of his age as there is, I don't care where. I'll show you the paper."

The document had a long list of signers, many of them, to my surprise, leading Secessionists. But Looper was a man of property, influence, energy, and courage; and when Southern public feeling does not forcibly rid itself of such an antagonist it will treat him fairly. If it does not blow his brains out, it will subscribe his petitions. It has a certain martial respect for a courageous opponent.

The case of young Looper, a lad of only eighteen, by the way, was as follows: A North Carolinian named Miller, said to be one of the desperadoes who were set loose by the surrender of the Confederate armies, came to the house of one of the Durhams of Pickens District and was entertained there. On his departure the son of the family sought out young Looper and an uncle of his own, named Andrew Durham, informed them that Miller was Largent, and induced them to join in an attempt to arrest him. When they found the North Carolinian he had fallen from his horse, intoxicated, and was lying in the road. It was dusk; none of them knew Largent well; the drunken man raised himself on his elbow; the younger Durham whispered, "Take care!" Looper, aware of Largent's quickness with the pistol, fired, as he supposed, in self-defense and with fatal effect.

Will it be credited that Largent visited Pickens jail to look at the two men who had sought to kill him, and that the jailer was so polite as to show him about the establishment without broaching the idea of arresting him? Young Durham stared in alarm through his grated door at the renowned desperado and pacifically, meekly, humbly asked him for a chew of tobacco, as a vanquished Indian might request the pipe of peace.

"No," replied Largent; "I don't mean to be stingy of my tobacco, but d————d if I give chaws to men who try to bushwhack me!"

Such is the sublime indignation of injured innocence—in Pickens District!

On the trial it appeared that young Durham knew Miller and could not have mistaken him for Largent; also that he had seen a roll of currency in Miller's possession and had subsequently transferred it to his own pockets, whence it was inferred that he had instigated the assassination for the sake of robbery. He was found guilty of murder and condemned to death; young Looper was found guilty of manslaughter and condemned to seven years in the penitentiary; Andrew Durham was acquitted. After a few months Governor Orr pardoned Looper and commuted the punishment of Durham to imprisonment for life.

A UNIONIST WIDOW

She was a woman I suppose of thirty-eight, but looking forty-five. Her form was middle-sized, square, and thin; her sallow face square, with strong jaws and large, dark gray eyes; her expression uncultured and—but for a certain earnestness—commonplace. When she came to Greenville, riding sometimes in an oxcart and sometimes in an open farm wagon, she always wore her best dress of blue checked homespun, narrow in the skirt—no crinoline, no gewgaws. At home her attire was probably of tow-cloth, or coarse, unbleached cotton. Her invariable headdress was the old-fashioned coal-scuttle bonnet, made of strips of pasteboard covered with calico, and having a cape to shield the neck and shoulders.

She had visited all my predecessors; she came repeatedly to see me; she called on the magistrates, the solicitor, the United States commissioner, the collector of the internal revenue; always with the same grim purpose—vengeance on the murderers of her husband. She stayed whole days in the village, going about from office to office, detailing her wrongs and asking counsel.

"My husband was drawn for the war," she narrated to me. "He was a good Union man and wouldn't go to fight agin the government. Besides, what was to come of his family if he went off to the army? So they sent a detail after him. I know several of the men in the detail; I can give their names when they are wanted; but one of them I'll tell you now, because you know him. It was James Parsons, of our settlement; he was one of the first and fastest to kill my poor man; and since the war they've made him a square!

"Well, they come down upon us before we knew it. My old man was out in the yard; he run a little ways, but they caught him. They took him into a holler where thar was a piece of woods, and there they set him up against a tree, some say, and shot him; others say they shot him as he was running— I don't know; I was in the house and didn't see it, but I heard the firing. Yes, I heard the firing! When I run out to see what was the matter some of 'em met me, and says they, 'Your old man is dead; we shot him for a deserter; you'll find him down there a piece!' Well, I ran down to the holler, but when I got thar it was over."

Such was the tragedy. Was it legally a crime? Two or three similar cases had been already presented to me, and I had in vain attempted to bring them before the local courts, the complainants alleging that it would be useless to appeal to a "Reb jury." As for military action, General Sickles had, by order, forbidden that, except where the civil authorities had refused to prosecute. So far as I knew no case like this one had anywhere been brought before a military commission. Thus I had no precedents to guide me.

"If I could git it before the United States Court I could git justice," continued the woman in her dreary monotone.

As the United States commissioner was next door, I took her in to him. He remarked that the affair was not between citizens of different states and that consequently he had no manner of jurisdiction over it.

"You must bring your complaint as other people bring theirs," I then said. "You must make your affidavit before a magistrate and thus have it presented to the grand jury. If the magistrate or the jury or the court refuses to act, then you can appeal to the military authority."

"But our square is one of the very men who killed my husband," she replied, raising her voice in natural indignation at such a state of things.

"Then go to the next squire. Try it. It is the only way. Let me know what the result is."

Over and over she returned to me; she absolutely haunted the district in search of justice; yet she could not be induced to make her complaint legally. "What was the use of going before a Reb square and a Reb jury?"

Once she informed me that several of those concerned in the tragedy had proposed to pay her a moneyed compensation, in case she would agree not to bring suit against them.

"By all means accept the offer," I counseled. "Even if you could get your suit before an unprejudiced court, it is not certain that these men would be found guilty of murder."

"What! didn't they kill my old man?"

"Yes; but they killed him as soldiers; they were acting under the orders of superiors; it will be hard to fix the responsibility on any individual. Moreover, if they can be tried for shooting him, other Confederates can be tried for shooting other loyal citizens. All the deaths of all the Union soldiers during the war might be brought into court. You are poor; you need money to enable you to live; if you can get it, give up the vengeance which you probably can not get."

Her reply was worthy of the hot blood and pugnacious education of the Southron, whether chivalrous or semi-chivalrous.

"Stranger," she said, "I would rather see the men hung that shot my old man than have lots to eat and wear. I want justice more than money."

I asked Parsons, the magistrate, for his version of this bloody story. He was, as I have described him in another chapter,[7] a plain and poor farmer, dressed in homespun, mild in expression, quiet in manner, with a slow, soft utterance, and evidently in feeble health. He showed me his right arm, withered to the shoulder by rheumatism.

"I was drawn for the army and sent to Virginia," he told me. "Then the surgeons rejected me as unfit for field duty on account of this arm. After that I was put into the home guards. Almost everybody was put into the home guards who couldn't do full service; it was made up of old fellows, boys, sick men, and wounded. Their duty was to keep order around home, collect stuff for the army, and hunt deserters. It was a detail of the home guard that went after this man. He had been summoned, and he had failed to join his company, and so they posted him as a deserter. I didn't make the law, and I couldn't help executing it. I was as much under orders as if I had been in the regular army. If I didn't shoot I might be shot myself. It would be hard to say who killed him. Several men fired as he was running, and he fell. I didn't want to hurt him; I had nothing against him. It was the war that did it."

Yes, it was the war that did it; and that impalpable monster will probably be the only one who will ever answer for it; there is no likelihood that the case will come before a court of justice. It is better so; let us bury the bloody past as deep as we can; the present has better and more pressing work on hand than vengeance.

THE UNIONISTS AS A PARTY

"Why don't you extend your operations into other districts?" I sometimes asked of the loyalists of Greenville.

"Yes, and run a mighty smart chance of being bushwhacked," was the usual answer.

7. Chap. I, p. 7 ff.

Even the pugnacious mountaineers of the Allegheny ranges had not thrown off the terrorism of the Confederacy and the domination of the "chivalry." Notwithstanding its military and financial overthrow, the old planter class, with its superior education, its experience in politics, and its habit of authority, was still the most potent moral force of the South.

"I want to join the League," said more than one intelligent citizen of Greenville to me or to others whom I knew. "But the Leaguers won't have me; they blackballed my application. Some of them tell me that I have too much land to get in. You know they are still in hopes of confiscation."

When I spoke to the Leaguers about such an applicant, their reply was usually to this effect: "We can't trust him. He has been too good a Reb; he served in the Confederate army. He's no true man; all he wants is to save his land or get office; if he should get in, he would betray us."

"But your party won't fill an omnibus if you go on in this style," I expostulated. "Of course, some people are guided by their own interests; but they may be valuable members of society notwithstanding. Here you go, rejecting men of education, political experience, social influence; you won't have a convert unless he is poor, ignorant, stupid, and of no value; you are making a party without money and without brains. You are turning lukewarm friends into open enemies, who in less than four years will outmanœuvre you and beat you. It looks as if you were afraid of clever recruits, lest they should seize upon the offices."

The invariable stubborn response was, "Well, we don't want no Rebs."

The result was that the Union party of Greenville District contained, so far as my knowledge extended, but one planter of family and culture; and that its next best man was a circuit preacher blessed with a common school education and an experience of living on three hundred dollars a year. Having heard him speak, I believed him to be a good preacher; but he was no fit opponent for Wade Hampton [8] or Governor Perry. As

8. Originally a supporter of President Johnson's plan of Reconstruction, Wade Hampton campaigned vigorously against the more drastic Congressional policy of 1867 and 1868. In 1876, as leader of the Home Rule forces, he was elected Governor of South Carolina.

a Republican and a lover of the Union, I was filled with wrath when I thought of the men who might have been and should have been in his place.

Solomon Jones, the sheik of the mountains, a man of unusual "horse sense" and moral vigor, the projector and builder of one of the best roads over the Blue Ridge spurs, wrote with so much difficulty that when he was president of a board for enrolling electors his signatures were all made for him by the secretary. In other words, he did not set pen to a single one of the hundreds of official papers which exhibited his name. Yet so bare was the Union party of character, talent, and education, so successfully had it repelled the penitent Rebels of the higher class who at one time would have rejoiced to join it—in short, so deficient was it in the proper material wherewith to fill responsible offices, that Solomon Jones was at one time spoken of as candidate for governor! Knowing the man's superior natural abilities, I have no doubt that, with a good secretary, he would have made a fair chief magistrate; but in this century one recoils from the idea of a governor who needs as much time to sign his name as Dexter [9] needed to trot a mile.

Of carpetbaggers, that is Northern adventurers hunting office, we had none in Greenville. They flourished in the low country, where the native Unionists were few and the Negroes were many and ignorant. It is a pity that revolutions, even the noblest of revolutions in cause and effect, will fling so much scum to the surface. However, the carpetbaggers were not "Southrons," and this book has nothing to do with them.

9. When this chapter was written, Dexter, a gelding, held the mile trotting record of $2:17\frac{1}{4}$, established on June 21, 1867.

CHAPTER IX

CHIVALROUS SOUTHRONS [1]

THEY certainly are, these "Southrons," a different people from us Northerners; they are, perhaps, as unlike to us as the Spartans to the Athenians, or the Poles to the Germans; they are more simple than we, more provincial, more antique, more picturesque; they have fewer of the virtues of modern society, and more of the primitive, the natural virtues; they care less for wealth, art, learning, and the other delicacies of an urban civilization; they care more for individual character and reputation of honor.

Cowed as we are by the Mrs. Grundy of democracy; moulded into tame similarity by a general education, remarkably uniform in degree and nature, we shall do well to study this peculiar people, which will soon lose its peculiarities; we shall do better to engraft upon ourselves its nobler qualities. [2]

Before entering this gallery of pictures which the abolition of slavery has destined to dispersion and decay, let me explain that by "chivalrous and semi-chivalrous Southrons" [3] I do not mean crackers, sand-hillers, and other low-downers. Let me add also that I shall draw largely for portraits on the district in which for fifteen months I performed the duties of Bureau Major.

SELF-RESPECT

"Southern chivalry, you see, Madame," said Mr. Calhoun Burden of Greenville, South Carolina, to the wife of a United States surgeon.

1. Published originally as part of the first installment of "Chivalrous and Semi-Chivalrous Southrons" in *Harper's New Monthly Magazine*, XXXVIII (January, 1869), 192–197.
2. It will be well to remember that this sketch of the Southern gentleman dates from just after the war. (De F.)
3. In the original article in *Harper's New Monthly Magazine* this section on chivalrous Southrons preceded the previous chapter; thus De Forest's qualifying statement now seems out of place.

Mr. Burden, a stoutish, middle-aged gentleman, richly flavored with Durham tobacco and Pickens whisky, and as proud of himself in his suit of homespun as if it were broadcloth, had called in a reconstructing spirit on the Yankee family and in the course of conversation had found it desirable to put a question to the colored servant-girl. Making a solemn bow to the mistress of the house, he said, "With your permission, Madame"; then added, in an impressive parenthesis, "Southern chivalry, you see, Madame"; then delivered his query.

That no such delicate behavior was known among the Vandals north of Mason and Dixon's line; that it could not easily be matched in Europe except among the loftiest nobility; that it was especially and eminently Southern chivalry—such was the faith of Mr. Calhoun Burden.

It was a grotesque and yet not a very exaggerated exhibition of the ancient sectional and personal pride of the Southerner. He never forgot that he represented a high type of humanity and that it his duty not to let that type suffer by his representation. In the company of Yankees and foreigners he always bore in mind that he was a triton among minnows, and he endeavored to so carry himself as that the minnows should take note of the superiority of the triton character.[4]

In men of native intelligence and high breeding this self-respect produces a very pleasing manner, an ease which is not assumption, a dignity which is not hauteur, consideration for the vanity of others, grace of bearing, and fluency of speech. In men of inferior quality and finish it results in such farcical pomposities as we have heard from Mr. Calhoun Burden.

"I can't stand this any longer," said a young Kentuckian of old Virginian blood, who had tried in vain to habituate himself to New York. "I can't respect myself when I am run against a

---

4. Here De Forest touches upon a characteristic that was already well recognized in the Southerner. Joseph G. Baldwin had written in 1853: "The Virginian is a magnanimous man. He never throws up to a Yankee the fact of his birthplace. He feels on the subject as a man of delicacy feels in alluding to a rope in the presence of a person, one of whose brothers stood upon nothing and kicked at the U. S. . . . So far do they carry this refinement that I have known one of my countrymen, on the occasion of a Bostonian owning where he was born, generously protest that he had never heard of it before." *The Flush Times of Alabama and Mississippi*, p. 75.

dozen times a day by Irishmen, Jews, Yankees, and all kinds of busy people. I am of no consequence here; nobody cares whether I am a gentleman or not—whether I am angry or pleased; nobody values me as I know that I ought to be valued. I must go South again—go where there is more elbowroom—go where I can make myself known. I detest a city where seven hundred thousand people tread on my toes and haven't a moment's leisure to apologize and don't even know that my name is Peyton."

It was indescribably amusing to watch a Charlestonian friend of mine during his first and last visit to New York. Dressed in a full suit of black, and bearing a gold-headed cane in his hand, he walked Broadway at the dignified rate of two and a half miles an hour. Some one brushed against his right elbow: he turned and glared, grasping his cane tightly: the intruder was gone. Some one brushed against his left elbow: another pause, glare, and settling of the cane in the fist: no antagonist visible. Every few steps he felt himself insulted, he prepared to vindicate his honor, and he failed to discover any one whom he could call to an account. At the end of six blocks, fuming with a consciousness of aggregated injuries, he took a carriage, drove back to the St. Nicholas, drank a mint julep, seated himself in a window of the reading room, and stared sullenly at the interminable crowd which hurried by unaware of his existence. He was like a cat who should be hustled and intimidated by a garret-full of scrabbling mice. Within a week he left the city, thoroughly disgusted with its multitudinous bustle, and never returned to it.

If you ever see a tall man in Broadway, standing stock-still, glaring about him and swearing, you may fairly suspect that he is a Southerner and that some one whom he can not find has run against him. If you ever see a tall man in Central Park, seeking the loneliest paths and surveying the mob of pleasure-seekers from a distance, you may pretty safely infer that he also is a Southerner and that he is mainly happy because he has found a little elbowroom. Should you address either of these bewildered personages respectfully, he will receive you with a cordial smile, cotton to you without difficulty, and presently ask you to take a drink. He feels like a man who has been abused and who unexpectedly finds sympathy; like a voyager who has been ship-wrecked and who unexpectedly gets food and lodging.

I remember a young Georgian on the Cascine of Florence,[5] who was disturbed in his position near the music by the prancing grays of an English family carriage, and who, refusing to move, called to the coachman, "D—n you, Sir, if you drive one step further I'll tear you off your box!" When the coachman replied, "I beg your pardon, Sir," and when the rosy old gentleman and the two handsome girls in the carriage looked respectfully at him, he was instantly appeased, lifted his hat in apology for his objurgation, and made way for the advance of the equipage.

Yes, it is a sensitive quality, this self-respect which has grown up in the solitude of great plantations and the quiet of small towns; it can not bear the dense crush of a busy world and is especially hurt by the friction of a hurried democracy. These things rub the down off its wings and make it sore and angry and miserable. Where it can have consideration it is gentle and charming; where it can not it is pugnacious or sullen, and socially inconvenient. How often, especially in the times before the war, have we encountered Southerners at the North who seemed driven by a mania to prattle perpetually concerning their sectional peculiarities, excusing them, vindicating them, and boasting of them! For instance, slavery: they would insist on touching it off under our noses; they would not see that our chiefest desire concerning it was to ignore it.

An Englishman, sailing from New York to Liverpool, found himself occupying the same stateroom with a clergyman from South Carolina, whose everlasting topic was the welfare and felicity of Negroes under the patriarchal institution. Parting with him joyfully on landing, he shortly afterward met him again in Oxford at a dinner of the high-mightinesses of the University. The reverend gentleman began a dialogue with his *vis-à-vis* on the happiness of Negro slaves in South Carolina. The subject received some delicate attention, suited to its fas-

5. During his European travels De Forest stayed at Florence for several months. In a letter to his sister-in-law, February 28 [1851], he described the Cascine and praised highly the band concerts which he heard occasionally in this park on the outskirts of the city. De Forest Collection, Yale University Library.

tidious nature, and then was dropped. At the first pause in the general conversation our countryman, who meanwhile h'ad said nothing, opened upon the happiness of Negro slaves in South Carolina. There was a word of civil response, and again the matter was gently superseded. Presently a change of courses produced another silence, and our friend reintroduced the happiness of Negro slaves in South Carolina. Losing patience, the *vis-à-vis* answered, "My dear Sir, if things are as you say, why not go back to South Carolina and become a slave?"

Our high-toned and reverend friend flew into a rage upon the spot and next morning sent his interlocutor a challenge, which was not accepted. It would be safe to wager that he very soon returned to South Carolina and that he did not attempt to get the Constitution changed so that he might enter into the joys of slavery.

The chivalrous Southron is great in his own eyes not only because he is what he is, but because he lives where he lives. In these modern times there is no other civilized creature so local and, if I may be offensive, so provincial, in sentiments, opinions, prejudices, and vanities, as he. The Turks are hardly more incapable of conceiving that people born afar off may be as good as themselves. At least a part of the contempt of the Southerners for Yankees arises from the fact that the latter drew their first breath several hundred miles from the land of cotton. Imagine the scorn with which they would regard an adventurer from the Milky Way! A friend of mine asserts that, if the South Carolinians should once become satisfied that the New Jerusalem is outside of their state, they would not want to go to it. Let us indulge a hope that this is an exaggeration.

"I'll give you my notion of things," repeatedly declared a sturdy old planter who bestowed much of his wisdom upon me. "I go first for Greenville, then for Greenville District, then for the up-country, then for South Carolina, then for the South, then for the United States; and after that I don't go for anything. I've no use for Englishmen, Turks, and Chinese."

To a Charleston friend, who was wont to boast of the high qualities of the "true Southern gentleman," I sometimes said, "Oh! you mean Texans and Arkansans, I suppose."

"Not in the least," he laughed. "When *we* speak of the

Southern gentleman we mean the product of our city and of the region immediately around it. All else is more or less spurious —a base imitation."

Of old the contrast between the Southerner's proud self-assertion and the Northerner's meeching humility was inexpressibly mortifying to every thoughtful inhabitant of the free states. On a Mississippi River steamboat there was once a little chance party of travelers who met there and then for the first time, and whom iced drinks incited to a temporary boon companionship. After many stories and some singing, the youth who had been chosen president of the conclave, a jolly, gracious, graceful, gigantic Virginian, proposed that each man should toast the state of his nativity. When every Southerner had glorified his own commonwealth to the best of his ability, a Yankee arose and stammered: "Gentlemen, I am ashamed to acknowledge that I was born in the abolitionist state of Massachusetts. I am now, however, a resident of Louisiana, and I beg leave, therefore, to drink to her."

No sooner had this pitiful recreant taken his seat than the Virginian uplifted his six feet four inches of stature, stood there erect, large-chested, head "full high advanced," and said: "Gentlemen, no man need be ashamed to come from the state of Benjamin Franklin and Daniel Webster. Gentlemen, I call on you myself to drink to the glorious old Commonwealth of Massachusetts."

If ever a "mean Yankee" felt himself to be distinctly and unequivocally mean it must have been then. Thank God that those shameful days—those days in which our representatives cowered in Congress and our private citizens ate dirt in every corner of the land—thank God that they have been ended, though at a cost of half a million of lives!

PUGNACITIES

Self-respect, as the Southerners understood it, has always demanded much fighting. A pugnacity which is not merely war paint, but which is, so to speak, tattooed into the character, has resulted from this high sentiment of personal value and from the circumstances which produced the sentiment. It permeates all society; it has infected all individualities. The meekest man by nature, the man who at the North would no more fight than he would jump out of a second-story window, may at the South resent an insult by a blow, or perhaps a stab or pistol shot.

I knew a middle-aged South Carolinian, at one time a representative of our country to one of the minor courts of Europe, who temporarily withdrew his connection from the church of which he was a member in order to give himself elbowroom for a duel.

I knew a clergyman of the same pugnacious little state who was the hero of another "unpleasantness." The Reverend James Clayton, as I shall presume to miscall him, had suffered under various disobliging remarks and irritating practical jokes from a fellow citizen whom I will venture to stigmatize as Mr. Tom Noddy. One sale day, that is, on the first Monday of a month, a number of people had gathered around the steps of the village courthouse, attracted by an auction of property sold for delinquent taxes. Amidst the magnates of the place, leaning backward upon the cane which he held behind him in both hands, discussing some grave subject (perhaps the nature of the Negro soul) with his usual blandness of aspect, stood Parson Clayton. While thus beneficially engaged, his cane was knocked from its hold in the earth, causing him to reel backward. Supposing that some intimate friend had done this thing, the reverend gentleman turned round with a smile and beheld the exasperating grin of that low-toned Noddy. In a second the cane was in the air, and in another the insulter lay on the ground. Next Mr. Clayton rushed to the office of a legal acquaintance; not, however, with the intention of taking refuge behind the legal code; no, but to plant himself in front of the code of honor.

"But, my dear Sir, your cloth!" objected the lawyer; "you certainly are not bound to fight a duel; your cloth relieves you from that obligation."

"I will not attempt to shield myself under my cloth, Sir."

"But—excuse my frankness—this is a grave matter, and you have placed it in my hands—but will not the public consider that your cloth prohibits you from appealing to the code?"

"Sir, I am a minister of the gospel; I am proud of my profession; I have sought to honor it. Had I been insulted as a clergyman I would have accepted it as persecution and would have endured it meekly. But I have been insulted as an individual. My family has a social status and a reputation which I must not allow myself to ignore. It will not do for a Clayton of Clayton District to suffer these impertinences as though he were a poor-white or a slave. I must act suitably to my name. I beg, Sir, that in arranging this matter you will not consider my cloth any more than the lowbred person who insulted me considered it."

"Nevertheless, you are not bound to take the initiative. You knocked Mr. Noddy down, it appears; and consequently it is his business to challenge. That is the code, Sir; you may rely upon it."

As Mr. Noddy was in every respect unchivalrous and did not at all regard it as his business to challenge, the affair went off without triggers.

Very curious in certain cases is the contrast between a man of turtledove disposition and the falcon-like ferocity which Southern public opinion can force him to exhibit. A citizen of New Orleans who had been repeatedly insulted by a bully and who was threatened with expulsion from society because of the meek manner in which he had endured his wrongs, found himself at last driven to appeal to arms. With a cocked pistol in either hand he entered an eating-saloon where sat his persecutor, and marched slowly to the attack, swearing viciously. He might have slain the foe at once; but he was too tender-hearted to shed blood except in the exigency of self-defense; his agonizing desire was that the other should run away. Fortunately the threatened blusterer had no weapons, and, after one glance at his plated table-knife, he skedaddled through a side door. There was a noisy chase down the street; the promenaders made way, followed on, applauded; the omnibus drivers stopped to see the issue of the affair; there was a general disappointment when the fugitive dodged into his boarding-house.

Then did the turtledove rampage up and down the pavement, defying his adversary to come out to mortal combat and blaspheming like a veritable falcon. The grandeur of the demonstration was somewhat diminished by the circumstances that he was as pale as a sheet and that in his nervousness he fired both his derringers into the sidewalk, very nearly amputating his own toes and leaving himself at the mercy of his antagonist. But, as the latter did not make a sally, the turtledove escaped with the palm of victory and was thenceforth passably esteemed in New Orleans as possessing at least a showing of the high-toned valor.

The average Southerner, however, was not like this man; he was quicker to fight, and when he fought he meant business. How quick he was to fight, how prompt at believing that the combat had begun, how disposed to accept an insult as an injury may be inferred from the charge of a Virginian judge in a case of trial for murder. "Gentlemen," said his Honor, "the lie is the first blow."

If this is not common law at the South, it is, I believe, common sentiment. In the early part of 1868 I heard a South Carolinian of respectable position relate the particulars of a recent rencontre, or, in other words, murder, in which the victim was a Northerner.

"The most remarkable circumstance in the transaction," said he, "and what struck all the by-standers with surprise was that the fellow made no attempt to defend himself. Every one supposed, from his giving a desperate man the lie, that he was prepared for a fight; but he allowed himself to be shot down without offering the least resistance; in fact, he had no arms about him."

Evidently the amazed narrator and his equally astonished listeners considered "the lie the first blow," or something so near akin to it that it was not worth while to speculate upon the difference.

"There is something miraculous about the geography of Dixie," said a Yankee to me; "the backwoods have always remained unnaturally near to the seacoast."

I am aware that Southerners will deny that bloodshedding is more common with them than with us and will point to the murders of New York and Philadelphia as a set-off to their combats of honor and passion. But the two things are not parallel: our tragedies are crimes, so regarded by the community and so punished; their tragedies are gentilities which the public voice does not condemn, and for which the law rarely exacts a penalty.

Moreover, duels and rencontres have been far more numerous south of Mason and Dixon's line, at least in proportion to population, than murders north of it. As Bureau officer, responsible for the peace of a large district, it was my business to know what acts of violence occurred in it; and in the course of my inquiries concerning the affairs of my day I necessarily learned much of what had happened during years previous. I declare positively that I was amazed at the number of persons who bore marks of frays, and the number of houses which had been rendered memorable by scenes of blood.

Opposite my hotel was a building where an old gentleman had sought to cane his niece's husband and, before he struck a blow, had fallen dead under the youth's ready pistol.

Do you see that tall and dignified man, a person of repute in the community and an ex-member of Congress, who pauses to salute an acquaintance with such an ingratiating smile, such a musical intonation of voice, and such fluent speech? He has been attacked with knives and bludgeons; he has fallen down wounded and been forced to scuffle for life; he has pulled trigger on three human beings, once with fatal effect; he will tell you of these things as "lamentable occurrences, which I very much regret."

That other gracious personage, portly in build, dignified in bearing, with the intellectual forehead and the benevolent smile, a man of probity, a citizen of distinction, has also killed his antagonist.

That young fellow with the dark eyes and the silvery utterance has in his hand a huge cane which will never be the solid stick that it was before it came in contact with a human head.

If you will ride with me up a certain road I will show you four plantations within a few miles of each other, the former proprietors of which have either been slain in single combat or have slain others.

Yet Greenville has been a nest of turtledoves compared with some other portions of South Carolina. There was once a famous "gentleman of the old school" in Abbeville who ruled his district with the pistol, who during the course of his long and high-toned life killed several other high-toned fellow creatures, and who consequently had himself elected to office whenever he pleased. Abbeville was renowned for its hundreds of shooting men, but this man shot straighter and quicker than anybody else. Yes, pugnacious Greenville is a haven of 'Quakers compared with Abbeville, Newberry, and half a dozen other districts.

Of the Carolinian of the seacoast who may pretend to dispute my statements I will ask whether he has ever heard of a bland and dignified old planter, who won in his youth, by dint of frequent fights and duels, the surname of Tiger Bill. In one specially famous encounter this antique worthy, disarmed, prostrate, and held down, doubled his legs over his adversary's back, and roweled him from loins to knees with Spanish spurs. And Tiger Bill was but the first among peers; he was a model for widespread and jealous imitation. Probably he had not an acquaintance who did not regard him with more respect than he would accord to John Howard [6] or any other hero of peace and good will toward men.

COURAGE IN THE FIELD

The pugnacious customs of Southern society explain in part the extraordinary courage which the Confederate troops displayed during the Rebellion. A man might as well be shot doing soldierly service at Bull Run or The Wilderness as go back to Abbeville and be shot there in the duel or street rencontre which awaited him. The bullet hole was a mere question of time, and why not open one's arms to it on the field of glory?

Fighting qualities result in a great measure from habit; and when the war commenced the Southerners were, in a sense, already veterans; they had been under fire at home or had lived in expectation of it. They went into battle with the same moral superiority over their Northern antagonists which a border militia has over an urban militia; which, for instance, the Highlanders of Prince Charles Edward, habituated to the dirk and claymore, had over the burghers of Edinburgh; a superiority

6. An English philanthropist and prison reformer, 1726–90.

resulting from familiarity with the use and the effect of weapons.

But this was not all: there was also the power of patrician leadership; there was also the sense of honor. The Southern troops were officered in the main by the domineering, high-spirited gentlemen who governed them in time of peace; and they were fired by the belief that the greatest glory of humanity is not learning, not art, not industry, but successful combat.

Even this was not all: they were defending their own native soil; they were stimulated by a long-cherished hate and encouraged by a carefully inculcated contempt for their antagonists; finally, they were guided in their operations by a superior knowledge of the country. Is it wonderful that a race educated under the circumstances which spring from that state of suspended war, slavery, should for a time foil and often defeat superior armies of men who had been gathered from a purely peaceful democracy? The result was as certain as that there is logic in history, although we had too much confidence in ourselves to expect it. Time alone enabled the higher civilization, the greater mass of population, the larger wealth, the more widely diffused intelligence, the superior capacity for organization, to overcome the military aptitude and feudal passion of a rebellion of aristocrats and low-downers.

Unquestionably a strong military tone is perceptible in the character of the "chivalrous Southron." Notably brave, punctilious as to honor, pugnacious to quarrelsomeness, authoritative to imperiousness, generous to extravagance, somewhat formal in his courtesy, somewhat grandiose in his self-respect, there is hardly an agreeable or disagreeable trait in him which you can not find in the officers of most armies. This is doubtless one reason why, at the opening of the war, many of our old regulars leaned to the Rebel side; there was a relationship of sentiment between the professional militaire and the feudal head of a plantation; moreover, the latter had always treated the former with distinguished hospitality.

Before the war this soldierly spirit flowered out in military schools, in a prodigious crop of governor's aides, and in enthusiastic militia musters. Since the war it is quiescent—it has had its fill of arms and glory.

VIRILITY

It seems to me that the central trait of the "chivalrous Southron" is an intense respect for virility. He will forgive almost any vice in a man who is manly; he will admire vices which are but exaggerations of the masculine. If you will fight, if you are strong and skillful enough to kill your antagonist, if you can govern or influence the common herd, if you can ride a dangerous horse over a rough country, if you are a good shot or an expert swordsman, if you stand by your own opinions unflinchingly, if you do your level best on whisky, if you are a devil of a fellow with women, if, in short, you show vigorous masculine attributes, he will grant you his respect. I doubt whether a man who leaves behind him numerous irregular claimants to his name is regarded with disfavor at the South. He will be condemned theoretically; it may be considered proper to shoot him if he disturbs the peace of respectable families; but he will be looked upon as a nobler representative of his sex than Cœlebs.[7]

The good young man, as pure as a young girl, whom one finds in the Abrahamic bosom of Northern Puritanism, would not be made a Grand Lama of in Dixie. The chivalrous Southron would unite with the aristocracy of Europe in regarding him as a sort of monster of neutral insipidity. I doubt whether even the women of our meridional regions admire that sort of youth. "I shouldn't fancy a hen-husband," said a lively Southern girl, alluding to a man without vices.

It may be taken for granted that a people which so highly prizes virility looks upon man as the lord of creation and has the old-fashioned ideas as to what is the proper sphere of woman. If the high-toned gentleman continues to be influential at the South, it will be a long time before the "strong-minded" obtain much of a following there, a very long time before they will establish female suffrage.[8] Next to our supposed passion

7. Charles, the hero of Hannah More's novel, *Cœlebs in Search of a Wife* (1809), is endowed, according to his mother, with "justness of . . . taste" and "rectitude of . . . principles." So equipped, he goes in search of the woman who will make him the ideal wife, perfect in the virtues his parents have commended to him.
8. This prediction proved remarkably accurate. When the Nineteenth or Woman

for putting the Negro on an equality with the white, there is nothing in Northern life so abhorrent to the Southerners, of both sexes, as the movement in favor of woman's rights.

"I do think," said an emphatic old planter to me, "that your free-love business and women's voting and all that is just the miserablest mess that ever was invented. I don't see what ails you to go for such vile nonsense. But then you always were as full of whimsies as the devil."

It would have been useless to tell him that he was binding in one fagot ideas which had no connection. I did my wisest by him; I left him unanswered.

COURTESY

There certainly is or was more suavity of manner at the South than at the North. It is delightful to see two high-toned gentlemen of the old Virginian or Carolinian school greet each other. Such gracious bows and insinuating tones! Such mellifluous compliments, particular inquiries concerning health and welfare, animating congratulations as to future prospects! Such sunny and, one might almost say, equatorial blandness! You feel as if you were in Paradise, hearing Dante address Beatrice as "gracious lady." The moral thermometer rises to summer heat; your humanities expand and bloom under the influence; you are a kindlier and, I think, a better man for the sight.

It is a pity that we Northerners have not been better educated in such gentilities and that we have not the requisite time for the exercise of them. If there were twenty-eight hours in a day the Northerner might possibly become thus urbane; as it is, he has barely opportunity to fill his pocket with the necessary greenbacks and his head with the necessary information to get on in the world; he is too much hurried by practicalities to make his manners. At the South there has hitherto been a leisurely caste which set the example to all the others.

But the high-toned gentleman, full of provincial prejudices, was not always civil to outside barbarians. He was not civil to our congressmen in the old days when he governed them; he

Suffrage Amendment was adopted the only states which withheld ratification were ten Southern states.

cracked the plantation whip over them as he did over his Negroes, and for the same reasons: they were not of his caste, they were his natural subordinates, and they were sometimes fractious.

Returning to my own experience with this grand personage, I must state that I have not always obtained sweetness from him. It must be remembered that to my native infamy as a Yankee I added the turpitude of being a United States military officer and the misdemeanor of being a sub-assistant commissioner of the Freedmen's Bureau. In the exercise of these atrocious characteristics it was once my duty to settle a dispute as to the division of a crop between an elderly Negro and a South Carolinian of historic name and French descent. The planter's accounts were admirably kept; the right was on his side, and I decided in his favor. Throughout the interview I treated him with all possible courtesy for the sake of the worth of his Revolutionary ancestor; but, alas! I committed the error of pronouncing his patronymic after the English manner instead of the French. When his Huguenot patience was exhausted he corrected me: "Sir, my name is ————," giving it the Gallic accent.

"I beg pardon," I replied. "We at the North habitually anglicize foreign names. My name is French by origin, but we use the English pronunciation."

He picked up the certificate of settlement on which I had just indorsed my official approval, glanced at my signature, and said with a half-concealed sneer, "Oh, I see that you put a *De* to it!"

Conceive my humiliation, thus charged with stealing a French particle!

A few days later I had occasion to approve a labor contract for a lady of another family, but likewise of Huguenot race. Her name I also anglicized, not in ignorance of the Gallic form and not with the purpose of giving offense, but solely because of Northern custom. Again I was corrected: "Sir, my name is ————."

Struck with the repetition of incident, I made the same reply as to the gentleman: "I beg pardon; we at the North habitually anglicize foreign names; my own, etc., etc."

The lady picked up the now finished contract, glanced at the indorsement, and said, "Oh, I see— De Forest. I knew a Mr. De Forest once; that is, he did some work for me. He was a shoemaker."

Conceive my second humiliation, thus crushed under this degraded De Forest, who was a shoemaker!

But before the war, before the days of rage and ruin, the High-toned was not thus peevish; he was, notwithstanding some superciliousness and imperiousness, our courtliest social figure.

I shall never forget the grace and kindness of a man who may yet be remembered in Charleston as one of its most finished social ornaments. I was at a supper of the Literary Club; we were standing or sitting around a table which would have pleased Brillat-Savarin; all the others were well-known citizens, reverend and respectable; I was the youngest and the only stranger. I had dropped out of the conversation and withdrawn a little aside, when Colonel John Alston observed me and divined my stranded situation.

He did not know me; it was the first time that we had ever met; but he instantly came toward me and begged leave to wait on me. It was not the deed so much as the manner which was so exquisitely ingratiating. There was an *empressement* in his expression which seemed to say: "Sir, your mere appearance fills me with respect and interest; you are obviously worthy of my attentions."

I have sometimes thought that it would be a fine thing to be a handsome young lady; and I felt at that moment as if I were one. Well, this hospitable act toward a perfect stranger, this courteous advance toward a wallflower, was characteristic of the man and, in general, of his caste.

CHAPTER X

MORE CHIVALROUS SOUTHRONS [1]

PROCEEDING with my sketches of our Southern and very nearly torrid brethren, I come to

GENEROSITY

It was not that Yankee generosity which sends pundits to convert Hottentots, founds school systems, hospitals, sanitary commissions, and endows colleges with millions. It was the old-fashioned sort, the generosity of the Arab and of the feudal noble, feeding every beggar who came to the door, setting bounteous tables and keeping full wine cellars. It was the profuseness not of philanthropy, but of good fellowship. Even before the war there were single states in the North which gave more to missionary, educational, and charitable organizations than the entire South.

But the Southerner was more than lavish; he was good natured and easy in his business transactions; he had such a contempt for small sums that he would not use pennies; he paid loosely at long credits and was careless in his collections. I knew an upright wretch in a Southern town who strictly settled his debts and sternly demanded his credits, and who was consequently very unpopular, in spite of many virtues and worthy deeds. I knew a jolly fellow who was not much astonished, and not at all angry, when another still jollier fellow borrowed a hundred dollars of him, treated him handsomely out of it, and never repaid him.

"Is that what you call generosity?" I asked with a Vandalic sneer.

"Well, I like it better than stinginess," replied the victim.

1. Originally published partly in the first and partly in the second installment of "Chivalrous and Semi-Chivalrous Southrons" in *Harper's New Monthly Magazine,* XXXVIII (January, February, 1869), 197–200, 339–341, 346–347.

"He thought he was doing what was handsome; he felt as if it were his own money. If it had been his own he would have spent it just as freely. It *was* just a little rough, though, that he should get all the credit of the bender when it was I who really paid for it."

Meum and *tuum* were a little mixed; people who lived on Negroes felt it right to live on each other and to help each other; what a man could borrow or get trusted for was his own until a neighbor asked for it. Happy-go-lucky planters settled their store bills once in seven years or after they were dead;[2] and the storekeeper settled with his Northern furnisher as soon after his notes matured as was convenient. When the war opened more than half the rice and sea-island estates were mortgaged to the verge of bankruptcy; and the personal debts of Southerners to Northerners were estimated at eighty-five millions of dollars.[3] The virtue of generosity had been prolonged into the vice of ruinous extravagance.

HONOR

Notwithstanding his thoughtless lavishness, there was a high sense of honor in the "chivalrous Southron." He did not mean to defraud any one. I have known an expensive, generous fellow to cut his throat because he could not meet a note which was coming due. I have known another bankrupt to put his wife and children into a buggy and drive with them into the sea, drowning the whole party.[4] I do not assert positively—I only give it as my strong impression—that such tragedies of wounded honor were more common in Dixie than in Yankeeland.

The honor of Southern students is not college honor as it is understood at the North, and perhaps in Europe; it comes much nearer to the honor of good citizens and the honor of the gentle-

2. Cf. Thomas Jefferson's statement about Virginia tobacco planters: that their debts "became hereditary from father to son for many generations, so that the planters were a species of property annexed to certain mercantile houses in London."

3. On the eve of the Civil War, the New York Chamber of Commerce made a careful estimate and concluded that the entire Southern debt to Northern merchants amounted to approximately $200,000,000. Philip S. Foner, *Business and Slavery* (Chapel Hill, 1941), p. 218.

4. He was said to be of Northern birth. (De F.)

man of society. The pupils are not leagued against the teachers for the purpose of passing fraudulent examinations by the trickeries of stealing the prepared lists of questions, carrying furtive copies of lessons into the recitation-rooms, mutual postings, and purchased compositions. A professor of the Charleston Medical College assured me that he had never detected such a cheat in thirty years of tuition. A professor of the university at Columbia, South Carolina, told a friend of mine that he had known but one such instance, and that in that case the two criminals were forced to leave by their classmates.

The "chivalrous Southron" undergraduate, at least while surrounded by his native moral atmosphere, considered himself a gentleman first and a student afterward. When one remembers the strength of college *esprit de corps,* these facts exhibit an individual self-respect and uprightness which is astonishing and which must, I suspect, fill the faculties of Yale and Harvard with envy. I should explain that my testimony on this point refers only to South Carolina, and I may therefore have drawn too large an inference in extending my eulogium to all Southern students. It is worth while also to note that in Dixie examinations are less severe than with us and that a failure in passing them rarely ends in expulsion.

"How can a race of traitors be called honorable?" will be the objection of millions of loyal citizens. It must be remembered, I answer, that the "chivalrous Southron" conceived himself as owing a closer allegiance to his state than to the Union; and that, furthermore, he, like the Roman patrician, like the aristocrat of all time, felt that he owed fealty to his caste. These questions have now been settled by the highest of earthly courts. If the South rebels again it will be traitorous even in its own eyes.

INTELLECTUAL TRAITS

One of the mistakes of the "chivalrous Southron" was to suppose that he was a great reader, and abreast of his age in science and literature. The truth is that while his reading was mainly good, it was venerable; he had a conservative taste for what had been considered improving and interesting by his grandfather; his shelves were loaded with the worthy though possibly heavy old "books which no gentleman's library should be without"; he was fairly sure to own Hume, Robertson, Gibbon, Addison, Johnson, Goldsmith, etc. In theology he was strenuously orthodox, holding fast by the English fathers in Biblical exegesis and distrusting all Germans without knowing anything about them. In science he was averse to admitting novelties, unless they went to show that the Negro is not a human being, and so not entitled to the benefit of the Declaration of Independence. In light literature he was cautious how he meddled with Northern and even with English publications, lest he should unawares become entangled in some "ism."

It was wonderful to hear an old-time Southern clergyman defending the deluge, ciphering at the ark so as to show how it might contain all the species of animals, asserting that the fossils on Mount Lebanon date from the time of Noah, and supporting a strict interpretation of Genesis by the traditions of the Potawatomies. The belief that the American Indians are the descendants of the ten lost tribes, and as such ought to be besomed off the face of the earth, still has more followers in Dixie than in all the rest of the world put together. There was a prodigious movement in the Southern mind in consequence of Dr. Cartwright's discovery that God created three kinds of beings, to wit, men, "living creatures," and beasts; and that the Negroes, being evidently "living creatures," are lower than "humans," though not so low as animals. This remarkable "reading," having been popularized by a writer signing as "Ariel," [5] was used with great effect by Governor Perry in his letters against universal suffrage, much to the confusion of certain Radical pundits, who did not know what the governor was talking about. In short, the learning of the South is (or was) what one might expect to find among solid, squire-like people addicted to farming. If the true savant wants a hearty laugh let him read the old numbers of *De Bow's Review*.

Before the war things were growing worse, instead of better. Bullied and reproached by abolitionism, scared at the prospect of losing two thousand millions of dollars invested in Negroes, the chivalry concentrated its intellect into a defense of slavery and actually thought of little else. The subject was dwarfing the

5. See p. 117 n.

Southern mind; it had infolded and partially stifled that fine genius which produced so many of our early statesmen and wrote no small part of the *Federalist;* it was like a theological dogma which insists on being taken for granted and, when so taken, destroys the freedom and power of logic. The Southerners, trammeled by admitting slavery, could no more reason on politics than the Jews, trammeled by the Mosaic dispensation, could reason on Christianity.

Indeed, they had begun to lose the power of thinking justly and brightly on any subject. An unprejudiced person who will glance over their literature will discover a vast declension since Jefferson and Legaré; [6] that is, after the period at which slavery was established as an axiom of Southern ethics and political science, not to be disputed under penalty of death or exile; in other words, since the intellect of Dixie ceased to be free. Its later condition was much like that of the natural philosophers of Putterum, who are obliged by law to preface every inquiry into the astronomical position of the earth by saying, "I believe that it stands in the centre of the universe, on the back of the sacred turtle." After that, it will be perceived, inquiry becomes needless; and the philosophical writers of Putterum always stop just there: hence a decadence in Putterum science and logic.

It is a curious instance of the power of prejudice that, with regard to the Civil War, the chivalrous Southron did not fully credit the evidence of his own senses. Although regiments from every Northern state marched over every Southern state, he still held to the idea of Yankees which he formerly established on an experience of subservient Congressmen, obsequious merchants, and non-combative peddlers, and believed that we conquered him with columns of foreign mercenaries. Having served three years in the field and fifteen months in the Provost-Marshal General's Office, I knew from sufficient authority the fallacy of this supposition and could state that our alien-born citizens

6. Hugh S. Legaré (1789?–1843), like Jefferson, had been both a public official and a man of letters. Politically, he served his state, South Carolina, in the legislature and as attorney general, and he was a member of President Tyler's cabinet as attorney general and, briefly, as Secretary of State; but he was also a co-founder and editor of *The Southern Review,* and author of articles in *The New York Review* on Demosthenes, the Athenian Democracy, and the Roman Law.

had scarcely furnished their fair proportion to our armies. I could remark that if *all* our able-bodied Irish and Germans had served they would not have made up one half of the twenty-five hundred thousand men whom we enlisted under our flag. I could suggest that if every Hibernian in the world had volunteered for us we should still have lacked a million and a half to our gigantic levy. It was useless; the Dixieite held fast by his venerable prejudices: "the Yankee could not fight and therefore had not fought."

The Southerners were equally wrong-headed, at least according to our view of the matter and "the sword of Brennus," in pointing out the causes of the war. Over and over they assured me that the contest arose not from the necessity of slavery to rule or ruin, but from the aggressive spirit of the Northerners and particularly of the New Englanders.

"They always were, you know, the most quarrelsome people that God ever created," remarked a Greenville planter. "They quarreled in England and cut off the king's head. They have been quarreling here ever since they came over in the *Mayflower*. They got after the Indians and killed them by thousands. They drove out the Baptists and whipped the Quakers and hung the witches. Then they were the first to pick a fight with the old country. It's my opinion, Sir, and I think you must agree with me, that God never made such another quarrelsome set. What in h-ll he made them for passes my comprehension."

As this was better history than one usually meets in Putterum I let it pass without controversy.

POLITICAL OPINIONS

There is an old traveler's story to the effect that in the highlands of Africa exists a race of monkeys who, during the cold season, gather into tight little knots, each one having for its centre a venerable senior of great wisdom and influence, and the business of the others being to keep him warm. The chief inconvenience of this organization is that, as there is a general desire to be the central monkey, much strenuous crowding toward the middle ensues, attended by an uncomfortable amount of scratching and squalling.

In consequence of the somewhat feudal, somewhat patriarchal, social position of the large planter, politics at the South have been conducted much on the central-monkey system, only that there has been a decent regard for the central monkey. Every community has its great man, or at least its little great man, around whom his fellow citizens gather when they want information, and to whose monologues they listen with a respect akin to humility. For instance, the central monkey of Greenville was Governor Perry. When he stood at a corner people got about him; when he opened his mouth all other men present closed theirs. Had he favored the "constitutional amendment" [7] Greenville would have accepted it; as he denounced it Greenville rejected it, without taking the superfluous trouble of reading it.

I found it so everywhere that I went, and during all the time that I remained, in the South. Not one man whom I met had read the amendment, yet every man scouted it with the utmost promptness, confidence, and indignation. He scouted it because he had been instructed to do so by his central monkey. The latter, the little great man of his district, had, of course, issued these instructions mainly because the third section of the amendment deprived him of the power to hold office unless a two-thirds vote of Congress should remove his disability, that Congress being then two-thirds Radical. In short, I found the chivalrous Southron still under the domination of his ancient leaders.

Political opinions had necessarily been somewhat muddled by the results of the war. The logic of events had been so different from the logic of *De Bow's Review* and the *Charleston Mercury* that men scarcely knew what to think. A soul which had been educated in the belief that slavery is a divine and reverend institution could not help falling more or less dumb with amazement when it found that there was no slavery to revere. On this point, however, the Southern mind presently accepted the situation, and I found a surprisingly general satisfaction over the accomplished fact of abolition, mixed with much natural wrath at the manner of the accomplishment.

"I am glad the thing is done away with," was a frequent re-

7. See Introduction, p. viii f.

mark; "it was more plague than pleasure, more loss than profit." Then would perhaps follow the Southern *Delenda est Carthago*—that is to say, "D—n the Yankees!"—always appropriate.

Just imagine the condition of a nation of politicians which sees every one of its political principles knocked into nonexistence! Slavery and state sovereignty had for years been the whole of Southern statesmanship; they had formed the rudder, the keel, the hull, the masts, and the rigging; when they vanished the crew was in the water. The great men and the little men, all the central monkeys and all their adherents—everybody was afloat like so much driftwood, not knowing whither to swim. Blessed interregnum! No wire-pullers, no log-rollers, no caucuses, no mass meetings; a time of peace in which every man could mind his own business; an opportunity for building and launching financial prosperity. How we at the North envied it! how glad should we have been to drown *our* central monkeys! how we hoped that the conflict of sections was forever closed!

I found it nearly impossible to converse ten minutes with a Southerner without getting on to the subject of politics. I saw the monster coming afar off; I made my preparations in good season to evade it; I dodged it, ducked under it, swam away from it; all useless. At the most unexpected moment it thrust out its arms like the *pieuvre* [8] of Victor Hugo, enveloped me in its slimy caresses, sucked me dry, and left me flaccid.

POLITICAL FEELING

Walking the streets of Greenville, I met a child of six or seven—a blonde, blue-eyed girl with cheeks of faint rose—who, in return for my look of interest, greeted me with a smile. Surprised at the hospitable expression and remembering my popularly abhorred blue uniform, I said, "Are you not afraid of me?"

"No," she answered; "I am not afraid. I met three Yankees the other day, and they didn't hurt me."

We of the North can but faintly imagine the alarm and hate

8. In *Les Travailleurs de la Mer* (1866).

which trembled through millions of hearts at the South at the phrase, "The Yankees are coming!"

The words meant war, the fall of loved ones, the burning of homes, the wasting of property, flight, poverty, subjugation, humiliation, a thousand evils, and a thousand sorrows. The Southern people had never before suffered anything a tenth part so horrible as what befell them in consequence of this awful formula, this summons to the Afrites and Furies of desolation, this declaration of ruin. Where the conquering army sought to be gentlest it still devoured the land like locusts; where it came not at all it nevertheless brought social revolution, bankruptcy of investments, and consequently indigence. A population of bereaved parents, of widows, and of orphans, steeped in sudden poverty, can hardly love the cause of its woes. The great majority of the Southerners, denying that they provoked the war, looking upon us not as the saviours of a common country, but as the subjugators of their sovereign states, regarded us with detestation.

I speak of the "chivalrous Southrons," the gentry, the educated, the socially influential, the class which before the war governed the South, the class which may govern it again. Even if these people knew that they had been in the wrong they would still be apt to feel that their punishment exceeded their crime, because it was truly tremendous and reached many who could not be guilty. I remember a widowed grandmother of eighty and an orphan granddaughter of seven, from each of whom a large estate on the sea islands had passed beyond redemption, and who were in dire poverty. When the elder read aloud from a newspaper a description of some hundreds of acres which had been divided among Negroes, and said, "Chattie, this is your plantation," the child burst into tears. I believe that it is unnatural not to sympathize with this little plundered princess, weeping for her lost domains in fairyland.

Imagine the wrath of a fine gentleman, once the representative of his country abroad, who finds himself driven to open a beer saloon. Imagine the indignation of a fine lady who must keep boarders; of another who must go out to service little less than menial; of another who must beg rations with low-downers and Negroes. During the war I saw women of good families at the

South who had no stockings; and here I beg leave to stop and ask the reader to conceive fully, if he can, the sense of degradation which must accompany such poverty; a degradation of dirt and nakedness and slatternly uncomeliness, be it observed; a degradation which seemed to place them beside the Negro. Let us imagine the prosperous ladies of our civilization prevented only from wearing the latest fashions; what manliest man of us all would like to assume the responsibility of such a piece of tyranny?

Moreover, "Our Lady of Tears," the terrible *Mater Lachrymarum* of De Quincey's visions, fills the whole South with her outcries for the dead. It is not so much a wonder as a pity that the women are bitter and teach bitterness to their children.

Of course there were lower and more ridiculous motives for this hate. Non-combatants, sure of at least bodily safety, are apt to be warlike and to blow cheap trumpets of mock heroism. Furthermore, it was aristocratic to keep aloof from Yankees; and what woman does not desire to have the tone of grand society?

When will this sectional repulsion end? I can only offer the obvious reflection that it is desirable for both North and South, but especially for the weaker of the two, that it should end as quickly as possible. For the sake of the entire republic we should endeavor to make all our citizens feel that they are Americans, and nothing but Americans. If we do not accomplish this end, we shall not rival the greatness of the Romans. It was not patricianism which made Rome great so much as the vast community and bonded strength of Roman citizenship. Let us remember in our legislation the law of solidarity: the fact that no section of a community can be injured without injuring the other sections; that the perfect prosperity of the whole depends upon the prosperity of all the parts.

This idea should be kept in view despite of provocations; this policy will in the end produce broad and sound national unity. As the Southerners find that the republic brings them prosperity they will, little by little, and one by one, become as loyal as the people of other sections.

FINANCIAL CONDITION

In Naples and Syria [9] I have seen more beggarly communities than I found in the South, but never one more bankrupt. Judging from what I learned in my own district, I should say that the great majority of planters owed to the full extent of their property and that, but for stay-laws and stay-orders, all Dixie would have been brought to the hammer without meeting its liabilities. When I left Greenville there were something like a thousand executions awaiting action; and, had the commanding general allowed their collection, another thousand would have been added to the docket. I have known land to go at auction for a dollar and twelve cents an acre, which before the war was valued, I was told, at seven or eight dollars the acre. Labor was equally depreciated, able-bodied men hiring out at seventy-five cents a day if they found themselves; at twenty-five cents if found by their employers. The great mass of the farmers could not pay even these wretched wages and were forced to plant upon shares, a system unsuited to a laboring class so ignorant and thoughtless as the Negroes.

It seemed unjust that debts should retain their full valuation when all other property was thus depreciated. Yet I doubt the practical wisdom of the stay-orders. I think it would have been better to let the whole row of staggering bricks go over; then every one would have known where he was, and industry would have resumed its life. As it was, there was a prolonged crisis of bankruptcy, in which neither debtor nor creditor dared or could take a step. It was a carnival of Micawberism; hundreds of thousands of people were waiting to see what would turn up; they were living on what remained of their property without working to increase it; why should they accumulate when the creditor might seize the accumulation?

This financial and moral paralysis fostered dishonesty. People who had in other days been honorable descended to all sorts of trickeries, in the hope of saving property which did not

9. In 1846–47 De Forest visited his brother and sister-in-law, then serving as missionaries in Beyrouth, Syria; and in 1854, during his first series of European travels, he spent a month or two in Naples.

seem to be covered by the stay-orders. I was teased with applications to use my authority in preventing the collections of debts,
the administration of estates, and the levying of taxes. In short,
the stay-system was transforming the chivalrous Southrons into
a race of—Micawbers.

There would have been more hope in the future of my district
but for the exhausted soil and the wretched agriculture which
had been bequeathed to it by slavery. Land which, under proper
cultivation, might produce two generous crops a year had been
reduced, by lack of manure and of management, to one crop,
varying from ten to two bushels the acre. The common plow-
share of the country was about six inches wide by ten long, and
this was used until it wore down into a "bull-tongue," a phrase
which aptly describes its shape and size. This triviality could
not turn a furrow; it scratched the earth like a harrow.

Here and there, at monstrous intervals, a planter used Northern plows and manure, gathering his forty and eighty bushels
of corn to the acre. His neighbors looked on with astonishment,
but without imitating him, as if his results were magic and
beyond merely human accomplishment. A German colony,
planted at Walhalla, in the northwestern corner of South Carolina, had converted a tract of some thousands of acres into a
garden of fertility. Among their Anglo-Saxon neighbors you
could not discover a sign of their influence. What is to become
of this bull-tongued and bull-headed race? I sometimes thought
that there was no hope of the physical regeneration of the South
until immigration should have rooted out and replaced its
present population.

In this same land numberless water privileges send their un-
gathered riches to the sea, and the earth is crowded with under-
ground palaces of mineral wealth. The climate, too, is admirable: the summer heat in Greenville was rarely too great for
walking, its highest point being usually eighty-four; while the
winter brought at the worst two or three falls of snow, which
melted in two or three days. Neither in Europe nor along the
shores of the Mediterranean have I found a temperature which,
during the year round, was so agreeable and healthful. You can
see its natural results in the remarkable stature of the men and in
the height, fullness of form, and beauty of the women. My im-

pression is that the entire Allegheny region, from Maryland down into the north of Georgia, is a paradise for the growth of the human plant. If bodily comforts and intellectual pleasures existed there, I should advise all New England to emigrate to it.

Yet it was poorer than Naples, and before the war it was not richer. So much for the political economy of the chivalrous Southron, and so much for his rule-or-ruin statesmanship, and, in one word, so much for slavery.

SOUTHERN INDIVIDUALITY

Whether chivalrous or semi-chivalrous, the Southerner had more individuality of character than the Northerner and was one of the most interesting, or, at all events, one of the most amusing, personages on this continent. He had salient virtues, vices, and oddities; he had that rich, practical humor which is totally unconscious of being humoristic; he in the gravest manner decorated his life with ludicrous and romantic adventures; in short, he was a prize for the anecdotist and novelist. Dixie still has thousands of high-toned gentlemen who suppose themselves to be patterns of solemn and staid propriety, but who would be fit to associate with the Caxtons and Doctor Riccabocca.[10] In that land of romance you will find Uncle Toby and Squire Western and Sir Pitt Crawley and Colonel Newcome and Mr. Pickwick and Le Chourineur,[11] all moving in the best society and quite sure that they are Admirable Crichtons.

In what other part of the civilized earth would a leading statesman write a ponderous political work in dialogue,[12] after the fashion of the essays of Plato and Cicero? Such a gusto of classical imitation might possibly be found in a Harvard sophomore; but at the South we discover it in an ex-United

10. In *The Caxtons* (1849) and *My Novel* (1853) Bulwer-Lytton turned to the domestic novel and to the description of English family life. Characters like the Caxtons and Doctor Riccabocca, portrayed in all seriousness, barely avoid seeming ridiculous in their effusive display of sentiment and correctness.

11. In *Les Mystères de Paris* (1842–43) by Eugène Sue, Le Chourineur, a murderer who has served a prison term of fifteen years, finally accepts the help of Prince Rodolphe and makes a melodramatic bid for the reader's sympathy.

12. *A Constitutional View of the Late War between the States* (1868–70) by Alexander H. Stephens is cast in the form of colloquies between the author and fictitious characters representative of various contemporary political factions.

States congressman and ex-vice-president of the Confederacy. Alexander H. Stephens was as redolent of Greeks and Romans, as verdant with lore, as Keitt or Pryor.[13]

Where else could you meet such a curious incarnation of the apostolic character as —————— ——————, a planter by profession and habitude, but a preacher by mission? He was a passionate religionist; if he met you in the street he buttonholed you and vented upon you his dogmas; chance passers-by were beckoned to until he had a circle; you listened because you dared not run away. One Sunday, exhorting in a little crossroads church, and having been annoyed by two Negroes stealing out of the house, he came to a solemn pause in his service and then spoke as follows: "Next Lord's day I shall hold worship in this same place. I shall bring my double-barreled gun; I shall stand that gun, brethren, in the pulpit, alongside of me; and, if any man gets up and goes out while I am preaching, by ———! I'll shoot him."

A half-fuddled planter called on me one evening and invited me out to a treat of stewed oysters. The restaurant was the back room of a bakery; we sat on broken chairs, among sticky pans, spilled flour, and loaves of dough; the oyster cans were opened with an old bowie knife. When the stews were before us my friend observed: "Come, don't let's eat this like savages. Major, can't you ask a blessing?" As I declined, he pulled his broad-brimmed felt from his muddled cranium and said grace himself.

I knew a worthy old South Carolinian, bearing a name of Revolutionary notoriety, who would not invest his money at high profits, holding that "six per cent, my dear Sir, is the interest of a gentleman."

I knew another worthy old person who raised a set of white and a set of black children, treated both with generosity and affection, maintained an excellent character in his church, and died in the odor of public esteem.

I knew a planter who, having said in a drunken spree that he would sell his plantation for twenty thousand dollars, would

13. Pre-war Congressmen from South Carolina and Virginia respectively, both Lawrence M. Keitt and Roger A. Pryor had reputations for being lawyers of wide learning and great ability as public speakers.

not revoke his words when sober, although it was worth thirty thousand.

I knew of another planter who beat his beautiful wife as long as he lived, and at his death willed her a considerable property, on condition that she should never quit the state, he knowing that her chiefest desire was to remove to the North.

I knew Southerners who taught their slaves to read in spite of severe prohibitory laws, and who labored for their growth in morality and piety as missionaries labor for the conversion of the heathen.

I knew of a Louisiana lady who flogged a Negro woman with her own hands until the sufferer's back was a vast sore of bruised and bloody flesh.

Audacity, vehemence, recklessness, passion, sentiment, prejudice, vanity, whimwhams, absurdities, culture, ignorance, courtliness, barbarism! The individual had plenty of elbow-room at the South; he kicked out of the traces with a freedom unknown to our steady-pulling society; he was a bull in Mrs. Grundy's china shop. Strangest of all, he believed that he was like the rest of the world, or, more accurately, that the rest of the world should be like him.

The chivalrous Southron has been too positively and authoritatively a political power to get fair treatment in literature. People have not described him; they have felt driven to declaim about him; they have preached for him or preached against him. Northern pens have not done justice to his virtues nor Southern pens to his vices.

The elder romances of Dixie, produced under a mixed inspiration of namby-pambyism and provincial vanity, strong in polysyllables and feeble in perception of character, deserve better than any other results of human labor that I am aware of, the native epithet of "powerful weak." The novelist evidently had but two objects in view: first, to present the Southron as the flower of gentility; second, to do some fine writing for his own glory. Two or three works by Kennedy [14] and by the authoress "Marion Harland" [15] are the only exceptions to this rule. Let

14. De Forest is probably referring to such novels by John Pendleton Kennedy as *Swallow Barn* (1832) and *Horse-Shoe Robinson* (1835).
15. Pseudonym of Mary V. Terhune, who wrote *Sunnybank* (1866).

us pray that a true Southern novelist may arise, for he will be able to furnish us vast amusement and some instruction. His day is passing; in another generation his material will be gone; the "chivalrous Southron" will be as dead as the slavery that created him.

INDEX

ABBEVILLE, S.C., 13, 182–183
Allums, Cato, freedman, appeal to Freedmen's Bureau, 1; shoots bushwhacker in self-defense, 2–3; witness for, 3–4; legal proceedings, 5–12; arrest of, 10; released by court, 12; and horse stealing, 13
Alston, Col. John, 188
American Freedmen's Union Commission, 116 n.
Anderson District, bushwhackers of, 7, 11
Ariel. *See* Payne, Buckner H.
Aristocrats, and free transportation, 37; at Greenville, 45; attitude toward Northerners, 46, 193–194, 197; and slaves and slavery, 55, 58, 176–177, 192, 203; charity of, 63; poverty of, 65–66; attitude toward freedman, 74; retain moral leadership, 171; characteristics of, 173, 176, 184, 201–204; conception of chivalry, 174; provincialism of, 174, 177, 186; in the North, 174–175; abroad, 176–177; militarism of, 178, 183–184; and dueling, 179–183; sense of honor, 184, 190–191; and manliness, 185; position of women, 185–186; manners and customs, 186, 188; affectations of, 187–188; and public charity, 188–190; financial position of, 190, 197, 202; as students, 191; allegiance to native state, 191; reading habits of, 191–192; and politics, 194; losses of, 197; future of, 198, 204; in literature, 203–204
Arkansas, labor migrations to, 130
Army, records on rationing, 70–71; accountability system, 71, 85–86, 88; red tape criticized by De Forest, 85–86

BANKRUPTCY. *See* Financial condition of South
Benson, Terry, Negro, wounded, 24 n.
Bigamy among Negroes, 102
Birkett, bushwhacker, 19–20; attack on

Col. H. R. Smith, 20; arrested and tried by military commission, 20–21
Blasingame, Berry, freedman, attacked by whites, 110–111
Bray, Captain, Freedmen's Agent, and Cato Allums, 2–3; and the Loopers, 166
Britton, Captain, Freedmen's Agent, 74–75
Brown, Texas, bushwhacker, and Ezra French, 15–16, 20; and Foster, 17; and Lewis, 18–19; search for, 21–23
Bryce, Unionist, 127–128
Burden, Calhoun, 173–174
Bushwhackers, and Cato Allums, 2–3, 11–12; and Union Leagues, 170

CARPETBAGGERS, 172
Cartwright, Dr. Samuel, physician and writer, 117 n., 192
Castle Pinckney, 3
Cauble, Peter, Commissioner of Poor, assaults Negro, 35–36; and the poor, 60
Charity, private, aristocrats and, 63
Charity, public, distaste for, 59; available to Negroes and whites, 59; subscription plan failure, 84; aristocrats and, 189–190
Charles, Sally, Negro, flogged, 11 n.
Charleston Mercury, 195
Charleston, S.C., De Forest at, 39
Child labor. *See* Labor, child
Children of freedmen, delinquency among, 105–106, 114; disciplined, 115
Citizenship and the Negro, assuming responsibilities of, 5; fitness for, 46
Citizenship and the whites, assuming responsibilities of, 5, 10
Civil law, restoration of confidence in, 5; authorized in South Carolina by General Sickles, 13; settlement of disputes by, 24, 29; restored, 31; Negroes encouraged to appeal to, 31; and confusion with military order, 32. *See also* Courts

places of, 36 n., 38; Negroes and new occupations, 94
Equal rights, 5
Ethnology of Negro, Southern viewpoint, 117 n., 118
Evictions of tenants, 69

FAMILIES OF SLAVES, illegitimately created, 58
Farming, lack of equipment, 200
Financial condition of South, prior to war, 132; bankruptcy, 190, 197; moral effect of, 200
Florida, labor migrations to, 130
Food, prices, 75
Freedmen, ignorance of law, 8, 31, 74, 107–108; schools for, 23, 116–117; complaints of, 29–30, 40; and wages, 30, 34; and division of crops, 30–31; and stealing, 32–33, 103–104; and transportation, 36; poverty of, 48; marriage and, 56–58, 133; and poor-whites, 72; and rationing, 80; indolence of women, 94; in business, 95–96; charity of, 98–99; social life of, 99; and Union Leagues, 99; and liquor, 103; dishonesty of, 103–105; truthfulness of, 106; children of, 105–106, 114–115; as witnesses, 106–108; pacifism of, 108–109; family life, 114–115; and education, 116–117; political future of, 126; and taxes, 129; as farmers, 130; as property owners, 131
Freedmen's Bureau, reports of outrages, 1, 109; protection and counsel of, 4; duties, 5, 29, 39, 41, 135; withdrawal from South Carolina, 6 n.; Educational Department of, 6 n., 116 n., 119–120; reports in National Archives, 6 n.; bureaucracy charged, 25; ridiculed, 26–28; authorized to approve labor contracts, 28; lacks authority over property, 30; official inspection tours, 39; reports, 39–41, 70, 86–87; census of handicapped and indigent, 41, 75; qualifications for agents, 41–42; distribution of clothing ordered, 69; rationed stores for freedmen and refugees, 71; authorized by Congress to issue corn, 83; official accounting for distribution of corn, 86; earlier corn rations, 88 n.

French, Ezra, farmer, quarrel with Texas Brown, 15, 20; flight to Mississippi, 20

GATES, GEN. HORATIO, and the South Carolina Militia during American Revolution, 155 n.
Gibbon, Dr. Lardner, 116 n.
Government agents, undesirable Northerners as, 43–44
Green, Gen. Nathanael, and the South Carolina Militia during American Revolution, 155 n.
Greenville garrison, transferred to Newberry, 42
Greenville, S.C., and bushwhackers, 14, 21; description of, 46; as resort, 44–45; social life, 45, 47–48; gifts of food for, 83; Loyalist advance on, 160–161; climate, 200

HAMPTON, WADE, campaigns against Congressional Reconstruction Program, 171
Handicapped, clothing rationed to, 72; census of, 76
Harland, Marion, writer, 203
Homestead Act, 130 n.
Hopkins, Charles, Negro teacher, 92, 118–124
Howard, John, English philanthropist, 183
Howard, Gen. Oliver O., limits transportation, 36 n.; limits rationing to hospitals, refugees and some freedmen, 60 n.; criticized by De Forest, 60, 86; and accountability system, 86; other attempts to curtail rationing, 88 n.; temperance plan for freedmen, 102–103
Hunnicutt, Miles, 24 n.; slain in outrage, 127–129

ILLEGITIMACY, among poor-whites, 50, 145; among Negroes, 56, 102, 133, 139
Illiteracy, 73, 82–83, 146
Immigration from Europe, as possible competition to poor-whites, 158, 200; invited by South Carolina Commissioner of Immigration, 158

of, 107, 109–110, 117, 122, 131–134; pacifism of, 108–109; affection for children, 114. *See also* Freedmen; Slaves and slavery

New England, industrial employment absorbs shiftless, 157

New York Freedmen's Union Association, 119–120

Newberry, S.C., Greenville garrison transferred to, 42

Niles, Brevet Lt. Col. A. E., Bureau Agent, 25, 91

North Carolina, bushwhackers escape to, 21

Nullificationists, 67 n.

ORPHANS, records of, 41, 54, 75, 197

Orr, Gov. James L., and bushwhackers, 20; appeal for aid, 75; forwards gift of corn and bacon from Maryland, 83; pardons Unionist, 167

Outrages, reports of, 1, 24 n., 40; number of, 24 n. *See also* Cato Allums, Terry Benson, Birkett, Berry Blasingame, Texas Brown, Sally Charles, Miles Hunnicutt, Joly, Largent, Bill Stigall, Jim Stigall, Sullivan, Thomas Turner

PARSONS, JAMES, magistrate, and Cato Allums, 6 n., 7–12; involved in shooting Unionist, 168, 170

Passmore, W. P., emigration speculator, 102, 130 n.

Payne, Buckner H., 117 n.

Perry, Gov. Benjamin F., and Congressional Plan, 5; supports civil authorities, 5; clothing of, 45; on ethnology of Negro, 117; opposition to Nullificationists, 159–160; as Unionist, 161 n.; as Rebel, 161 n.; liberates Unionist, 162; opposition to Congressional Plan, 171; and suffrage, 192; as political leader, 195

Petigru, James L., 159 n.

Pickens Court House jail, 9–10

Pickens District, 3, 11–13; description of, 7; receives gift of corn and bacon, 83–84

Planters. *See* Aristocrats; Landowners

Poinsett, Joel, 159 n.

Politics, Southerners' ignorance of, 194

Poor-whites, and free transportation, 37; and rationing, 50; illegitimacy among, 50, 139, 145; poverty of, 51; origin of, 52, 137, 154 n.; effect of slavery on, 50; effect of emancipation on, 53–54; in Confederate Army, 54, 156; war widows and orphans, 54; encouraged to work, 61; vagrancy, 61–63, 142–145; ingratitude of, 63–65; irreligion among, 64, 146; and freedmen, 72; ignorance of, 78; morality of, 135–139; and prostitution, 137; and drinking, 139; improvidence of, 139–140; and begging, 140; desire for land, 141; profess Union sympathies, 142; wanderings of, 144; illiteracy of, 146; quarrelsomeness, 145–152; value of human life, 152; history of poor-white family, 154–157; war casualties among, 157; future of, 157–158; and respectability, 157; European immigration as threat to, 158

Poorhouse, fear of, 59; available to Negroes and whites, 59; aided by Governor's order, 60; aided privately by Commissioners of Poor, 60

Press, and Cato Allums, 11

Prisoners, condition of, 60; food ration to, curtailed, 60; labor contracts in Florida and Louisiana offered to, 103

Prisons, condition of, 60. *See also* Castle Pinckney, Pickens Court House jail, Tortugas

Prohibition of liquor. *See* Temperance

Prostitution, 59, 137, 144

Provost Court, abolished, 30–31

Pryor, Roger A., Congressman, 202

Public opinion, Northern, 10

Public opinion, Southern, and Cato Allums, 7, 10, 12–13, 19; in Miller-Looper case, 166; fairness of, 166

RACE PREJUDICE, magistrates and, 31

Rationing, reports of, 40–41; corn distribution, 42–54; appeals for, 49–50; moral effect of, 58–59, 66–67; limited to institutions, 60 n.; clothing distribution ordered, 69–73; De Forest opposed to corn distribution, 69; vagrants and, 80; method of determining most needy, 76–85; distribution of

Unity, need of post-war, 198

WAGES, De Forest on, 29; lack of capital to pay, 29; retention of, by employers, 30; all labor entitled to, 34; ignorance of wage system, 96; daily wages as possible solution, 97

Walhalla, S.C., German colony at, 52, 200; receives corn and bacon ration, 84

War Department, red tape criticized, 71, 88

Whites and Negroes, relations, 74, 108, 115. *See also* Aristocrats, and slaves and slavery; Aristocrats, attitude toward freedman; Freedmen, and poor-whites

Widows, 54, 75, 137, 157, 197

Williams, Joseph, bushwhacker, 6 n., 7–8, 11–12

Williams, Wallace, freedman, 109

Women, position in Old South, 185–186; and suffrage, 185–186

YOUTH AND CRIME, De Forest's comment on, 14